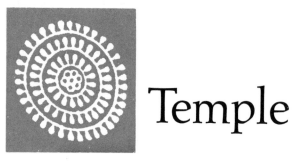

Temple

The Mind of India:

Yogis, Swamis, Sufis and Avataras

of the Phallic King

by PAGAL BABA

Edited and with photographs by EDWARD RICE

SIMON AND SCHUSTER • NEW YORK

ACKNOWLEDGMENTS

The author is indebted to Edward Rice for editorial assistance, photographs, notes, and graphic material, to Mr. E. C. H. Edwards, an American businessman who has kindly turned over portions of his Indian journal for use in this book (he has been especially interested in our astrologers), and to Jayati Gupta, Rajit Gupta, Maya Bahadur, Kishan Bahadur, Mrs. D. S. Guha, Sudhir Mitra, Neepa Bagchi, Jharna Mitra, Vishtu Mitra, Shura Cohen, Colonel Lal, S. Kumar, Arthur Avalon, R. N. S. Duda, Srila Chatterji, Edward and Marian MacDowell, and to a number of other people who prefer to remain anonymous. Special thanks to Ujjala Deb and Mishti Rani.

The reader is cautioned against a seeming duplication of characters. There are two Babajis (one of them at least five hundred years old), plus Dadaji, Babuji, and Sidhi Babu, two Swamijis (Calcutta and New Delhi), and Sant Maharaj Ji and Sant Ji Maharaj (father and son, respectively).

I refer you to the Editor's Note for clarification of certain themes running through this book.

An asterisk after a word or phrase refers to a note at the end of the book.

Pagal Baba
Ballygunge
Calcutta, West Bengal

CONTENTS

EDITOR'S NOTE

I first went to India out of curiosity. I had some slight knowledge of it: a favorite uncle (a kind of Delinquent Cha Cha) had lived there and in Ceylon for ten years and there was a certain slight Indian ambience at home when I was a child. Later some close friends adopted a wandering Indian sadhu, called merely Dr. Bramachari (the name means monk), who hung about the Columbia campus for several years, subsisting on (or should I say, putting up with?) the vegetarian plate at the local Child's, leaving his purse, the mouth open, on a table when he was broke. Dr. Bramachari eventually returned home, and soon afterward his country was partitioned into India and Pakistan. Dr. Bramachari, who was a Bengali, found himself in East Pakistan, which was carved out of the Muslim section of Bengal. As a Hindu in a Muslim nation, Dr. Bramachari was in a very precarious position, since the authorities automatically assumed his sympathies favored India, though the fault lay not so much with the Bengali Muslims but with the West Pakistanis, who treated the eastern portion of their country like a colony.

I visited Dr. Bramachari in East Pakistan shortly before it revolted, tracking him down in an obscure Hindu settlement south of a town called Comilla. His people welcomed me with an hour-long chanting of the Hari Krishna, a performance that touched me deeply and irrevocably. A few weeks after I left, Comilla and the neighboring countryside were ravaged by a great hurricane, which killed tens of thousands of people. A second hurricane came soon afterward, and then the Bengali uprising against the West Pakistanis, in which something like a million people were killed and nine or ten million fled as refugees. Freedom was won in a series of bitter battles and peace was established, the new nation being called Bangladesh, the Land of the Bengalis. Dr. Bramachari was swallowed up in the holocaust and I have not heard from him since, though he may still be alive. While few men want to die, I suspect that he would not have fled from death, for death is not an end but a gateway into the future.

I mention Dr. Bramachari because he is a Bengali, and I find that after five stays in India my conditioning has become more and more Ben-

11

gali. Bengal is India in all her multitudinous characteristics to the extreme: the most spiritual, the most sensitive, the most abject and poor, the most savage, arrogant, refined, revolutionary, beautiful, the most compassionate. It is known as Sonar Bangla—Golden Bengal—by Bengalis. And when I saw the first rough draft of Pagal Baba's manuscript, I was not at all surprised to find that (though he himself is not a Bengali) it was largely Bengalis who populated his world.

This long aside has brought me face to face with the book. It is one of those curious, almost enigmatic works that fit into no category. It was written mostly by Pagal Baba, with various contributions by other people. As editor, I have pulled together a large mass of material and have shaped it according to Pagal Baba's wishes. It has a form, but it is an eastern form, which is cyclical and not linear as in the West. Even with my Westernizing touches, *Temple of the Phallic King* is still enough of an oddity for the publishers to have asked me to write this introduction as a brief guide to the reader's understanding of what is to come. From my slight knowledge of other works with Indian themes there is no antecedent for the book in English, probably not in any of the Indian languages, though it draws upon popular epic, devotional and tantric works, and folk motifs to illustrate its interweaving themes. *Temple of the Phallic King* brings us into the mind of India, into the minds of certain individuals, and into a portion of the Indian psyche which is not normally probed, except from a distance by anthropologists and sociologists, who have little commitment except to their research. But this is not research: it is a *search* into reality, and it is a reality of a kind that the rationalist western world knows little about except through hearsay and is likely to dismiss as superstition or fantasy.

On a purely physical level India is very little like the West, and yet very close, as a couple are in sexual union (a concept which runs throughout the book). It is very poor—but poverty is not the subject we are concerned with, except the obvious poverty of the Western soul. And India also lacks, and is ignorant of, what is so necessary to our lives. The daily press barely exists; there is very little radio programing and no television except in two small areas, beamed at some twenty or thirty thousand communal sets in villages. India has few of the luxuries we take for necessities, like a car for every family, beds, three meals a day, shelter from the elements, universal education, and so on. But it has a fantastically good railway system which binds the country together like the nerves and sinews of a huge body, enabling the people to fortify their normal psychic ties physically with ease and economy. Most interesting of all, there is a huge movie industry (the largest in the world), which operates on a kind of mythic basis, drawing heavily upon the ancient epics like the Mahabharata or upon traditional moral, ethical, and religious codes and concepts (fate, duty, love) which underlie man's existence. The daily life of the ordinary Indian is, more or less, one long cycle of work and prayer. It is hard manual labor for the average man, his wife and children, but throughout the day man, woman, and child are in touch with the Divine. The day starts, when possible, with a trip to some source of water (for water is sacred)—a river, a tank, lake, stream, the ocean—where one defecates, has a ritual bath, and prays. A Brahmin, who is a member of the priestly caste, may pray frequently during the day. Other men are not so committed or may not have the time, and people in the lowest castes are in fact denied the privilege of the same prayers as the Brahmin, though they may be allowed to hire a Brahmin to pray on their behalf on some occasions. But whatever, the mass effect is that India is almost totally absorbed in the Divine. However, this is not a book about prayer. It is a trip into another world, in which mind and body take different paths.

At the risk of leaving myself subject to commitment by some literal-minded psychiatrist, I will try to emphasize that the human mind does not work the same in India as in America. I am convinced, after a few personal experiences which I at first tried to deny, that it is quite possible for a yogi (to name one type of individual with such powers) to enter the mind of another person. This entry, you should understand, is done in most cases for positive and beneficial reasons. I have been told over and over again by highly educated, clear-minded, and unsuperstitious Indians that this does happen. I believe them. I had also been warned against a certain swami who was notorious for entering people's heads with diabolical intentions, and after looking into this man's activities and having two or three confrontations with him, I am certain that he could use his powers for destructive purposes. Such warnings are not to be dismissed as superstition, and my normal Western skepticism vanished in the light of the facts. It is possible to reject or fight such mental intrusions. One can often "feel" a yogi's probing, and I have had several psychic struggles with yogis whom I did not trust or wanted to confound, but at other times I was willing to let my mind be used as a kind of amanuensis or I was caught unawares. But it was for a purpose, as I learned.

In a certain sense Pagal Baba's book will do this to you. If you are receptive, it will fill your mind with themes that reach back into the dawn of time and soar as high as the sky, flowing upward to the source of the celestial Ganges. *Temple of the Phallic King* will bring you into the "mind" of India, and India into your mind. And, as I have insisted when talking to people about the book, you must open your mind and try to discard the rubbish of the West (though there is much good to keep). There is no "correct" way to read *Temple of the Phallic King*, except to let it absorb you and flood your head with light. Some of it will be laser-sharp; some will at first seem diffuse and then clear. You will receive what you are ready for and no more. Part of the light will come from people who at first glance may seem fatuous or stupid or grasping (and some are), but they serve merely as catalysts for the knowledge they transmit. They may speak directly, or warmly, emotionally, angrily, calmly, subtly, or even insiduously. Some of them may tell you what is not true, eventually your heightened perceptions will enable you to separate true from nontrue. But whatever they say, they are getting into your head.

Which is what Pagal Baba wants.

We are left with a final question: *Who is Pagal Baba?* (Incidentally his name means, roughly, Crazy Daddy and is pronounced Pāgal Bābā.) . . . Americans, so say Indians, ask too many questions, often when there is no question to be asked, and want definitive answers. Like those individuals—Indian or foreign—who are especially touched, marked, seared by India (a little bit crazy, that is, because there is something in the atmosphere that burns like a ray from God the Sun), Pagal Baba says there *is* no answer. He can reply only with a secular paraphrase of a response of the Bengali saint Anandamayee Ma, "I am *who* you think I am, and no one else."

EDWARD RICE

FOREWORD

This is a book of darshan.

Darshan (sometimes written darsána) means: presence, vision, literally "sight," and is what one receives from sitting in the presence of a spiritual being or even from hearing or reading his words. Darshan thus equals insight plus blessing. One may obtain darshan from casual visits to holy men or women, but better yet, from constant attendance. The best way to receive darshan is by becoming a chela or disciple and following the strict regime under the teaching of a guru or master at his—literal—feet.

Most of you are unable to become a chela, but in the following pages I hope to direct the Western reader into the *mind* of guru. Guru is not only master but God, and God is guru, and guru is you and you are guru —statements which you may find puzzling at first but which will gradually become manifest as you read further. I refrain from saying "become clear" or "be understood," because these are Western conceits. One becomes part of, is absorbed into, what these pages tell you.

The westerner must try to dissociate himself from western modes of thinking, with their logical progression from beginning to middle to end, and let himself be absorbed into the great Self, the Calm Ocean of Our Consciousness, the Ground of All Being, which is manifested in Shakti, Eternal Energy for the pedant, but for the people, Mahadevi, the Great Mother who is the Temple of the Phallic King. Discard reason, conditioning, ambitions, fears, forget the automotive, technological, nuclear world and proceed on foot like any pilgrim to guru. In the heavenly, sportive playground, where the active female principle, Shakti, couples with Shiva, the otherwise passive male, in a shower of seed that fecundates the earth, there is no dualism of divine and human. The Creator and the created are One, both full, both complete. The transcendental is the transcendent. There is no separation, no linear flow. All comes and goes, all returns, is born dissolves only to be re-created. It is an eternal continuum without parts.

You will realize that *Temple of the Phallic King* exists on a multitude of levels: there is an endless flow of meanings—mystical, erotic, practical (as in the exposition of traditional yogic techniques, which I hope will simplify what is becoming unduly mysterious), reportorial, joking, analytical, critical. I have added a number of passages by others to supplement certain ideas that absorbed me, and I have reworked various traditional prayers, chants, sayings, and incantations and invocations to mirror the basic theme of Shakti in different facets. But everything is connected: this shifting subjective approach becomes objective and then reflective—all calculated to dis-locate the mind and open it to the flow of energies released by Mahadevi.

I feel a brief explanatory note about Mahadevi might be in place. The Great Mother is most popularly experienced as Kali whom Westerners (due to a nineteenth-century misunderstanding perpetrated by missionaries and Germanic scholars) erroneously believe to be the goddess of destruction. We observe Kali (who is also known as Durga, Sati, Bubaneshvari, Mahakali, Uma, and so on) in many moods, from that of the patron of the heavily sexual, sensual tantric yoga to her present incarnation as Anandamayee Ma, the Bengali woman mystic whom many of my people see quite literally as an avatar of God. There are interweaving currents: the great mantra OM and other mantras, yantras, Kundalini the Serpent Power, mystics, saints, gurus, and yogis. I am especially fond of Sai Baba, who though "dying" in 1918, is very much alive today as a number of people in this book will tell you. The body is merely a shell for the jiva, the living person. These themes are set against the tragedy of the Kali yuga,* the last age, which is a long downward trend in the lives of men from the golden past to the present times of viciousness, weakness, disease, and general decline of all that is good. But the Buddha avatar, as we know, has already appeared and the Kalki avatar the tenth and last incarnation of Lord Vishnu, is still to come, to save us from ourselves.

You may wonder why so many Indians—yogis, swamis, gurus, and even musicians, dancers, poets, and writers, to say nothing of numerous students (I except our businessmen)—are now at work in your country. There are hundreds of centers of yoga, vedanta, and Hinduism all over America, perhaps dozens in some of the big cities like New York and San Francisco. Our first contemporary missionary, Swami Vivekenanda, went toward the close of the nineteenth century to the World Congress of Religions in Chicago. He found America open and eager to learn from the East and in need of guidance. However, the first "converts" to our ways of thinking were (like those Indians who went over to Christianity in India in the sixteenth century) mainly the lonely, the aged, and the dispossessed. An esoteric faith appeals initially only to those who are rejected by their own land. Now we find that the East (and I include the Buddhists, who are, after all, nothing but another kind of Hindu) is reaching Americans of all ages, social types and dispositions. What we have to offer is important because America's tremendous energies and talents, unguided and misdirected, can destroy the world. Ram Chandra warns that salvation can come only from India: "A type of civilization based on spiritualism will spring forth in India and it shall, in due course, become the world civilization. . . . Every nation must sooner or later adopt the same course if it wants to maintain her existence." Obviously, as our seers tell us, America can survive only through India.

Pagal Baba
Ballygunge, Calcutta
West Bengal

There is the god
Swayambhu
in the form of
fire
and there is
the god
Pingaleshwara.
There is the
god called
Vindunadeshwara
and there is
the god called
Bhadreshwara.

OM
original
all-containing
sacred
everlasting
sound
symbol of God
Infinite
Power

OM, the symbol of the three in one: the three worlds in the Soul.
The three ages: time past, time present, the eternal future.

The three divine powers: creation, preservation, transformation in
the One Being;
The three essences: immortality, omniscience, joy in the One Spirit.

Sudhi Babu is a sadhu. He is a slim, black-haired man. He is said to
be sixty but looks forty-five or forty-eight, brisk, straight-backed,
alert.

"OM is the universal sound," he tells me. "All sounds are contained within OM."

He says OM in a long, drawn-out resonant voice that comes
from deep within him and echoes throughout eternity, "OM."

It goes on and on, slowly fading away. The earth shakes, the
heavens cloud over and clear. Wide gulfs appear in the land, the seas
heave and churn, drought, monsoons, the relentless sun burns the
earth, lightning strikes the wooded slopes of the Himalayas. When
all has been destroyed, the world is re-created and sun, laughter,
joy, eternal bliss, fill the land. OM. His voice fades away into the
centuries, into the countless eons.

There is a long period of silence. "There are seven sacred
sounds," he adds. He makes a tch tch tch sound, like crickets in the
grass, then another sound, like the wind rustling in the primeval
forest. "There is the sound of sea shells, the sound of the conch as
when you cup your hand over your ear. And the cry of the peacock."
(The peacock is a sacred bird.)

Silence.

"I forget the rest," he says softly, "but there are seven sacred sounds, all of them contained within OM. That is the first, the primordial sound, the original, the everlasting sound within which all other sounds are to be found. But OM is the only sound you need know."

SWAMIJI

✤

I used to see Swamiji walking rapidly through the garden to visit Sunita's sister in the house next door. He came in an old car—it must have been thirty years old, and looked like a European copy of a 1930's Studebaker. I should have found out what it was, but never did. Sunita said from time to time, "Swamiji wants to see you." So one day I went over to the sister's house and talked to Swamiji for ten minutes. The sister had a great big Doberman, rather friendly for that kind of dog, but Swamiji was terrified of it. I found the dog a nuisance because it was one of those beasts that are always sniffing your private parts. For some reason it kept after me rather than Swamiji. Maybe it just didn't like yogis. Swamiji always wore a white tunic over his orange sannyasi robes and a hood over his head. The hood made the damnedest impression, turning him into a kind of medieval Christian monk. I never saw him without it.

We sat down to talk, with the dog still sniffing. Swamiji pulled out a bunch of tattered photographs. There was Swamiji, stripped down to a loin cloth and without the hood, in the usual yoga exercises, his long full beard and long wavy black hair flowing in all directions. He had been photographed in the standard asanas (postures), the lion, the lotus, the serpent, etc. He looked about thirty-five to me, but Sunita said later he was believed to be eighty. I grunted politely over the photographs. Swamiji then said that he wanted me to become a disciple of his. It meant an hour every day or so studying hatha yoga. I wanted to, and thought about it, but studying yoga wasn't practical at the moment, as I was about to leave Calcutta on a trip and there was no point in beginning something as time-consuming and demanding as hatha yoga if I couldn't do the exercises faithfully. So I said no.

But Swamiji kept after me, sending messages. Finally I returned to Calcutta and had the free time, but by then Swamiji had disappeared. He was in the habit of seeing two or three families, going from one to another, giving them yogic instruction and listening to their problems, and then when he had had enough or thought they were in good shape he would suddenly disappear. The family would have to swallow their disappointment and accept the fact that they had graduated from Swamiji's course.

So I began to call around for Swamiji. The trouble with running him down is that he lived in Dum Dum, in the northern section of the city. It was rough territory because it was Naxalite* country and the underground were always shooting one another and shooting the regular Communists and Socialists and the cops and getting shot at, so no one went there willingly. And anyway, Swamiji would never allow anyone to visit him at home. He always came to the disciples and clients. You located him by phoning around and leaving messages, and eventually he would turn up, either at your flat or at a friend's. But he had this habit of dropping people when he felt he was becoming too attached to them, or the people to him, and then, whammo, no Swamiji and you knew that he had cut loose.

I was about to take another trip, but first I wanted a talk with Swamiji. He got my message finally, and we met at Sunita's flat, in a big, quiet, rather disorganized room. We shut the door to keep out the kids and the servants and the dog (Sunita also had one of those sniffing dogs), and after Swamiji had shown me the same ragged photos again I began to pump him about the Other Life. He was a man of facts, or unfacts, as I had already suspected. Anyway, I'll put down what he said and you can add your own salt. Or take it straight. He started by talking about yoga:

Yoga has six-fold advantages. Purification of the internal and external organs of the body; removal of viruses, auto-immunization; longevity in the sense of living beyond old age (up to one hundred years you will be looking as if still young); and mental, moral, and spiritual sublimation, culminating in the Ultimate Absoluteness. In yoga the stomach, heart, lungs, and brain are made fit.

There are three things on which you can judge a man's health: bowels, appetite, and sleep. Proper evacuation of the bowels is important. Bodily filthiness is the root of all illnesses. What are also important are the circulation of the blood, circulation of the glands, proper breathing, purification of the blood, control of the breath, and peace of mind. The more you slow the rate of breathing the more you'll have peace, one-pointedness of mind.

When you meditate, select a posture which enables you to have peace of mind. The lotus position is the best, but it is not necessary if it is uncomfortable. There are other positions.

What is the ultimate end of yoga? Why should we practice yoga? . . . Someday we will all be One. No separateness of you and me. Hatha yoga is that which concentrates upon the body. Without a perfect body you cannot concentrate, you cannot meditate. When you have perfectness inside, everything will come. First and foremost you must have the body.

Food is of the utmost importance. If the body is not assisted by proper diet it is nothing. Think of an elephant—he is vegetarian. You can control him. But an animal that lives on flesh and blood you cannot control. Food should be cooked because there are so many poisons in it. Vegetables and fruit, of course—how can you put decayed meat into your stomach? Take the animals as your guide. Sitting in the cobra position will give you a strong back. Birds never suffer from stomach trouble, because they live on fruit. A peacock can eat any kind of poison and live. When you exercise, try the crocodile posture, the tiger posture, the swan posture.

Now about sleep. How much should you have, how much is necessary? . . . None, not even one second. You can always sleep standing, sitting. Lying down is not required. And medicine is more injurious than anything else in the world. It is dangerous. Especially foreign drugs. That's what leads to heart trouble, constipation, bad thinking, wrong birth.

The first step in yoga is cleaning, then everything else follows. To start you must wash out your system with forty to fifty glasses of water. It will take forty-five minutes to an hour to go through your system. (For me, ten minutes.) Complete cleaning outside is lightness inside. It is a thing to be felt—I cannot make you understand. One must experience it himself. Once you are clean you will be able to meditate.

The trouble is that people want to jump, to begin at once, to attain the One on the initial step. You must be in good condition first. Then you move on. And so long as there is worldly desire there will be no peace. No-attachment, no looking, no-desiring, no-wanting. Your attention must always be on the atma, the soul, which is everlasting. If you will go to the Infinite you will be infinite.

Attachment is bad. You must be like the lotus leaf. Water is flowing by, but it is itself. That is like society. Everything depends on the will of God. Man has got nothing to do with it. But his ego, his fighting, his anger, passion—they cause trouble. If you've got faith in one who is running the world, that is good, whatever happens is good. Naxalites, goondas [hooligans], whatever. God is good. That is the thing.

You will not age. There is a man who is five hundred years old*—his name will come to me [it never did]—but everybody knows about him. Then there is a man one hundred and eighty years old, Sant Hans Ji Maharaj. He lives in Gaya. Just go to the railway station and ask: they will tell you where he lives. Such a holy man! And there is another holy man, Shri Sathya Sai Baba. When you see a photo of this saint, ashes come out, nectar comes out, honey comes out. A marvelous thing! See these three men and go into the jungle. In the city there is a purely artificial way of living, in the jungle there is the native way, natural food, the practical things—simplicity, greatness, one-pointedness of mind, good body, good physique. I know you are curious why I stay in Calcutta when the jungle has so much to offer . . . One day I must go—but now it is the design of God to keep me here. Who can go against that?

In the Himalayas there are many saintly men, great saints, great souls. There is a lady there who sits in a temple. She will be in meditation all day before the goddess, power will come upon her, she will be able to tell people about themselves. She can predict what is to happen, illness, good fortune. And there are other powers. Can people really levitate? If the yogi thinks you are the proper man he will levitate for you. Automatically, if you do things right, you will have the power. Any man can gain it. In the jungle there are men who can turn themselves into animals, into tigers and bears. They sit before their caves on bolsters. That I have seen myself.

Concentration and meditation in the nighttime—that is, in the predawn hours, not before midnight—is the only way. Go with your mind directed toward simplicity. Meditate, meditate, meditate. Sitting in a corner you will be able to know everything. Everything! God is in the heart of the devotee. First you must realize, then you can teach others. Self-realization first. God in the heart.

Who is interested in all of India? Everybody is interested, to learn the fitness, to learn, to meditate. We have much to teach you. The world [the West] has nothing for us. We must realize that, you must realize that.

Shortly afterwards I visited Gaya and tried to find Hans Ji Maharaj. A man in the local tourist office, a Mr. Singh, graciously ran down the facts for me. The sant had never reached one hundred and eighty but had died in 1966 at the age of seventy. Shortly before his death he called his four sons together and, laying his hands upon the youngest (I believe he was nine at the time), passed his soul into the boy. I never found the five-hundred-year-old man, though he is mentioned frequently in Sri Yogananda's interesting work, *The Autobiography of a Yogi,* and after talking to some friends about Shri Sathya Sai Baba I decided against a visit to him, having been warned that he is a fraud (though he is the subject of a major adulatory work by an American. He claims to have taken the soul of a previous (and authentic) Sai Baba and says of himself that he is a very holy man. He performs a lot of impressive tricks. ("He pulls watches out of the air, things like that," said one of his critics, "stuff anybody can do. The usual bit—mysterious scents, jasmine petals suddenly appearing.") It was the showman aspect that put me off, as the sacred books continually caution one against magic, and displays of any kind are not said to be indications of saintliness.

When I returned to Calcutta I got in touch with Swamiji again, and we met at a mutual friend's house for dinner. He showed everyone his photographs. At the table he began to question me about my trip and told me that the next time I went away there were certain holy men I must visit, among them a five-hundred-year-old man whose name he could not recall, and Shri Sathya Sai Baba. "There is a man who is very holy named Santji Maharaj in Benares. He is one hundred and eighty years old. A very great man, very powerful. Just by touch he can cure, even cancer. Just go to the railway station and ask: they will tell you where he lives."

Swamiji has copped out. He refuses to let R photograph him (I wanted a new set of photos of him in those ghastly, obscene yogi poses, with his stomach withdrawn and the muscles—or is it the intestines?—protruding). He is still talking about the hundred and eighty year old man. Each time he mentions Hans Ji Maharaj he places him in another city. This particular evening we are at the Z's, a Canadian couple. Swamiji says, "You should not eat curd at night —it's a medically proven fact." Who proved it? I ask. He looks annoyed. An air of tension has arisen. Right before dinner an Indian businessman had come to see Swamiji and had fallen on the floor and groveled before him. As the man became more and more obsequious Swamiji began to puff up and turn on his arrogance, all the while muttering yogic platitudes. At dinner Mrs. Z remarks loudly that when she has her Indian friends in the house she asks the servants to watch them to see that they don't steal anything. Is this a warning for Swamiji?

Swamiji had objected to the curd because it was cold, but then he ate chilled papaya without comment. Mrs. Z has some beautiful peasant candlesticks made out of red baked clay. They cost a few cents in the bazaar, but they are slim and graceful. I admire them, but Swamiji wrinkles his nose and says, "To me they are valueless. Only gold and silver and jewels have any value. Not clay." "But they're so beautifully made," both Mrs. Z and I reply. "Clay, they are clay! How could beauty come of clay!" I mention the photographs again: May R take some pictures of Swamiji? He pouts and acts as if he wants to be coaxed. OK, so I'll coax him. He becomes very coy. He stands up and begins to edge out of the room, sideways, taking little dancelike steps. Mrs. Z tells him to stop acting like a girl. He simpers and fades away through the door.

Hari Krishna*
Hari Krishna
Hari Hari
Hari Ram
Hari Ram
Ram Ram
Hari Hari

HOW WE THINK

I don't think the West will ever understand us. I know you are convinced that we really don't believe certain things we talk about, which are the core of the Hindu way of life. You must realize that there are two basic facts in Hinduism—call them keys, clues, whatever you will—which are maya and karma. Maya is illusion. Nothing is real—poverty, wealth. For example, a rich woman may pass a beggar in rags. Her jewels and the gold in her sari are no more real than his leprosy. Karma is your destiny. Whatever you are today is the result of what happened in a previous birth. I can conceive of an all-powerful Creator (by any name you want to call Him), but he doesn't intervene in a man's life. On the other hand, it is incorrect to suppose that God in His aspect as Brahma created the world some millions of years ago and has since done nothing. Brahma is always creating and re-creating the manifested substance which Shiva as Rudra is ever breaking down.

On the full moon (and on the new moon) a man or a woman will go to the temple with clothing and money and food for the poor, not out of charity (this must be clearly understood) but to propitiate the gods. For the self alone. Compassion for others does not exist. This is ingrained in us, just as a sense of social justice is ingrained in Westerners. You cannot change your heritage. And you must accept the fact that social justice is not a particularly admirable quality: you cannot interfere with another man's karma.

In thinking about India you must try to comprehend our psychological background. Christians—the West, that is—want sanctification of the holy. Hindus want deification of the living. We have been a subject people since 1100, when the Muslims invaded us. All our great men, thinkers, creators, philosophers, lived before then. There have been a few flare-ups, like the bhakti or devotional movement, but nothing significant. Indians are no longer original. We

Indians copy but don't understand. We wear English clothes but
don't know the reason—we don't know if we're imitating clerks or
the governor. We have no way to identify caste and social position
in the foreigner. Underneath our western veneer we are still Indian.

[A Bengali Brahmin woman] I was walking down the street when a
yogi said to me, "Why aren't you saying your mantra?" It had been
given me by my guru at initiation, but I had not said it for a long
time. A mantra is secret, of course, and you must never tell anyone
what it is. But the yogi knew it. Everything is planned. I cannot do
anything but what is meant to be done. Why ask about the future?
If you *know*, you will be unhappy. It is better to sit quietly and be
content with what *is*. Calm resignation to the god. God is a con-
solation. God is a feeling, one you can't define. You cannot *will* the
future. Will power depends on the stars; if they are in a certain
position, they give you a certain kind of will power.

You cannot do what you like. Duty and obligation are the rules
you must follow. Society means that all is intertwined, each person
looking after the other, each caste with its responsibilities. My rights
should not harm another person's liberties. Self-control is very much
practiced in India, each of us working within his or her own path
and not infringing on others.

There is a generous attitude in our blood. In the old days the
rajas always used to feed the poor. To feed the poor is to feed
Narayan [a form of Vishnu, one of the three great gods]. His name
means savior. He is the symbol of kindness, the preserver. During a
puja, at the time of a marriage, after the death of a relative, we feed
the poor. When my father died, on the tenth and on the thirteenth
day I called in the beggars, even the pariah dogs, from the street. I
had to feed them before I myself could eat.

God is worshiped by doing good to others. God is not in the
heavens, God is within us. If I am bad, if I am brutish, is that not
hell? "Know thyself"—we say "ATMANAM VIDDHI"—that is the liberation of the soul, that is the manifestation of God. Every living thing
is a manifestation of God. Nothing is without God. God, that is
Brahman, IS. Brahman IS. This means that we don't have the mono-
theism and duality of the West, nor do we like to be called "poly-

theists," because all these terms are nonsensical. Do you follow me? Brahman IS.

Do I have doubts? In everything I have doubts. But what is to happen will happen, whether you say it or not. My knowing or not knowing is not the limit of everything. When you give a present it is how much you are thinking of the present. It is the same way with God. The best things must be taken in very little amounts. That is why we cannot take God in one big gulp. God is One but we worship Brahman in different moods, as in Ganesh [the elephant god], just as a man has different moods.

I would like to go abroad but cannot because of my mother. My father had made me stop working—I had been a teacher—and he would not let me accept a scholarship in Europe. It's still open to me, but since my mother depends on me I must stay with her. Five years abroad would be a long time.

My father died two years ago. He was cremated at the Kalighat, the most sacred spot in India, which is on the most sacred branch of the Ganges. I had to walk along with the body. No son, no brother, no living male relatives. I put the fire to his mouth with a jute wand. Lighting the fire is a legal act as well as religious— whoever does it is recognized as the dead one's successor. After the body was consumed I immersed my father's stomach in the Ganges. The stomach is the part that does not burn.

Out of nothing comes nothing.

In the beginning was the One, Who willed and became many.
Man cannot imagine, cannot name, cannot describe the nondual
    Immensity called Brahman.
Brahman is indivisible existence, knowledge, eternity.
Brahman is other than all that is known, is above the Unknown.
Brahman cannot be called non-Being, cannot be called Being,
is neither one nor many.

Formless Immensity, Void, silence, absolute darkness,
beyond mind, beyond intellect,
the substratum of man's own nature, his own self, his Atman,
the individual Self small as an atom, vast as the universe,
"not This, not That,"
ungraspable, indestructable, unattached,
beyond injury and anguish,
unborn and undying,
not slain when the body is slain.
From nowhere and not from anywhere.
Form resplendent, unthinkable,
hidden in the hearts of seers,
the Invisible Continuum.

Inactive, beyond grasp, without qualifications,
inconceivable, indescribable, Brahman is the essence
aimed at through the notion of Self,
ever aloof from manifestation,
yet manifested.

Calm, peaceful, auspicious, Brahman is the fourth unmanifest stage,
    beyond the three stages of existence (gross, subtle and causal),

beyond the corresponding stages of experience, waking consciousness and deep sleep.

This Immensity, this Void, this Unknown, this Non-Existence, this
    non-dual Absolute,
is the innermost nature of everything.
All the gods are this one Soul
and all dwell in the Soul.

From Brahman comes Brahma, the Immense Being who constructs
    the universe,
Shiva, the Father, the possessor of the organ of procreation,
Krishna, the Protector, who descends as avatar to redeem angels
    and men.

Brahma is the fount of all rhythms, forms, intellect.
From his thought the world's egg, the Golden Embryo, is born.

From Shiva, the boundless void, the silence and obscurity
of deep dreamless sleep when all mental activity stops, comes
Shakti, manifest Energy, expressed as Mahakali, Mahadevi, Kali,
Parvati, Mahalakshmi, Gauri.

Vishnu shows the way to supreme enlightenment,
is the transcendent divine experience, has manifested himself
nine times; his tenth avatar is still to come: Kalki, riding on a white
    horse
and wielding a sword blazing like a comet, will re-establish
    a golden age.

The Baroness tells me that there is a tree—only one—in Tibet whose leaves have mantras on them. "How do you know?" "Oh, I know." The Baroness (hereafter referred to as B or the B) is a thin, wiry, energetic Bengali woman, the wife of a successful Indian business-man. The husband is strongly pro-Western and specifically pro-American, to the extent of being a fervid supporter of the right-wing Establishment and preferring American to Indian friends. He re-marks from time to time that he doesn't believe in all that Hindu nonsense, though I have seen him drop on the floor before the B's father and touch his feet, as any good, respectful son-in-law should. The B, on the other hand, is deeply religious and is a sincere Hindu according to her own lights (and mine, too, I might add). I think she is one of the few truly authentic mystics I have come across, a natural mystic, who cuts through the mumbo-jumbo. The B medi-tates regularly and observes a full-day fast each week (on Mon-days). Every morning she has the driver take her by car to the nearby Shiva temple and often to a local shrine dedicated to the goddess Kali. Usually B's children and I accompany her. But she prays alone in the Shiva temple and brings us some fresh bel leaves (wet, usually, with Ganges water), which she gives to the children and me to eat and to the driver as well, though he is a Muslim. When we visit the Kali temple we leave the car outside and walk down a long tree-lined alley to the shrine. We remove our shoes. The B enters to pray and I wait outside by a small Shiva lingam, where there are usually two or three teen-age girls standing in meditation.

At the evening hour, when the conch shells sound and the temple bells ring throughout the city, B stops for a moment (even in the middle of a sentence), bows her head, and puts her hands together in a gesture of prayer. She is a great devotee of Kali, though two days ago she was mad at Kali for not delivering according to her prayers. I had been spending some time in parts of Calcutta where there had been a lot of civil strife and frequent political murders. B says I have been saved by Kali from being beaten up or even killed. "You are under Her protection." "But Kali destroys," I say, knowing that this is a Western myth spread by missionaries and that the B is going to snap back. "To create one must first destroy." This leads into an argument about Vietnam (and about the Nazi murder of the Jews). "Vietnam is quite necessary. It must be destroyed so a new world can be created. Destruction of evil and good both so that good can be created. If good people have to die to be reborn, that is right." "What about the Americans?" "Their turn will come too. They will die only to be reborn. I believe that. They will be reincarnated." "You really believe that?" I ask. "All practicing Hindus believe in reincarnation." I mention two I have met who don't, one a sweeper and the other a rickshaw wallah (both are at the bottom of the caste system and are beyond hope). "They must be Communist influenced." "What does your husband think about reincarnation?" "Nothing."

"What is a Hindu?" I ask. "To a Hindu everybody is a Hindu." She had once remarked that she didn't know a certain person from Adam. I mention this—"What do you mean, Adam? He wasn't a Hindu." "Yes, he was, everybody is a Hindu." "Christ, too?" "Yes, Christ, too."

I ask her if she meditates. "Yes." When? "Morning and night. When I wake up and right before I go to sleep." Does she read anything first, just to get in the right frame of mind? "No, I just meditate. It is very easy for me. Basically I am an escapist."

I talk about throwing things out and simplifying my life. B: "Everything you have is necessary. When it isn't necessary you throw it out." She would like to take LSD to go on a trip, but—"I have such an active fantasy life that I don't need drugs."

Another day: She is complaining about her astrologer. He made a prediction that hasn't come true. She asks me to see the astrologer as she is afraid she will lose her temper with him, to find out what went wrong. The astrologer gives me a shady story and says he will check with his preceptor. B asks me: "How can you ask people what is God? God is so personal. First of all, how can you say He?" I reply that "He" is just a term of convenience and tell her a story

I had recently heard from an American: A man died but three days later came to life. His friends want to know what happened. He replies, "Well, I saw God." The friends want to know what God is like. "First of all, She's black . . ." The B snorts in indignation. "Of course She's black." Americans, who are on a level with untouchables to her, have sunk even lower. Of course God is black: Kali, the Great Mother, the All-Pervading Energy, the Destroyer and Creator, is black.

We talk further about God. Her father had told me, "You don't have to believe in God to be a Hindu." I mention this to her. She says I have misunderstood. But I hadn't. We are continually at cross-purposes. She remarks rather sarcastically that I won't ever lie, even on the telephone. I say that I try not to lie under any circumstances, we Indians never give a direct answer, we're incapable of saying yes or no, and I think that is bad. Life is difficult enough without falsehoods. The B: "Life's no fun without lying."

A week later: How do you meditate? What happens when you meditate? "I lie down and cover my head with the sheet." What about the lotus position? "Oh, that's a lot of nonsense. I just lie down and think about what I want to think about." I reply that I thought you were supposed to empty your head of thoughts. "My head is empty most of the time." She tells me (as she has very frequently) that I ask too many questions. "Accept what is." She adds: "There's no such thing as good or bad. What will be, will be."

[Mokund Chatterji, an astrologer] Astrology is the same as darshan. It means "to see," to know, to be acquainted with Truth. The whole world is contained within astrology. Thus I know the whole world by inference. Astrology is very intricate, very spiritual, the only worthwhile subject. The stars contain everything—science, art, philosophy, botany, philology, ordinary life, politics, birth, and death —all knowledge beyond comprehension. All comes within the direct influence of the planets.

Astrology is basic to Hindu philosophy. Astrology places the human being into the perspective of the stars, the planets, the sun, and the moon. The universe, mind, body, soul, heart, are all ruled by astrology. It is a basic law of physics. Astrology is considered an empirical science. Jyoti, the Indian name for astrology, means to know the truth, the truth of anything pertaining to the earth, planets, animals, human beings, and all that governs the life of the earth.

If the proper time, longitude, latitude, place of birth, year, the month, day, hour are correctly known, then all aspects of the province of human life and the style of its stay on earth can be correctly ascertained. The planets influence the life of animals, plants, and human beings directly. Each planet has its own sphere, relating, as the case may be, to physiology, psychology, to wealth, to the prosperity or decline of a man. Take, for example, the satellite moon, and her influence on human beings. Moon relates to mind. She has a definite influence over water and on the mind and on the tendency of the subject to good or to evil.

This is a scientific fact, this influence of moon. She is the nearest to earth of all celestial objects. In Hindu astrology the science of living beings is determined by moon. In the Zodiac, over the entire 360° the place of the moon is in Cancer. Moon covers the whole cycle of the Zodiac with twenty-nine days and a few hours—that means two and a quarter days or less than one orbit. Now take, for example, anyone born when moon is in Cancer—he or she must be a person with a very solid character, very much established, naturally balanced.

Astrology is not static: it grows every day and we know more and more about it. Since astrology explains the relation of the individual to the stars, and vice versa, the angular relation, we can chart the influence of the planets in almost all the affairs of an individual, from birth to death. The man who will become illustrious can be predicted, if his horoscope can be properly measured. It of course depends on the accuracy of the data. This is not to say that astrology makes a man a fatalist, but with proper calculations and predictions it can make a man more sanguine, more dynamic and optimistic.

But we are human beings. We are not always perfect in our calculations. We can make mistakes. This is why there sometimes arise doubt and uncertainty in the science of astrology. The fault lies not with the subject or with the stars but with the astrologer, his ignorance, his credibility—these are factors to consider. Basically, with a correct reading, there is nothing to do with what is called the chance factor. Chance has no place in astrology. The previous life, the present life, the future life, the afterlife, everything can be predicted. Given this, it is up to the individual to make the most of his astrological chart, and through meditation and various yogic practices to develop the innate spirituality within himself. What changes occur then will be from the individual's own development.

Astrology shows us some very interesting things about India and America. Both countries have Gemini as their symbol, their sign. A number of people have pointed this out. They affect each other, are parts of the same whole. You might say it is a kind of mystical marriage. And if India, the feminine partner, goes beyond the influence of America—CATASTROPHE! Gemini and Gemini deserve to be linked. That is why you find a similar, mutual understanding between India and America. India is the opposite side of America, America the opposite of India. You will find the best of Indians in America, the best of Americans in India. India and America can, together, contribute a lot to a lasting "no war" on earth. India, unfortunately, is badly affected by the malefic influences of Mars and a bad moon.

India and America must come together, come closer. This should be and will be. My prediction is that they will. But we must first pass through a great trial. My prediction for the near future is that within a year or two or three there will be the possibility of a great global war. And that socialism will be sponsored by America, because Americans are more materialistic even than the propagators of materialism in the world, the socialist countries like India and eastern Europe.

KALI

Kali and Shiva

Earth, water, fire, air and ether,
mind, atma, the supreme, nothing
is greater than Kali.*

Goddess of the full breasts, hers is the milk with which
she nourishes the world with the drink of immortality.
She gives birth to the world and protects it.
She is without childhood or old age,
she is primordial
but her youth is ever-fresh.

Her swelling breasts express great motherhood.
Her golden girdle supports her waist, which bends under
the burden of her breasts,
thrice-folding the skin beneath her bosom.
Heavy-hipped, she is naked, terrific, with fiery eyes, erect nipples,
hair disheveled in sign that her mind is free from all restlessness.
Naked because she is stripped of all maya,
is awakened.

It is said that Kali destroys. The Goddess does not destroy.
Man does.
The Goddess takes back what she has put forth.
At the end of a kalpa all things
from Brahma to a blade of grass will be dissolved
        in Mahakala.
She is in and One with that Mahakala.
O Mother of the world, obeisance!

Kali is without beginning or end.
She is blue, black and white.
Blue like the sky, because she pervades the world.
Multicolored like a cloud which appears blue, white and black
because of the sun's rays.
She is said to be black because she is colorless.
She is pure consciousness, massive, compact, unmixed.
She has the Sun, Moon and Fire as her three eyes.
She is the witness of the world, past, present and future.
She is the sole creatrix, preserver and destroyer
of infinite millions of worlds.
Her yoni signifies creation,
her full breasts preservation,
her terrible glance
    the withdrawal of all things,
    their ultimate destruction.

She has large teeth and a lolling tongue,
blood dripping from the corners of her mouth.
The dead bodies of two boy-children are her earrings.
She wears a garland of severed white heads
which are the fifty letters.
In her hand is a cup made of a human skull.
She wears a belt of human hands
and stands on the breast of the corpse-like Shiva.

In coition with Lord Shiva, hers is the dominant role.
Kali—Shakti—is active, Shiva passive.
Blissful, she is united with Shiva
    in the pleasurable world of creation.

I know the Goddess
    Kalika.
I meditate on Her
who dwells in the
    cremation ground.
May that meditation
and the knowledge thereof

                save me
        from
        this dangerous
                    world.

OM. O Goddess Kalika, goddess of terrible form, who fulfils all
desires, who are good and are worshiped by all the gods,
May you kill my enemies!

Shakti is manifest energy, the energy of creation, of the universe. We picture energy as female, the active principle, the passive principle being male. The quality of the divine expresses itself in the form in which there is most energy, in other words, in the female principle. Shiva, in his aspect as Lord of Sleep, cannot act, cannot create or destroy without the cooperation of the liberating female principle. Expressed as Devi, the Great Mother, who is in turn manifested as Kali and a number of other goddesses, Shakti is revealed to the world. The eternal energy is released by the union of Shakti/ Devi and Shiva. In this act of coition, which we call viparita-maithuna (the form of intercourse in which the woman assumes the dominant role), Shakti is active and Shiva passive. As the eternal Lord of Sleep, Shiva is merely the form of the Void. That is, he has no form. He is a corpse. What can you expect from the worship of nothingness? Nothing!

When Shakti's yoni clasps Shiva's lingam, the result is a cosmic orgasm from which creation springs forth. The universe is shaken and set in motion. Without Shakti the world is quiescent, and quiescence leads to dissolution.

As Kali—possibly the most common form of Shakti—we see the embodiment of energy, the source of all, the universal creator, consciousness, knowledge, the Immensity from which the world arises.

[SUDHI BABU] Kali is absolutely black. She is absolutely naked, as our mind is naked. There is nothing within our mind, except as Kali fills it. This she does as Bhuvanesvari, the Lady of the Spheres, in the saharasa chakra, or brahmanandra, at the top of the head, beyond the plane of the body. Blackness is a symbol of the void. You can put anything into that void. "From darkness comes light," we say. When you have achieved this primordial nakedness, you can put in any image that will take shape, will take form, just as a blank film will contain an image once it has been struck by light. "Out of formlessness comes form." What you obtain from filling the void with the power of Kali is the strength you need. You can use the power any way you wish: dacoits [robbers] used to worship Kali for power, the tantrics for liberation. There are numerous ways of worshiping Kali, depending on your mood and will.

Her image is symbolic. The four arms represent the four sides of the compass, North, South, East, and West: evil comes from all sides. One of her hands is raised with a weapon to cut off evil and another holds the head of a man representing evil, decapitated by her sword; one is outstretched in giving and the fourth is raised in blessing and protection. "You just help us, O Mother Kali!" we pray. We pray to her as a mother for peace of mind.

Kali stands on a man, Mahadev or Shiva, however you want to call him. He is not dead but sleeping. He sleeps because goodness doesn't come willingly. You are drawn to goodness by thought, prayer, meditation. Our mythology says that man has no power within himself, he needs a symbol. By thought he develops power within himself.

You may wish to take the symbolism in another manner. Kali is standing on her husband's chest. The goddess springs from Lord Shiva's body—actually his mind—and combines with the Supreme Energy. Kali is the force or energy which is the root of all creation, the Divine Nourishment. The idea that Kali kills or destroys has often been misunderstood. What she kills are the demons of anger or avarice or any of the other six qualities that must be uprooted from man. Kali destroys these demons and out of such destruction comes the creation of the good.

You may sometimes wonder why we haven't seen Kali in a more beneficent form, as Christians see the Virgin Mary, smiling, gentle, calm, and a bit enigmatic. You must try to understand our land, the fierceness of life here, the all-devouring sun which sears our souls, the heat, dust, poverty, the foreign invasions, the natural disasters.

You may have noticed the starkness of our sky, a sky so empty and lacking in color (except during the monsoons) that it does not seem to exist. And the bareness of our land, all faded browns and grays, withered greenery, farms cracked with the heat of famine, the soil wrinkled and lined like an old man's skin, the river beds which for most of the year possess not even mud. Even at night we explore a different sky from yours because we are in another latitude, a sky almost devoid of stars. Above us is the primordial blackness, the eternal night. This is Kali's sky, the empty black sky. We understand Kali's fierceness but we are not afraid of it. When she destroys it's in order to create. What she destroys is evil, ignorance, our enemies, our own sins, passions, lusts, lies. When she creates it is good, we are absorbed into her, into her great nourishing breasts, into her mothering womb, into her intelligence, energy, consciousness, above all, into her love, her love, her all-consuming nourishing love. We are part of her and she of us. Kali, Shakti, is in the Brahma Randhra, the asrasa chakra at the top of the head, beyond the fourth unmanifest stage. Kali is Kundalini, the serpent, awakened, rising through the chakras into the thousand-petal lotus which is Shiva, Brahma, Brahman.

MANTRAS AND YANTRAS

OM is a mantra. To make the pronunication clear, the sound is often written as OM though it is properly spelled AUM (which foreigners tend to pronounce, incorrectly, as *auwm*). OM is called the mantra which leads to the other shore. It is considered the source of all mantras. This mystical syllable incarnates the essence of the entire cosmos. It is the theophany itself—nothing less—reduced to the state of a phoneme. OM is the greatest of all mantras. It is composed of five parts, A, U, M, the stop (bindu), and the resonance (nada). (Beyond the realm of the five dwells the Lord.)

OM (AUM) is composed of the guttural A, the labial U and the nasal M. These letters comprise a triangle which physically delineates all the possibilities of sound.

The mind, the Bhagavad Gita tells us, is the prisoner of form and cannot reach the Formless. Devotees of the Unmanifest, bound by the body, face great difficulties in attempting to grasp the ways of the Unmanifest. The Unmanifest can be gained only through manifestation, that is, through certain forms and symbols. These forms and symbols are expressed as mantras,* or thought forms, and as yantras, or elementary graphic figures. Pictures and statues are not yantras, and are far less efficacious. In fact, as we have seen with OM, mantra is God, or god. Mantra is an independently existing, living, conscious sound-power equated with the divine. Each deity is represented by a distinct mantra. There are known to be seventy million mantras, which are called mula (root) mantras or bija (seed) mantras. Since there are three hundred and thirty-three million gods and an even greater number of demons, Nagas and other

57

celestial beings, the possible number of mantras is beyond calculation. A man is incapable of mastering more than a small fraction
of mantras in his lifetime.

Each mantra has its devata, or deity. The queen of all mantras
is OM (or AUM), the mantra of Brahman. OM is the Brahma-bija
(Seed of the Immensity); it is also known as the Brahma vidya
mantra (Knowledge of the Immensity). The mantra of Mother Kali
is KRIM. The mantra of Maya (Seed of Illusion) and/or Shakti (the
All-Pervading Energy) is HRIM. Other seed mantras include KLIM
(Kama-bija, or Seed of Desire), AIM (Vag-bija, or Seed of Speech),
SRIM (Laksmi-bija, or Seed of Fortune), and so on, beyond count.
Each element or category of the universe has its own natural sound,
which is also called bija. For example, the sounds of the five elements are (ether, air, fire, water, and earth) HAM, YAM, RAM, VAM,
and LAM. These sounds are eternal, as is the relation between them
and their subjects.

Mantra is senseless to those who do not know its meaning.
Westerners are likely to dismiss mantra as meaningless jabber. But
thought itself is every bit as real as an eternal object each being only
an aspect of one conscious Self from which both mind and matter
proceed. The Upanishads tell us that what a man thinks, that he
becomes.

Patanjali, in Yoga Sutra, points out that mantra (along with
drugs, austerities, and divine contemplation) can give "uncommon
powers of the mind." There are four basic types of mantra which
employ such powers, Sure, Helpful, Accomplished, and Enemy. The
first three categories are beneficial and are used for beneficent purposes. The fourth will destroy the mantrin, the person who utters
Enemy mantra, if improperly employed. The posture assumed for
reciting a mantra is important. Some should be said in the puraka
position, with the fingers raised and the thumb placed on the right
nostril; others in the kumbhaka position, in which both nostrils are
closed and breathing is suspended; and still others said in various
yogic postures.

I might give some instructions for the use of mantra. Above all,
under no conditions should one simply recite a mantra without
knowing the deity to whom it belongs, the seer to whom it was revealed, and the rhythm in which it is to be said. There may be
no great difficulty with a mantra of a single syllable, but when

the mantrin approaches more complex, multisyllabic mantras there is great danger. A mantra must be said with the perfect accent and rhythm. A careless or indifferently spoken mantra can have the opposite effect and can destroy the mantrin. I might add that a mantra in translation is no mantra at all. Mantras must be recited in the original tongue, which is Sanskrit. Some simple mantras are the following: NAMASKAR, to be used in connection with all mantras intended for peace and prosperity of the individual; VASAT, for the good health of a person; PHAT, an astra (weapon) bija, meant to injure or dement an enemy or to create dissension between friends or between husbands and wives.

It is commonly accepted that mantra can be learned only from a guru, who in turn has learned it from his guru, and so on back in an unbroken line to the seer to whom it was given and who first uttered it. Mantra taken out of an unbroken, direct verbal tradition is not alive. Mantra cannot be learned from a book, and an overheard mantra has no power. However, it is also said that the book itself is guru, and the mantra is transmitted via the book. Another theory is that since mantra is in the universal consciousness, it is the Great Guru himself who bestows the mantra on the individual. I leave the decision to the reader to make.

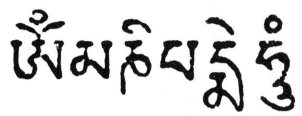

Mantra of Chenresig

OM MAN-NI PAD-ME HUM. This is the mantra of Chenresig, the four-armed herdsman, incarnation of Lord Buddha in Tibet. The mantra is pronounced OM MA NI PAY ME HUNG (ending in a nasal sound). The repetition of it, both in the body and in the world of the dead, can bring an end to the cycle of birth and rebirth and thereby bring one to the gate of nirvana. The literal translation is: "Om! The Jewel in the Lotus! Hum!" But these scant words are the emblem of infinite universes reverberating into eternity.

The Mani-bhak-hbum (which means "History of the Mani [mantra] of Chenresig") says this mantra is "the essence of all happiness, prosperity and knowledge, and a source of great liberation." An analysis of the mantra uncovers the following: OM closes the door to rebirth among the gods; MA, to rebirth among the asuras (titans); NI, among mankind; PAY, among subhuman creatures; ME, among unhappy ghosts or pretas; and HUNG, among the inhabitants of hell. Each of the six syllables has the color of the light path corresponding to the six stages of existence: OM, the white light path of the deva loka, or world of the gods; MA, the green light path of the titan world (asura loka); NI, the yellow light path of the human world (manak loka); PAY, the blue light path of the brute world (tiryaka loka): ME, the red light path of the ghost world (preta loka); and HUNG, the smoky-black light path of the underworld or hell (naraka loka).

[Sir John Woodroffe]* As I write . . . hard by the ancient and desolate Temple to the Sun-Lord at Konāraka in Northern Orissa, a continuous rolling sound like that of the Mahāmantra is borne to me from afar. I heard the same sound many years ago at the Pemiongchi

monastery when some hundred Buddhist monks rolled out from
their bodies the Mantra *Om*. Their chant then suggested the sea,
as the sea now suggests the Mantra. Here where the sound is heard
are green woods, bushes of jasmine, cactus in bloom and the rose
and yellow of the Karavīra and Kalikā flowers. Travelling however
whence it comes some two miles seaward, the eye surveys a wide wild
waste of land, with here and there coarse clumps of Ketaki, stretching from the world-famous Temple of the "Lord of the Universe" in
the South to the Golra jungle on the north. On the eastern edge the
surf of the Bengal Ocean in great waves, marbled with foam with
creaming crests, whipped into filmy vapour by the wind, ceaselessly
beats upon a lonely shore. The waves as all else are Mantra, for
Mantra in its most basal sense is the World viewed as—and in its
aspect of—sound.

"Yantra has mantra as its soul. The deity is the soul of the mantra.
The difference between mantra and deity is similar to that between
a body and its soul." Thus the Kaulāvalīyam yantra is the visual form

Two versions of the most celebrated of all yantras. It is known either as Sri
Yantra or Sri Chakra of Devi (or Tripurasundari, the resplendent beauty).
Representing cosmic dynamics, this yantra is identical with Shakti, the supreme
deity of yantrins. When called Sri Chakra, it is the Wheel of Fortune.

of mantra. Yantras are said to be the basis of all writing, through the original ideograms by which man first put word to a surface. Though two-dimensional, yantras must be conceived of as having depth and full dimension. A yantra expresses the inner aspect, the soul of any form of creation, animals as well as men. "There are in the world innumerable yantras," says a commentator on the Kalyana Upanishad. "Every shape, every leaf, every flower is a yantra which, through its shape, color and perfume, tells the story of creation to us." A Vedic book says: "Vishnu should always be worshipped in water, fire, a heart, discus or the yantra which represents him." All the basic geometric figures (point, triangle, straight line, square, circle, hexagon), along with the lotus, can be combined in a yantra to represent particular forces or qualities inherent in the cosmos. Just as each diety has a mantra, he or she also has a yantra. The mantra is the soul, the yantra the body of the deity, and the three are considered inseparable. The yantra is drawn with a diamond-tipped gold needle by those who can afford it, using a metallic substance as the surface. The poor do the best they can with a thorn on parchment or a leaf. The effectiveness of a yantra can be increased if the needle or thorn is dipped in Kula pushpa.*

Yantra is but a corpse without mantra, and
mantra is the jiva of yantra.
Devata is her jiva. Worshipped in yantra she is instantly pleased.

And why is this form called yantra?
Because she regulates, subdues all misery arising
from desire, anger and lust and other failings.
As the body is to the soul
yantra is the home of all the deities.
Therefore draw yantra
        meditate upon her auspicious form
know everything from the mouth of guru and worship according to
        rule.
If worship is done without proper yantra
then it can only bring down the curse of the devata.
Each deity is to be carefully installed in her own yantra
and worshipped with all the proper attributes.

Should you be light-headed and call one devata but worship another
you shall receive the curses of both.
Each deity is to be received with the proper honor,
with the mantra and yantra proper to its order.

The human body is the city of Brahmam, Brahma-pura, enlivened by three and a half crores of nadis (a crore is ten million). A nadi, in ordinary usage, is a nerve artery, but in yogic teaching it is a subtle channel of energy. There are fourteen principal nadis, three of which concern us now. The most important is sushumna, which lies in the hollow of the cerebral-spinal axis. It extends from the muladhara lotus, or chakra (which I will describe presently), to the sahasrara padma, or thousand-petaled lotus, in the top of the skull. Outside and coiled around sushumna are the nadis ida and pingala. Ida exists in the left nostril, and pingala in the right. Ida is pale and moonlike and contains nectar, while pingala is red and sunlike and contains venom, the fluid of mortality. The three nadis, each of which represents a sacred waterway—sushumna is the Sarasvati, ida, the Ganges; and pingala, the Yamuna—flow like rivers into the ajna chakra, the Third Eye which is also the Tenth Door.

There are six (major) dynamic centers in the body, the chakras, which are capped by the thousand-petaled lotus, the sahasrara padma. Each chakra is connected with a particular section of the anatomic nerves and controls its subconscious activities. Since the chakras are vital to spiritual development, it is necessary to control and purify them. When they are thoroughly cleansed they resume their original glow and the properties lying dormant within them are released. This is known as "awakening of the chakras." With the chakras cleansed and alert, our passage to the higher and finer states of superconsciousness is possible. A forceful awakening of the chakras, however, negates the ascent, and the result is brute power and the practice of trickery—walking on water, flying in the air, standing unhurt in fire, and other extranormal capacities in place of subtleness.

The six Chakras

The chakras are generally described as follows:

Muladhara is a triangular space in the midmost part of the body, situated between the base of the sexual organ and the anus, with the apex turned downward like a young girl's yoni. It is described as a red lotus of four petals, pointing in the four directions and containing the four forms of bliss—yoga bliss, supreme bliss, natural bliss, and vira bliss. In the center is the svayambhu linga, ruddy brown like the color of a young leaf. Muladhara is the root of sushumna and the base on which Kundalini rests. The goddess Kundalini, luminous as lightning, lies asleep coiled like a serpent around the lingam and closes the door of Brahman with her body. Kundalini pervades, supports, and is expressed in the form of the entire universe. She is the Glittering Dancer, and it is She who gives birth to the world made of mantra.

Svadhisthanan is a six-petaled lotus at the base of the sexual organ, between muladhara and the navel. In the six petals are the vrittis credulity, suspicion, disdain, delusion, false knowledge, and mercilessness.

Mani-puri-chakra is a ten-petaled golden lotus in the region of the navel. On the petals are the vrittis shame, fickleness, jealousy, desire, laziness, sadness, dullness, ignorance, disgust, and fear. Within the lotus is the red, four-handed figure of Agni, Lord of Fire, seated on a ram, and before him is Rudra (a form of Shiva) and his Shakti, Bhadra-kali. Rudra, old and vermilion-colored, is smeared with ashes and has three eyes. Near him is the four-armed Lakini-Shakti, the color of molten gold, her mind maddened with passion. Above the lotus is the abode of Surya, the Sun God, who drinks the nectar dripping from the region of the moon.

Nanata is a deep red lotus with twelve petals in the region of the heart, with the vrittis hope, anxiety, endeavor, possession, arrogance, languor, conceit, discrimination, covetousness duplicity, indecision, and regret. Within the lotus is Ishvara, the Overlord of the lower chakras, and His Shakti, Bhuvanesvari. Isvara, the color of molten gold, grants blessings and dispels fear. Adjacent to him is Kalini Shakti, lustrous as lightning, with four hands holding the noose of desire and a drinking cup, and making the sign of blessing which dispels fear; she wears a garland of human bones and is excited, though her heart is softened with wine.

Vishuddha chakra is the abode of the goddess of speech and is located at the base of the throat. The lotus is the color of fire seen through smoke. The lotus contains the regions of the full moon and the ether, and of the gods within, the foremost is Shiva, white, with five faces, three eyes, ten arms, dressed in tiger skins.

The sixth chakra is ajna, the two-petaled lotus situated between the eyes and slightly above them. Ajna chakra lacks an element, as the five known to man (earth, water, fire, air, and ether) are situated in the lower chakras, but it contains the celebrated mantra OM. Also resident in ajna chakra are the triad Brahma, Vishnu, and Shiva. The deity enclosed is Kali as Hakini, with six heads and four arms. In three of her hands she displays a skull, a drum, and a rosary; the fourth is held up in the jnana mudra, the gesture of knowledge, with the first finger raised and the others closed. It is through ajna chakra (known also as Third Eye) that the soul leaves in samadhi and, as the Gita tells us, in death.

Above all chakras is sahasrara padma, the Thousand-Petaled lotus of all colors, which hangs downward from the brahma randhra. This is the region of the first cause, and of the great Sun which is both cosmic and individual. Here the Supreme Guru resides. Here the atma, resplendent as ten million suns and deliciously cool as ten million moons, is united with the Devi Kundalini in the joy which is known as the supreme bliss: it is the union of Shiva and Shakti.

Kundalini is awakened in the following manner: The yogi sitting in asana stops the ears, eyes, nostrils, and mouth with his fingers. Meditating upon the chakras in order, beginning with the lowest, he arouses Kundalini by the mantra HUM HANSA and raises her to the sahasrara. Pervaded by Shakti and in blissful union with Shiva, he meditates upon himself, being the result of that union, as Bliss itself and the Brahman. This coition of Kundalini with Shiva produces nectar which floods the human body. Thus the yogi, forgetful of all in this world, is immersed in ineffable bliss.

[Ear and eye, the esoteric teachings of Sant Mat, Radha Soami Satsang, or the yoga of sound, known as shabad yoga.* Meditation begins by concentration on the space between the eyebrows. The first sign that shabad meditation is valid is when the sound of a bell is heard. The adept is likely to experience a sensation of ascent.]

The True Name of God is not a word or phrase but a transcendent Celestial Music or Divine Harmony called Nam, Bani, or Anhad Shabad—in other words, Name, Word, or Limitless Sound. Only a living contemporary saint, that is, a perfect guru, could connect our soul with this Divine Music which is God's True Name. Guru is equal to God; we should give our deepest and most profound love and devotion to him.

The manifestation of God in the Astral World is in the form of a Flame of Light with one thousand tongues. By the practice of shabad yoga, the mind realizes its oneness with the transcendent Flame. Above is the Causal World, in which God manifests Himself in the form of the Reddish Sun of Brahma or Om. Our mind in its finest root-form originated there.

But our soul is still higher: it is in essence the same as Satnam (True Name) in Sach Kand (known also among orthodox Hindus as Satya Loka, the Heavenly Sphere). Body and mind are merely covers over the soul and are used by it as means or instruments for its work in the physical and mental spheres. As we move about the material world with our gross material body, so, similarly, with the astral body we work in the Astral World and in the Causal Region with the causal body. Above that, in the realms of Parabhrama and Sach Kand (beyond Niranjan and Brahama) we work with pure Soul or Spirit.

If we want to go out of the delusion and darkness of maya and attain salvation, we should try to find this transcendent shabad. ("Without Shabad the soul is blind," said Kabir.* "It cannot find the way to Shabad; again and again it wanders in delusion.") Shabad is true kirtan. Kirtan is ever going on inside the head of man and can be heard if we concentrate our consciousness on the Third Eye behind the two external eyes. Then only can we be said to have real kirtan. In Kali yuga (the present age) it is especially effective, and no other sort of kirtan or any other spiritual practice is so suitable.

It is more or less the nature of our mind to wander about and not to sit still for a moment. If we enter the Tenth Door (the same as the Third Eye), which can be achieved by the practice of shabad, then it can become still and motionless. We shall then behold in it the face of the Lord, just as still water reflects trees, buildings, and so on, standing on the bank. The clearer the water, the clearer shall be the reflection. Similarly, the more motionless the mind, the clearer the vision of God.

When, after initiation by a perfect guru, we begin practicing the Word, i.e., shabad, we listen to internal sounds. First we hear confused sounds like those of a flowing river, a running train, or showers of rainfall. Gradually the sounds change into those of the insect cicada (binda) and of small tinkling bells; that is, a metallic ring is heard. Finally, when our concentration has reached a high pitch we hear the clear sound of a big bell, resounding and reverberating. That is the first real sound of shabad. It has a great power of attraction: it draws the soul up and into the Third Eye in the Astral Plane. From plane to plane the sound changes, until the soul reaches the Fifth Stage of Sach Kand, which is our True Home, and where it appears as the notes of a transcendent bagpipe.

When the soul of a man reaches Sach Kand, it merges with Sat Nam and becomes one with Him. It then goes forever beyond the quality of opposites that is found in the world of phenonomena. The soul itself becomes the ultimate Absolute Lord. In that state of eternal Bliss, Good and Evil, Right and Wrong, Pleasure and Pain, Worry and non-Worry, and all such distinctions vanish.

God and saints are one to such an extent that nobody can distinguish between them: and no one can say which is which, i.e.,

which is God and which the saint. Both become identically the same. "In me hath my Father manifested Himself. Inseparably have the Father and son been united. When the son hath known the Father, O Nanak, the Father and the son have got colored in the same radiance," we read in Bhairo.

Sat Nam is the final Lord of all creatures and beings. Ultimately it is by Him that all universes are created, sustained and dissolved, and it is under His final command that countless Brahmans, Vishnus, and Shivas do their work. "Millions of Vishnus take incarnation; millions of universes are His temples; millions of Shivas are created and destroyed; millions of Brahmas are put to making worlds. Millions of Dissolutions and Creations in an instant." (Thus Bhairo again.)

In our body there are various focuses. By concentrating on them we make contact with different planes of consciousness or regions of creation. In the spiritual practice of shabad yoga we first collect our consciousness in the focus of the Third Eye and then take it up to higher, subtler centers. Thus we cross the portal of death while still living in this world. (Sri Rag: "Where goeth man after death? O die thou in that place while living.")

When a man is on his deathbed, first his conscious current is withdrawn from his hands, feet, etc., and then it comes into his eyes and goes behind the eyes toward the Third Eye. By the practice of shabad yoga we achieve this state while still alive. Although the conscious current leaves the physical world and goes into the astral and higher, subtler planes, our connection with our body is not snapped, and our breathing, though slowed, continues uninterrupted, unlike the samadhi in pranayama. Thus by shabad yoga we learn to take our soul out of the body—how to die while still living—moving about in subtle transcendent planes, and then come back into the body. (Maru: "Who dieth by Shabad, perfect is that man; the brave Satguru uttereth and maketh him listen to this transcendent music. Within the body is true Amritsar [tank of nectar, the Sikh's sacred center of worship, a symbol and copy of the Heavenly Nectar], and with love and devotion doth the mind drink of it.")

To make contact with Shabad we have to withdraw our consciousness from the Nine External Openings of our body (eyes, ears, nostrils, the mouth, the urinary organ, and the anus) and then open the hidden Tenth Door (which is midway between the eyes and a little inward). Through Shabad which is heard inside our body, we come to know the Reality of all things and beings. (Mahj: "In this body are innumerable things. He who hath Truth—i.e., Shabad— bestowed upon him by a Guru, he does behold them. Nine doors are manifest but Salvation lieth in the secret Tenth, where ringeth Anhad Shabad.")

When the soul of a man is concentrated in his eyes, he begins to see lights, first like the glow of a burning charcoal, then of lightning, and finally a big shining star appears. Everyone who goes inside sees it as he enters the Astral Region. After that other stars appear, and we see a whole starry sky. Then appear the sun and the moon, beyond which our Guru stands in his Astral Radiant Form, waiting for us. Then we see a lotus, which opens up, and sheds beams of light which shows us the Inner Reality of things. (Maru: "Blossometh the Lotus and out cometh a ray of Light, which showeth us Reality made manifest.")

This flame is called Jyoti or Jyoti Saroop Bhagwan, that is, God in the form of Fire of Light. This spiritual Flame is so charming that it at once captures the mind. Everyone who goes inside himself and reaches this point shall see this Flame. It has one thousand wicks, with the chief or biggest in the center, and it sustains all creation that lies below. It is a superconscious Being, the astral form of God. Inner transcendent Lights are all due to the Anhad Shabad. We listen to this, its Divine Harmony, then we behold the inner Lights also; and in that Light we see the spiritual objects of subtle planes and attain transcendent knowledge.

The spiritual sound of the Bell of God in the Astral Flame draws the soul up. We have to undergo, while living, the process of death (so far as conscious current of the soul is concerned), if we want to have access into these subtle planes during our lifetime. We have to die before our death, so to speak, and shabad yoga teaches us that method of doing so. Shabad is the essence of all Reality; it is the Life of all lives, and the inner Being of all beings.

WHO YOU WERE,
ARE NOW
AND WHAT YOU WILL BE

From time to time certain interested and sympathetic Westerners, charmed by our cosmic vision and our grasp of the eternal, want to become Hindus. What they cannot understand, and what we seem to be incapable of expressing clearly for fear of hurting their feelings, is that there is no way to become Hindu but to be born Hindu. There is no such thing as conversion. A man is born Hindu because he has earned the honor as the result of his past karma, a reward for good actions and for propitiating the gods.

If your actions are evil, even as a Hindu, you are likely to be born something else lower down on the scale, perhaps as an American.

[The Baroness] Well, on Tuesday I went to see someone who interprets Brighu—let me explain—a muni, that is, a sage, 4,000 years ago or so they say, so wise that our Lord Krishna took his foot impression on his chest (but that is another story). Anyway, Bannerjee's calculations are fantastic, obviously done in the Sanskrit alphabet. He says everything about me. My name, ancestry, Prabhu's name, my children, our marriage [not happy, from outside appearances]. My present set-up, and what is so fantastic, Norben. He features much more prominently than Prabhu in my life, because he is a connection, says Brighu, from my previous life.

My last life reads like a super-romantic short story and is quite logical as a preface to the merits of this life. (You'll think I made it up, but my uncle [a sadhu] was with me and he'll bear me out.) I was born near a river in Bengal—in the same sort of home and same caste, etc., as I am now. I was married very early to a very cruel and rakish husband who died the year of our marriage. We had no children, and I took up religion. A foreign merchant came that way. He was also very spiritually inclined, and I fell in love with him. He went to a Buddhist country near China and took up Buddhism. I followed him and he asked me to leave because I was acting against society, but finally he succumbed and we lived together for a short while. Then he got word from home that his parents had died and his house had burned, so he left to settle his affairs and died on the way. This left me absolutely desolate and grief-stricken and I took up religion, but since my meditations were not free from desire I had to be reborn, and since we never really said goodbye he too was reborn. So this is now a life of renouncement for us both, and with proper meditation we can be released.

You know it is quite logical—you know how much I wanted children—my indifference to Prabhu and this peculiar attachment to Norben [he is a Buddhist from Bhutan]. I have never found him strange. In fact, I've always told my friends that I felt he was a part of my previous life. I know you won't laugh like my husband, and I hope I get an opportunity to tell Norben.

[Theresa, a Christian woman] I have some friends, like me, Indian Christians, who have a boy who was crippled by polio when he was very young. A very desperate situation. The doctors could do nothing. The parents went to a Brighu reader who said that by the age of twenty-two the boy would be cured and by twenty-six no one would ever know that he had been sick he would be so robust. This boy is now twenty and almost cured.

In my own case I met a Hindu boy named Suresh. We fell in love and wanted to get married. His family fought the idea bitterly, since I am from another community and they are very orthodox Hindus. So his mother finally went to a Brighu reader, who told her that it had been written that her son would marry a woman from another community, would have two children, and that she would fall into poor health early in marriage but would have an operation and would recover. As the results of the reading, Suresh's parents saw that it was all foreordained and that nothing they could do would stop us from marrying. So far everything the reader said has come true.

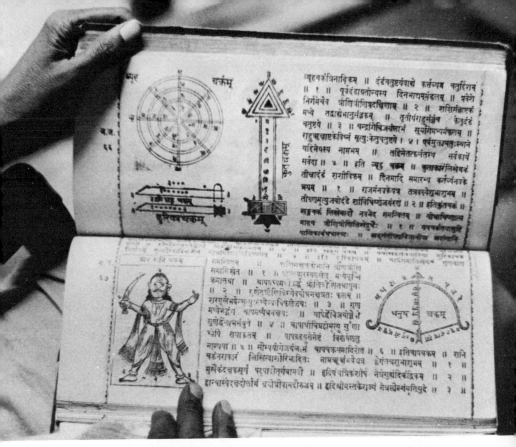

A page from the Brighu Samhita

Mr. Biswanath Bannerjee is a reader of the Brighu Samhita. The Baroness says he is one of only two such readers nowadays in India, and is the better one, the other (who lives in the Punjab) not being very skillful. However, I have heard about others beyond Bannerjee and the Punjabi (there must be half a dozen in Benares alone) and wonder who is really expert and who is imitation. Bannerjee has a small office near the Kalighat in Calcutta, where he receives clients and interprets their lives in the light of Brighu's teachings. The Baroness has been bringing all her friends, even the foreigners, to Bannerjee, and everyone seems to be impressed by what they have learned. Bannerjee begins with a blank slate—he doesn't even know the client's name, but finds it, and all other pertinent material, in the Brighu books. He can do this even with foreigners; for example, he found the name of a Polish woman in Brighu, spelled out in phonetic Sanskrit.

According to Bannerjee, Brighu lived ten thousand years ago. "He was God in disguise," says Bannerjee. "He sat on his haunches for twenty years in a room, and then everything came to him, the wonderful vision of everyone who was to be born, no matter where or when. He had an insight into all mankind to live until the end of time. Everything was an astronomical calculation." Brighu wrote it all down, in a series of pages which are to be read in the light of one's horoscope. There are some two hundred printed volumes, though some readers work with loose manuscript pages. The text is in Sanskrit. Bannerjee would like to have the Brighu Samhita translated into Hindi, Bengali, and English and published, but there is no interest in the project and he fears that with his death (though he is trying to teach a disciple to read the book) the Brighu Samhita will be a lost art. He admits that there is a "not so good" interpreter in Benares named Pandit Muranarali Ghar Shastri, but he feels that the book will disappear. In the past, Nepal was the storage center for the many volumes; the main seat of study was Benares, and its propagation spread from Bengal, Bengalis, apparently, being the most skillful interpreters.

[Biswanath Bannerjee] After taking birth, some people make no progress. God corrects a man at each of the seven births. Eventually everyone will go into the One. Moksha, the final emancipation, comes from the Omnipotent. Only the One is there—from the many comes the One. Our Vedas say, "I am only One but I divide myself into many." This is called Vishnarupa. In the Gita, Arjuna received that vision. He realized that all his kith and kin would die, and said, "If they die, what futility there is in taking life!" But Krishna says: "You are from me, and from me there are many. Every man comes from me and goes to me."

As soon as our duties are over, by one birth, two births, many births, then we come to Him. All the universe goes to a sea. We are coming from that ocean and we are going to that ocean. You can see the light, jyoti, but the light has no shape. When a man realizes that stage, he cannot describe it.

We are nothing but maya. When illusion goes, we come to Him. That is the reason we remain in this life. As soon as we take birth, maya comes to us, overwhelms us. Our philosophers say that when a baby takes birth, as soon as he cries, birth is perfected. His cry comes—Why? He is coming from the One. Now he is many. "O, God, why have You sent me here?" Then maya comes and he forgets everything.

Maya is nothing but the Divine Force of God. But God has no shape. There is no shape to God. Whatever shape of God a man likes he can take.

Why is the cycle necessary? This cannot be answered fully. It is the Lord's wish. It is His play, what we call lila. He likes to play.

I suffer, the Lord suffers. You suffer. Within you the Lord is there. Nobody can explain His wish, can tell us why things take place. The Gita says, "Who takes birth must die. He who comes must go. You have no choice." That is clearly said by Lord Krishna in the Gita. God stays within the heart of everyone. A man has no choice for himself. God has come to play here—the earth is His playground—and when He has played, He goes.

All this is charted by Brighu, one birth, two births, many births, He tells us what is our past, our karma, and with this knowledge we can be free of the cycle and become the One. This is why Brighu is so important. From our past we know our future.

[E. C. H. Edwards] The Baroness brought me to see Biswanath Bannerjee. He lives in a little cubbyhole on Sadananda Road, off a main avenue near the Ujjala movie house, in the general direction of the Kalighat. He sits bare-chested (with the sacred thread draped around him) behind a huge leather-topped desk, surrounded by an incredible mess of books, pictures of saints, holy men, and astrological calendars. He's very serious, like a kind of professor of an obscure subject, but there are little twinkles in his eyes. He's quite broad-chested and broad-shouldered. The Baroness tells me that he was once, as a young man, a good oarsman and swimmer, a rarity among Indians, who frequent rivers but can't swim. We sit there in the semidarkness, in the light of a fifteen-watt bulb. The Baroness stays for a few minutes, to get the reading moving. But she is afraid something too personal might appear, so after a while she slips away. Bannerjee doesn't know my name when I appear. The B had

merely said she was bringing a foreign friend. He pulls out a few old books and shuffles them about. Then he looks at my hand and asks the date of my birth. He wants to know the hour when I was born. I don't know. He decides: three A.M. How do you know? I ask. "You were born at night. I can tell. Three o'clock." Sounds like early morning to me, I remark. "Three A.M. is night for us."

Bannerjee shuffles the books again and opens up one, full of crumbling, torn pages taped together. He draws up my horoscope, with a lot of cross lines and little secret notations, and confers with the book. He seems pleased. Then he says he will tell me my name. He tracks down the initial syllable, then comes to the full name: Edmund. This is from the Sanskrit, I realize. He announces he will find my father's name. A longer search, as he becomes puzzled, then he realizes we both have the same name. "Father's name is Edmund, too?" says Bannerjee, looking pleased with himself. Yes. Mother's next. Takes longer. I am becoming impatient. He says, "Mother's name is Elyse." No. But he sticks with Elyse. I tell him he is close (it was Elsie) and think he can change the syllables slightly and be correct. But he sticks to Elyse and suddenly says: "It was Elizabeth." Which it was, actually; she had been baptized Elizabeth but changed her name to Elsie as a teen-ager. Then, he finds my ex-wife's name, Pearl. This search has taken half an hour. I think: I'm paying this fellow fifty chips for him to tell me what I already know. But the information flows rapidly after this.

Tells me I am divorced, giving the dates of separation and final papers quite accurately. Says P has a quick temper. (Who am I to deny that?) All the while he is flipping through the book. Now he pulls out another. The pages are torn and stuffed back into the binding with tape. Behind him are dozens, perhaps two hundred volumes, of the same set, but he seems to work with only two or three. Are the others relevant? Is it all a big hoax?

Says I was cheated by people I trusted. Yes, that is true. Some acquaintances of ten years' standing bought into my business. When it was all over, they had all the assets and I was out without a cent. "Sorry, Edmund, but that is life." Drinking pals.

Tells me the years 57, 58 will be good. The peak will be 56. (A long time to wait.) I will meet a woman who will first be an intellectual companion. Then marriage. We will be together the rest of my life. I will die suddenly, at 70, 72. No pain. "It is better that way," says Bannerjee. "If you are sick you cannot even get a glass of water for yourself." Number-two wife will live five years beyond me. My work will bring me "fame and fortune."

In my previous incarnation (this is the part I always like to hear) I was an Indian. Not all of what he says is clear. (I went back another day to ask him for details, but by that time he had forgotten, or said he had, and I suspect he was afraid of contradicting himself. What goes on, eh Bannerjee?) So I was an Indian. (Later, the B asks, what caste? It was a question that never occurred to me, the caste.) Brighu/Bannerjee tells me I was torn between marrying and caring for my parents and becoming a sannyasi. The eternal Indian dilemma. Instead I threw over all the options and became involved with a foreign woman. A bad woman, says Bannerjee. The woman may have been English. This would set the date of my previous birth within the past three hundred years, perhaps within the last century, when English women appeared more frequently. As punishment for my sins I was reborn an American. Such bad luck! I can see that Bannerjee feels sorry for me. His gentle features assume a look of compassion.

But not all is lost. He informs me that I can remove the curse by doing eleven days' puja or sacrifice, otherwise I am likely to go on suffering for many rebirths before I work out my karma. If I propitiate the gods, all will be well. That is, I can be reborn an Indian in the next birth. Now is the propitious time for puja, Bannerjee says. (We are in the feast of Durga Puja; Durga is a form of Kali, the great goddess.) Bannerjee tells me a few more inconsequential things (one being that my son had an accident to his leg recently; in checking about, this seems to be standard, one's son banging up his leg), but both of us return to the subject of puja. Bannerjee has made me very nervous. Do I want to go on suffering as a Westerner when I can be reborn an Indian?

Puja, says Bannerjee, will cost four or five hundred rupees. If I know mankind, it will be easily five hundred, and up. There are always those unexpected extras, even in puja when one's soul is at stake, one's eternal happiness by being reborn an Indian and not a Westerner. Five hundred chips would be about sixty-five dollars, if you are honest and deal at the official rate. Otherwise about $50 on the street. Isn't one's eternal future worth $50? "Puja is very expensive," says Mr. Bannerjee, confirming that it will be at least five hundred rupees. "We will need silver plates and brass pots, and since you don't know the prayers we will have to hire two priests to pray for you for the first ten days. You must be present on the last day." One can't be a cheapskate when his soul's fate hangs on such a slender thread. I pick up the Baroness and tell her the whole story. She says, "No, no puja," when we discuss it. First sensible thing I've got out of her. But I do worry about my next birth.

[E. C. H. Edwards with another Brighu reading] Just to check one version of Brighu against another, I went to a reader in Benares whom I met through a Mr. Gosh, a disciple of the yogini Anandamayee Ma, at her ashram. This reader is Pandit Devakinandan Shastri. He has a cubbyhole on Swarsati Phatak, which is one of the most crowded tiny streets of the old city. It is about the width of a man's outstretched arms and is jammed with people, cows, cow dung and urine, marigold petals strewn all over, Shiva phalluses, children, lepers, and pilgrims. Bannerjee had told me that there was only one reader in Benares—he hadn't mentioned this Shastri—so I was surprised to see signs for several.

Shastri's office is on a platform about waist high, opening onto the alleyway. There are large shuttered doors, which are pulled back during the day. We sit cross-legged on large white cotton covered mats. Shastri is a slick cat and radiates insincerity. A marked contrast to Bannerjee. He wants fifty chips for the reading. His Brighu book is not bound like Bannerjee's collection but is a loose collection of single sheets handwritten in Sanskrit. He shuffles them about, looking, I suppose, for the right phrase to fit any ESP he picks up from the supplicant. I insist, much to his annoyance, in writing down the reading word for word. I won't repeat it all for fear of boring everyone—much of it is quite repetitious—but the salient points will follow.

This Brighu reading takes the form of a dialogue between a sage and his son, who asks questions about the man born on the date and time of the particular horoscope, according to what Brighu, son of Lord Brahma, has said about him. Shastri got my birth date and set the hour at three-thirty A.M., then drew up the following chart. Each number refers to a particular planetary influence, but I will skip such details.

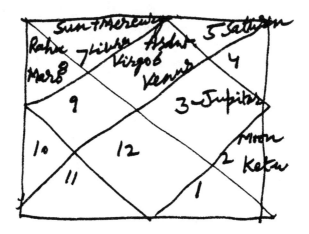

Shastri tells me that according to Brighu I was born in a Western land, which is America. Our hemisphere had not yet been discovered by the civilized world in Brighu's time, but Brighu knew about it because an asura, a kind of god or antigod, had been there to bring it within the scope of ancient India. The land was referred to as Maya, which, as everyone knows, is also the term for illusion. Make of it what you will. "But we know Maya and America same place," says Shastri. He then tells me that my "grandfather was famous in his village" (New York—some village!), etc. Father poor but hard-working. Tells me, "You are man of good character, kindness in heart, sweetness in tongue," and so on. (If you want to be well flattered, see Shastri.)

Family problems are foreseen by Brighu, but "without worship of goddess Durga there will be no happiness." I must admit he gets some facts right: two children, a divorce, etc., the effects of my past births giving me a lot of ups and downs in life, successes, failures, a rocky road. Various key dates turn up correctly. "At age twenty-eight you were married," Brighu/Shastri says. "You wife very beautiful, fair in color and health and education and very fickle, and by her fickleness there was the frenzy of ideas between you and wife. Only two childs by first wife but if you do the puja of Mother Durga you will get happiness from other or second wife. Without worship there will be no happiness through your wife's side. By worship you will get six childs, three son, three daughter." Various problems are added, but "If you wear talisman prepared according to Brighu, then you will get some peace of mind." This seems to be the point of the reading, because he hammers away at it, or Brighu does. "For your mental peace you should wear the talisman and worship the goddess Durga, and then you should try to remarry with a widow and then your life will be happy. That widow will be a tall figure and there will be no child with her and she will be simple educated with sweet health and charming and attractive qualities." And so on. And, "There will be starving and penniless position, but the fame will always be with you."

Now the previous birth: "Born in Persia in family of Persian king." But—the inevitable—I made "illegal connection with that girl your friend's sister and that girl became with baby and killed herself." As did the girl's parents from shame, who died cursing me so badly that I was reborn an American. Shastri looks shocked at the magnitude of the sin and the punishment, and I assume Brighu must have wept when he wrote those lines. My transition into the New World came when I was killed while hunting. There is no way out of the bad karma but to wear the talisman and worship the goddess Durga.

Brighu/Shastri continues: "This person [me] would go to the bank of the holy river in India and till worshiping period he will lie on the earth and he will take the fruits in his pudding after taking the cow's dung and urine and milk and curd and ghee." This is known as Panch Gauya, the five materials obtained from the cow, which of course is sacred. Panch Gauya, by way of explanation, is a common method of propitiation for sinners, such as those people who lose caste by going overseas and want to be restored to their caste. Brighu says I must obtain a gold image of Durga weighing one or two tolas (a tola is one thirty-second of an ounce) and repeat the following mantra:

OM. EM AM HRIM KLIM AM CHUM CHANDIKAYAI NAMAHAN PURWA PAPM NASAYA NASAYA DAR PUTRADIKUM SOUKHYAN DEHI DEHI HANI-CHINTA DARI DRUM KADARPI MADAHI MADAHI SARWAN KAMAN DEHI DEHI MUDHE MARKANDIDAN KORU KORU SARWAN KAMAN PURE PURE SARWAH OM CHUM AM KLIM RIM EM. OM.

Shastri was very scratchy about my writing it down, and it may not be completely correct. It translates roughly as follows: "We pray to goddess Durga you should excuse my past sins and you should give me happiness of wife and family and make disappear my poverty and loss of wealth and don't slow my progress in life and fullfil my heart's desire. O Mother Durga, I bow to you." The mantra is to be said twenty-five thousand times. After that there will be hawana, which is a sacred libation poured into a certain type of fire; the embers are read for auspicious or inauspicious signs. Then, "pleadings to the Brahmins." I should take a bath from water brought in a pot from Kailasa, a sacred mountain in Tibet. If I do this puja there will be but two more births. I will die in my eighties and be reborn in China—an upward move—and then will be born in India in a family of Brahmins. "After that there will be no birth."

Nirvana.

Then we get down to business. What is to save me from the endless chain of birth and rebirth in America, with its depressions, wars, pollution, housing shortages, rent gougers, materialism, greed, corruption, X-rated movies, divorces, credibility gaps, and so on? "Goddess Durga will save." One hundred and twenty-five chips for the talisman is what Brighu/Shastri wants. It is to be a container of copper, silver, or gold. "I put mantra in it. Two thousand rupees for puja. We do puja in room my house or in hotel or cellar. I chose five pandits to pray. I wear silk dhoti and chadda [shawl], pandits same." They will fast each day until the puja is over. I must sleep on the ground—no bed or cot. I will eat only fruit, milk, "corn"—no rice, meat, or fish—and a halwah made of pani phal, which is water chestnuts. The pandits will get twenty chips a day, Shastri one hundred.

I pay Shastri the fifty chips we had agreed upon. He asks for another ten. "You set the price," I say, "why should I pay more?" I tell him that I am a poor man, as Brighu has said. Would he take money from a poor man? "Rich man, poor man, I take money." Even from a poor man? "Even from a poor man."

Mr. Gosh reappears. He wants to know the news. "Such poor karma," he says. "You must do puja. My brother had bad karma like yours, but I did puja for him. Nine hundred rupees, but now he is a happy man." I said I would have to think about it. "Isn't your happiness worth two thousand rupees?" demands Mr. Gosh. Two thousand rupees is only two hundred dollars on the black market, and I couldn't make up my mind if I should pay it and be reborn a

Chinese and then a Brahmin and attain nirvana, or go on suffering as a miserable American or worse. I still don't know.

[S.C., an Englishwoman in her thirties] Shastri was very funny, I thought. He got most of the past facts wrong and waffled an awful lot about the future. I was there three hours and left bored and 50 rupees less. The only interesting part of the whole experience was the insight one got into Indian hopes and aspirations. He kept going on about my brother's wife and other such trivia. Hell, she lives seven thousand miles away and has no influence on my life at all!! A very Indian concern that would be for an unmarried woman. Told me to do a five-day puja on the banks of the Ganga. Drink cow piss and all that to Durga, and then I could find happiness through husband and child. Said these things were lacking because in last life I'd been a very Don Juanish German who had impregnated many ladies and not married them. Treated my wife badly, etc., so one impregnated virgin cursed me and that is why in this life I am an unmarried woman! Next time around I shall be an Indian.

[Editor] Being born a foreigner is a step down. Don't kid yourself: the ideal, the only way to salvation, is to be born an Indian, a male Indian of the Brahmin caste. Just to proffer an objective opinion, I asked an Indian woman (a Brahmin) which was worse, being born an American man or an Indian woman as the result of one's sins. "Indian lady worse than American man," she said. To be born an Indian male is the height of everybody's ambition, *everyone*, including insects, cats, dogs, cows, women. Americans (so Indians think) are dying to be born an Indian.

[E. C. H. Edwards] Juhu Beach, north of Bombay. Sikh—burned black by the sun, right incisor missing, bloodshot eyes, about five feet six in height, wearing a flowered turban, blue shirt, dark trousers, yellow plastic sandals, and the usual Sikh bangle on his arm—comes up from the side as I walk northward along the sand and says, "You are a lucky man." I reply, "Yes, I know," having talked to him the previous year. I continue walking, dropping him behind. On my return he comes alongside again. "Lucky man," he says again. I have nothing to do, and know his routine, so I decide to go along with him. Tells me to think of a number between one and ten, meanwhile writing something on a tiny slip of paper, which he puts in my hand. I am thinking of seven, and sure enough, when I open the paper there is the number seven. Last year he had also told me to think of a flower. I thought: nirgiz, which is both the name of a flower and a common name for Indian girls, but I couldn't think of what flower it would be in English. My mind was turned, forced, overpowered into thinking rose. And when I opened the paper it said rose.

Now he looks at my palm. Will live to eighty-four. Health, not wealth. Make money but can't keep it (how right he is!). I am thinking of a lady, he says (am I not always?). He will tell me her name. He brings out a battered business card, with his name, Mohan Singh, and a list of prices printed across the bottom. Seventy chips, fifty chips, forty chips, depending on the reading. No, not interested, I tell him, knowing that he will press and I will bargain. He keeps referring to my palm. In the hospital once, he tells me. Right. Whenever he is correct we shake hands. He asks me to think of a fruit. I think, pomegranate (last year it was orange, which he guessed). I keep my mind steeled, determined not to let him force me from pomegranate. He remarks that I am not concentrating. I am thinking of the lady and not the fruit, he says. "How many letters in the fruit?" I count on my fingers. Nine. He writes on another scrap of paper and places it between my fingers. He asks if I believe in God. Sometimes. "Only God and I know what I have written on this paper." He is doing several things at the same time; it becomes confusing.

He asks for forty rupees, then thirty. I tell him I will give him five. Ten if he gets the lady's name. We bargain. I am firm. Lady has a round face and a small mark on her right cheek. I know she has a round face, but I can't recall any small mark, much as I try (though last year's lady also had a round face and did have a small mark on her right cheek—am I a freak over round-faced ladies with beauty spots on the right side of the face?). He says there is another man in the picture (there always is, I suspect), but tells me I will win out (I didn't with last year's lady). Meanwhile he has his little packet of tiny slips of paper and is writing. There is some aimless chatter about my age and the lady's. What is lady's name, he wants to know. I tell him. How spelled? I tell him. "Two J's?" Yes, two J's. He seems puzzled. Again he wants to bargain for a better price, but I stick to five rupees, ten if he gets the lady's name. "Open the paper," he says, poking at my hand. I open it up, and there is the lady's name and my age and hers.

I give him ten rupees. He draws a talisman on a scrap of paper and asks for more rupees. I refuse but take the talisman. How can I give him more money when he told me I have none? What about the fruit? I demand. He looks hurt, he cannot tell me. "Stars have changed." Tells me when I go home I will get big money from sweepstakes. Yes, sixty thousand dollars, I say, because this was the figure he gave me last year. He is beginning to look uncomfortable, suspecting I have some psychic powers stronger than his. Lady has pain in chest, is sick in chest, no hospital but sick. Tells me I have four children. I say no, trying to make him guess the right figure. "You have two, lady has two." Right. Tells me about the lady's ex-husband. Right again. Says I am a businessman but is unable to say what business. A lot of handshaking throughout. Wants more money. Shows me some dog-eared grimy letters from other foreigners, one a Dutchman, who wrote thanking him and saying his predictions had come true. I give him a few more chips.

We have been sitting on the sand, talking. People come up and Mohan Singh chases them away. A kid with a monkey won't go. He stays safely out of the reach of Mohan Singh's hand (the old boy seems a bit decrepit, though I learn he is only thirty-six), asking for baksheesh for Charlie. Beat it, I snarl, but the kid and Charlie stay. Mohan Singh says he will take me to his guru. "Nah-ked." The guru has a lock on his left middle finger. "No sleep with ladies. He is yogi."

The next day, along with R, I go to visit Mohan Singh at his flat. He lives in the heart of Bombay near the main post office. He is waiting at the street corner for me and comes up as I am trying to decipher the sign, which is in Devanagari characters. We enter the building. He has rooms on the ground floor on both sides of a damp, poorly lighted corridor where some people are doing their laundry under a weakly running water tap. His wife is waiting, as are his sons and some other people, who go in and out. He takes me into a room which contains a shelf with a shrine and pictures of Guru

Nanak, the founder of the Sikh movement, and some other holy people, and sticks of burning incense and little pots of water and oil. "You pray," orders Mohan Singh. I try to think Cosmic Thoughts, without success. "You give some money." I put ten rupees on the altar. We go across the hall to another room, which is better lighted. Several people are waiting for us. Mohan Singh is not feeling well, that is obvious. "Shits," he says. "Got shits." He is too ill to take me to see his guru, but instead we go by taxi to his temple, a Hindu temple on the edge of the Muslim quarter. It is crowded with men offering puja over a large image of a lion. We take off our sandals and walk up the steps to the lion. Mohan Singh has asked me for money to buy an offering for puja. He scatters a handful of flowers over the lion. The floor, as is usual in Hindu temples, is sopping wet. The lion is covered with orange and white flowers and water and oil, and sticks of incense are burning next to him. Mohan Singh prays and I offer Cosmic Thoughts, wondering about the lady's chest. Then we walk around the interior shrine, where a priest is sitting on the floor in the lotus position and working a fan before the idol, and finally go back to his flat. He is very lethargic. I pick up some Lomotil from my hotel for his shits and return. He seems well enough to carry on a conversation, so I ask: "Who is God?" "God . . . God is everywhere. You believe in God, there is God. No believe, no God. God is in your heart. No need temples, shrines, churches. Only love-sick people go to churches. Not to pray. To find ladies." Meanwhile he keeps begging more money from me. I give him substantial amounts with each major progress in obtaining information. His eyes look very bad, so I tell him he must go to a doctor to find out what is wrong and to have them treated. He says he has been to an aryuvedic doctor. "A Western doctor," I urge. "Will cost three hundred rupees," he says hopefully. He looks at me slyly, his watery eyes blinking.

Another day. I return with R. Mohan Singh says he is offering yogic prayers for the lady's recovery. Says she is not in my country. Where? I want to know. "Philippine side?" he offers tentatively. No. "Germany side?" he says, watching my face. No. I say she is in my country. "But far away." How far away? "Two, three hours . . ." Two hours is close enough. He will pray. We discuss God. "What is God? No people have seen God. If your heart is clear, you pray. God will be happy. You pray honestly. You pray at home. God is

One. Religions are different." He stares at me with his blurred eyes. "Are only two religions. Ladies' religion and gentlemen's religion." My efforts to get this engaging concept clarified are not too successful. "God has given the girl and the man. God has made only two kinds of people." Meanwhile he gets more money from me. He wants me to take a Sikh bangle (I refuse), but I find myself with a yogi stone, cost ten rupees. He tells me he prays (in Hindi) to Guru Nanak. "Man will die. Who makes nice things goes to heaven. Not make nice things, goes to hell. When you are alive God will show you what happens in afterlife so you can choose." His father enters, a wiry old man with flashing eyes. He wants five rupees to be photographed. Then another yogi, Nihal Singh from Orissa, appears. He is a Nanak yogi, from a long line of yogis. In explanation he adds, "Like a padre in the R. C." He wears two bangles in place of the usual one and carries a brass water pot on a cord around his neck. The conversation collapses. Nihal Singh collects five chips from me. None of them seems like a truly "holy" man but more like people who have barely survived and are gurus because that is their profession. Like a padre in the R. C.

[E. C. H. Edwards] On the outskirts of New Delhi. I am visiting a colony of yogis. One of them, identified only as Swamiji, a little old man in a dhoti and kurta with long hair and the albino-like skin ailment called leukodermia, comes up to me and tells me he is seventy-six years old. He looks at my face: "You are searching, searching, searching! You haven't found yet, but you are searching!" As he speaks, he walks back and forth, turning away and then facing about. He asks the date of my birth. I tell him. Since I was born in the twentieth century, the first two figures are a one and a nine. "You take the first numbers, one and nine and you add them together and you get ten," he tells me. "And since you were born on the twenty-third day of the tenth month, you add two and three, which is five, which is half ten and ten is twice five. You see the importance of the number ten in your life?" All the while he has been walking away and spinning around and returning, like a little albino toy. Swamiji informs me that a year before Nixon was elected President he wrote and predicted victory. Now, says Swamiji, "I

have been invited to the White House to stay with Mr. Nixon." I urge him to go, thinking that a little eastern numerology might help stabilize American foreign policy. "Searching!" he exclaims, "you will find!"

Another swami, somebody's relative, insists on reading my palm. Yass, I will be married four times in all, will live to eighty.

Still another reader, this one a sadhu and the Baroness's uncle. We are visiting relatives. The sadhu goes over my palm, delivering a rapid stream of Bengali. A lot of ribald laughter from the women. Am satiated with worldly experiences, he says. A very strong spiritual life. "Will I ever marry again?" I ask.

"No." More rapid Bengali. "What the hell is he saying?" I ask the Baroness. Another burst of ribald laughter. But no translation.

ON THE ROAD
TO NIRVANA

Don't just do something, stand there!

Attributed to Buddha by Baba Ram Dass

Sudhi Babu tells me to sit cross-legged on the couch facing him, eyes open. Says to look at the end of his first finger, to think of nothing else. Holds finger eighteen inches away from my forehead, moves it slowly toward me. Touches my forehead, says to close eyes. I sit for a long time, conscious of nothing but some twitching in my fingers and the sounds in the room and people breathing. Mind seems empty. None of the usual crowd of distracting and irrelevant thoughts and images. I sit for what seems a long time, slowly open my eyes. The room has not changed. Everyone is still there, watching me. (The room is furnished in abominable Bengali: marble sacred cow, on which J's children climb, imitation Western furniture, imitation Indian paintings, including some by a popular artist named Roy in which all the figures have big Kali-like eyes stretching outside the face, very poorly done; but he is a Bengali cultural hero and highly respected.)

Sudhi Babu: "You can practice on a dot. You are not able to begin at a high point. You need to have a symbol or an image to start with, and after that you don't need it. Later on, gradually, the image fades away. That is self-realization. That is God." [?] "Yes, that is God. Any living being is an expression of God. Every person is a separate entity."

Sudhi Babu has high blood pressure. Bunny and Neepa break out laughing when he mentions it and tease him, rather cruelly, I think. How can a sadhu, an enlightened being, suffer such a mundane ailment?

Later I try to sit again in the peace I had attained. Useless.

Tinzhi Gyeltsen, Lama Rinpoche (the latter phrase is a title of respect accorded Tibetan holy men), was a member of the mission of
lamas who found the child identified as the fourteenth Dalai Lama.
In Tibet virtually every monastery is the home of an incarnate lama
or guru who is the descendant of the original founder. A lama who
attains his own liberation often renounces it to be reincarnated for
the benefit of others. Thus the Dalai Lama, whom the Tibetans
prefer to call Gyalwa Rinpoche—who is the incarnation of Chenresig
himself, the deity, the refuge and center of all Tibet—is now in his
fourteenth incarnation. When the greatest of all lamas dies, it is
customary for him to reappear within the next twelve months as a
newborn child. The search for the new Lama,* consequently, is one
of the greatest importance and is bound by an elaborate system of
safeguards against error and fraud (in the last search, at least two
families put forth their children as the new Lama but were rejected).

Tinzhi Gyeltsen's mission was directed to eastern Tibet; other
missions went to other parts of the country. But the east seemed to
be the likely place, because the then regent had seen in the depths
of the sacred lake Lhamo Latso a vision of the village where the
Lama had been born. The mission disguised themselves as plain
pilgrims and set out on foot. In a very poor farming village called
Tengster they asked for shelter in a cluster of houses belonging to
a farm family. An older boy in the family had already been recognized as the incarnation of an ancient and highly honored monk
named Tagster and had been sent to Kumbum monastery to take
Tagster's seat. The family and the village fit the vision exactly, even
to the mottled brown and white mastiff which greeted them. The
lamas stayed briefly, knowing in their hearts that their search was
concluded, but to allay suspicion they pushed eastward and then
returned. The child they had instantly recognized as the fourteenth
Gyalwa Rinpoche had been kept in the background by his parents,
but now he came forward and greeted the lamas as old friends,
talking to them in detail about events at the lamasery at Lhasa, the
Tibetan capital. The lamas had brought with them certain ritual
objects belonging to the previous Great Lama, along with identical
copies. The child immediately picked out the correct ones, demanding to know what the lamas were doing with his own possessions.
The mission's suspicions were confirmed, and the child and his

family were brought to Lhasa. Further tests were made, including the drawing of his name in a kind of lottery, and oracles were consulted. Each time the child was confirmed as the true Lama. He was installed as the fourteenth Dalai Lama and began rigorous training with Tinzhi Gyeltsen as his guru.

In 1940 Tinzhi Gyeltsen came to India, *the* great spiritual and intellectual home for Tibetans, as Tibet is for Indians. He now lives in the Tibetan lamasery in Bodh Gaya, the sacred site where the Lord Gautama Buddha received enlightenment. Tinzhi Gyeltsen (his Indian name is Shasan Dar Dwaj) is now close to eighty and his movements are restricted. He spends most of his time in an upper room in the lamasery, on a cot with his books around him, in meditation. He is slight, almost fleshless, with a bald head. The impression one receives is of a translucent being, radiating an inner light.

There are seven rules to follow in meditation. The best asana is the lotus position (though you may sit any way you like. But lotus is best). Right hand over the left on the lap. Arms straight.

At the time of meditating you should think.

Control your breathing.

Chin in, pushing against the Adam's apple.

Shoulders back.

Eyes slightly opened, so that you see the tip of your nose.

Tongue against the roof of the mouth—"touching upstairs." Then you can control your speech. Mouth closed. Don't grate your teeth.

Breathing: first, three times expel air at high pressure. Second, expel it at low pressure. Lastly, breathe slowly. Inhale as little air as possible. Breathe through the nose, not the mouth. "Breathing is coming outside. Then you take it as it is"—ordinary breathing. (An important point: do not speak even a single word.)

Mind: your mind should be controlled. You should not think about the past, present, or future. So many things from the past will flood your mind; your parents, your wife, children. Ignore them. And the present also. And the things before you, like the mosquito net, the table, books. And don't think about the future either.

You should not think about such things as the statue of Buddha which might be lying before you, though in the beginning, only as an aid to control and concentration, you can keep something before you. If you are a Hindu you can use the Shiva lingam; if you have no god, you can make something of clay.

It is not essential to keep the statue there, even in the beginning, but in your *mind* it is there. In the higher stages, the rupa stage, you remove the statue. If your mind is going to slip out of control, keep the statue.

If your body is healthy, if your character is good, automatically your mind will be controlled. If you are bad, then automatically your mind will go . . .

At the time of meditation you see the entire body of God. You think about what you can: His head, His body. Think about what you can, but the whole body is best. It is essential to think about His whole body. If this is not possible, then his half body.

After two or three years your mind will be controlled. You won't think about past or present. You will always think about the God who is in front of you.

The aim of meditation is to attain nirvana. Nirvana means the end of ignorance, of desire. You can attain it in four or five years. The word comes from ni, meaning "not," and vana, "wish" or "desire." The result is no anger, no attachments. Nothing in the mind. It's a kind of supraknowledge.

Once you attain nirvana you are finished with ignorance. The Lord Buddha says that nirvana is the last aim. You need not come to this world again. Monks can reach nirvana more easily, because of the kind of lives they lead. For the layman it is more difficult: since the mind must be controlled it is better to leave your family and become a monk, a disciple.

There is no soul in Buddhism. What others call the soul (atma) dies and comes back. Mind is not mind, because the past is mind, present is mind, future is mind. The present is half past and half future. The child's mind "walks" into the adult mind—and then dies. If it is not mortal, how can you have mind? Body, soul, mind, all die. Water is flowing in the Mississippi, but it is always the Mississippi. Not for a single moment is it still, but neither is it anything but the same river. It is eternally "sitting" but at the same time always flowing. So it is with the mind. What is born and reborn is your karmic energy, accumulated over the past lives.

Mind control, not exercise as in Hinduism, is yoga, the true yoga. In Buddhism yoga is for the mind. Mind is the driver. Moreover, mind is real, mortal, changing. Everything is changing, so how can what changes be immortal? Like a river into the ocean, the water evaporates into the sky and returns in the form of rain. So it is with the mind.

"The Wheel of Life" is what we call the cycle. The universe is a wheel. If we follow the Lord Buddha, do as he did, the wheel stops turning. We must change: if we do good work, we return on a higher plane. If we go down, we end in hell. If we ascend, we become Lord Buddha. *All of us.* We become the real Lord Buddha.

In the beginning one should not meditate long. The primary time is ten to fifteen minutes. We Tibetans focus on something to start, but eventually remove the object as the mind is better and better controlled. Eventually—after, say, twenty years of practice—one will be able to meditate for much longer periods. Control comes naturally with practice. One hour, two hours, a day. A week at a time, two weeks, three, a month. Then a year. In time, time.

As you ascend, the mind becomes controlled. Eating and sleeping become a part of meditation. And then you should have a very good guru. It is necessary to have a guru. Very important. What you must do, must know, is not written in books; it comes out of the guru. The choice depends on yourself: you should ask many people and experience many people. Some have knowledge, some education, others general popularity. You have to experience and learn.

Lord Buddha is supreme, real God. He has supreme power also, though he could not make the universe as he is not the Creator. Lord Buddha is just like God, but he is not a killer, not a creator. You were not born with the help of God. Lord Buddha is real God but not a god who kills or creates. Nor will he help you to attain nirvana. Nirvana comes only through yourself. According to Lord Buddha you will have rebirth only with the help of cause and effect. If there is cause there must be effect. We believe that all "making" is due to karma.

There are various kinds of yoga, such as hatha yoga, which is physical and involves rigorous training of the body. It is often followed by japa yoga, which begins with controlled breathing and leads into meditation—dhyana—and ultimately to samadhi. (In its migrations through Buddhism, dhyana became Ch'an in China and Zazen or Zen in Japan.) Samadhi is union with the divine. There is also kriya yoga, the science of using extra oxygen to halt the decay of bodily tissues; kriya is said to give the yogi special powers, like levitation, bilocation, and so on. Sincerely enlightened people are likely to look upon kriya with scorn. Another form of yoga is tantra,* a very difficult and virtualy inaccessible path which culminates in the physical worship of Shakti. And there are still other forms of yoga, which need not concern us now.

Practically speaking, you should start with hatha yoga and slide ever so imperceptibly into japa, which is the basic science of meditation. What follows is the common method practiced by many yogis and their chelas. It is the method outlined in Chapter Six of the Bhagavad Gita. (There are simplified forms of japa, like the Mahesh Yogi's Transcendental Meditation, and the Sahaj Marga, the Easiest Path, founded by Sri Ramachandraji of Fateghar and developed by Sri Ramachandraji of Shajahanpur. But japa yoga is easy enough; what is required is patiehce and self-control. Don't try to gobble it all up at once like a Yodel.)

Japa is the repetition of any mantra or name of God. In the present age, the Kali yuga, only the practice of japa (say the yogis) can give eternal bliss, peace, and immortality. Ultimately japa dissolves into dhyana and thence into samadhi.

Sitting. Arise at four in the morning, if you can. The hours before dawn, when all is quiet, are the most favored for contemplation, study, and certain other activities. Mind is then free, calm, pure, and relaxed. Also, there is an especially mysterious, magnetic, spiritual power present at sandhi, the junction of time at sunrise (and again at sunset). At sandhi the mind is quickly elevated to sattva, reality. The most favored locales for meditation, according to most (but not all) masters, are holy places like the bank of a river, a lakeside, the seashore (or any other water, even a well), under a tree, in a garden, a temple, or a cave, at the foot of a mountain or atop its summit. It is good to meditate near other yogis, since one absorbs their aura. Some masters suggest the building of a kutir, which is a small hut made of bamboo or wood and palm leaves or grass (again near other yogis if possible). Failing all these places, a room of one's own reserved solely for meditation will do. Other people should not be allowed to use it. The room should be plastered with cow dung (an antiseptic) or whitewashed.

You should wear clean clothes when sitting for japa, and have washed your face, mouth, hands, and feet. You should be neither hungry nor satiated with food.* Sit on the floor or the ground, either on a blanket, folded in four and covered with a white cotton sheet, or on a grass mat. A deer skin is said to be a more preferred seat, but, says Swami Sivananda, the best is a tiger skin complete with claws. "A tiger skin has got its own advantages," says the swami. "It generates electricity in the body quickly and does not allow leakage of electric current from the body. It is full of magnetism."* Face the East, toward the rising sun, or the North, where you will be in communion with the rishis of the Himalayas.

In the beginning concentrate on a black dot (about half an inch in diameter) drawn on a piece of paper pasted on the wall or the trunk of a tree at eye level, or on the flame of a candle, a bright star, the moon, or a picture of your favorite ishta devata. Select your ishta devata—Shiva, Krishna, Vishnu, Kali, Gauri, Durga, etc.—according to your own wishes or on the advice of a guru or even of a good astrologer. Because you have worshiped a certain devata in a previous birth, you will have a subconscious yearning for the same one now. Close your eyes and keep an image of your devata in the area of the ajna chakra, that is, between your eyes. Sri Ramachandraji suggested that the aspirant concentrate on the heart, where the Divine Light is present.

Yogic posture

The padma asana, or lotus position, the most famed of all yogic postures (it was practiced at least five thousand years ago), is the preferred one, but it is difficult. Guru is likely to recommend that you select the asana that is most comfortable and creates least strain, otherwise you will find yourself wrestling with your body and not concentrating your mind. You must keep your head, neck, and back straightly aligned. The spinal column must be straight but not rigid. Let your hands relax upon your lap. Before beginning japa you should say a few prayers or recite some songs (kirtan or bhajan); otherwise you may hallucinate from not being sufficiently relaxed.

The word japa means repetition. What is repeated is a mantra or a prayer. There is a divine power within each mantra which is released through faith and will power. The chanting of mantras generates powerful spiritual waves or divine vibrations or both. Mantras penetrate the physical and astral bodies of the sick when you pray for them and destroy the root causes of suffering. It is necessary to aim the mantra with one-pointedness. When it is awakened and becomes active, its invisible power will begin to operate.

In every mantra there are invisible forces hidden beyond our ability to see. OM NAMAH SHIVAYA is a mantra which means simply "I pay honor to the Lord Shiva," but if you analyze it in the light of esoteric science and occultism, you will know that every syllable has a definite meaning and a different range and frequency of vibrations. All mantras, whether intelligible or not, were first said by saints after full realization. You can meditate on the form of the mantra, on the sound vibrations, or on the guardian deity within it.

The following mantras are basic to japa yoga. Some masters advise their practice only with a guru, others allow their use in the case of a mature chela, since all of them are well known and there is no mystery as to their existence.

The most important of all mantras is OM. The syllable is the name and the symbol of God. OM is also your real name. OM represents all the worlds and all the universes, and the world comes from OM, exists and rests in OM, and dissolves in OM. As soon as you sit for meditation, chant OM loudly three, six, or twelve times. This will drive all profane thoughts from your mind. Then begin mental repetition of OM. OM arouses and transforms every atom in your physical body, setting up new transformations and awakening the inner powers of the body.

HARI KRISHNA, HARI KRISHNA, HARI HARI, HARI RAM, HARI RAM, RAM RAM, HARI HARI. The repetition of these six names of God destroy the evil effects of Kali. They remove the veil of ignorance over mankind. Whoever utters this mantra three and a half crores (30.5 million) of times atones even for the sin of the murder of a Brahmin. He becomes purified of the sin of stealing gold, from the sin of cohabitation with a low-caste woman, and from all other sins. He is released immediately from all bondages and attains salvation.

A devotee of Lord Vishnu should repeat OM NAMO NARAYANAYA; of Lord Shiva, OM NAMA SIVAYA; of Lord Krishna, OM NAMO BHAGVATE VASUDEVAYA; of Lord Rama, OM SRI RAMAYA NAMAH or OM SRI RAMA JAYA RAMA JAYA JAYA RAMA. Of all these mantras, select one and stay with it.

The Gayatri mantra is one of the most important of all mantras, next to the mantra OM in significance. Every caste Hindu must utter it at dawn, noon, and sunset. It should not be said by women or men of low caste. The mantra: OM! BHUR BHUVAH SVAH! TAT SAVITUR VARENYAM BHARGO DEVASYA DHIMAHI; DHIYO YO NAH PRADCODAYAT. OM! This is a solar mantra and is to be said twelve times at each sitting. The meaning: "OM! On the glory of God who has created the universe, who is fit to be worshiped, who is the embodiment of knowledge and light, the remover of sin and ignorance, we meditate. May he enlighten our minds. OM!"

There are four stages in the process of japa. The first is verbal, that is, loud chanting of the mantra. The second, more powerful, is repetition in whispers. The third, more powerful than the first two and not for beginners, is mental japa, in which you must meditate through the mental vibrations of the mantra and feel it within you. The fourth stage, for the most advanced, is ajapa, "repetitionless repetition," which is from the heart.

It will take the novice several years before he is ready for ajapa. There are three important points involved: deep breathing, relaxation, and total awareness. Not a single breath should go unnoticed.

There should be nothing automatic about breathing: you must have a total and unceasing awareness of every ingoing and outgoing breath. You must inhale and exhale consciously and not automatically. You must also notice how far in the breath goes—it should go to the navel—and when you exhale, it must come from the navel.

You must be able to sit in one asana for at least forty-five minutes. On the incoming breath the sound is so, on the outgoing breath, HUM. There should be no mental pause between so and HUM. Concentrate your thoughts on the ajna chakra. Think of nothing, let your mind become blank. Whatever thoughts enter your head must be gently removed, so is the sound of the inhalation, HUM that of the exhalation. Soon you will have a steady unbroken rhythm of so/HUM, HUM/so.

Again think of nothing; let the mind go blank. Concentrate on the ajna chakra. Centralize your awareness. During ajapa you must retain a complete and unceasing awareness of what you are doing. Create a mental vacuum; stop thinking.

During ajapa you may suddenly see a light in your mental plane. It will appear for a moment. In yogic language this is known as "locating the consciousness." We normally do not know the whereabouts of our astral bodies, but it is through this process of locating the consciousness that yogins transmit their consciousnesses.

Now we approach a more difficult stage. It consists of rotating the consciousness in the spinal column. The process of concentration and meditation consists of two factors: annihilation of the external consciousness and the expression of a calm and quiet atma within us. Meditation helps us destroy the sense-consciousness and awaken self-awareness, and thus remove impurities of the mind. The light manifests itself when the physical consciousness, the mental consciousness, the intellectual consciousness, and the personality itself are all completely annihilated.

It is a psychological fact that when you want to control the mind it wanders ruthlessly and you fail to control it. But if you watch your mental activities they will immediately cease.

In the beginning stages, you were asked to inhale with the breath going as far as the navel and returning. Now the process is to be changed. Circulate your consciousness in the spinal column, the sushumna, through the six chakras, starting with the ajna chakra and down through the others to the muladhara chakra. Retain your consciousness in the muladhara chakra for a few moments. Locate the inverted triangle, and within it Kundalini. Her tail will be upward and her mouth down. Meditate on Kundalini for a brief period. Now exhale through the spinal column and the six chakras. Repeat the process, breathing so/HUM continuously and rotating the breath through the sushumna and the chakras, down to Kundalini and returning, over and over but stopping short of exhaustion. Take a rest. At this point you will find that self-awareness is beginning to develop. Repeat the process at will, until your breathing is completely rhythmic, your imagination heightened but controlled, your mindfulness perfect and one-pointed, and your relaxation and awareness complete.

There is one more stage, for the highly trained adept. As always, sit in a comfortable but controlled asana. Interlock your hands and place them either in your lap or on your knees. Breathe so/HUM in a relaxed manner and let peace and joy flood your soul. Now raise your hands and with your thumbs plug your ears. Close your eyes and your lips with your fingers. Breathe deeply, and after a fully satisfying deep inhalation, close your nostrils with your fingers. Now, rotate your consciousness in the spinal column, plunging deeper and deeper with a mental so to Kundalini and then ascend with a mental HUM. Release your breath and rest, retaining your self-awareness and mindfulness. As you become more and more practiced, it will not be necessary to plug your eyes, ears, nostrils, and mouth. Inhale and descend into the region of Kundalini, relax there like a diver on the bottom of the ocean in langorous play, and ascend gracefully. This form of yoga, which is called pranayama (that is, energy control), is in effect a trip, and should not be done without the attendance of a guru. Swami Sivananda says that "gradually one should be able to retain the breath for three ghatikas (one hour and a half) at a time." The reward for this, as for all forms of yoga, is "a good appetite, good digestion, cheerfulness, courage, strength, vigor, a high standard of vitality, and a handsome appearance."*

In the East, one does not rush through this kind of meditation. A guru might keep his chela a year at each stage. But you Westerners, I know, are always in a hurry. My advice is to go slowly. If you are

white-skinned or black-skinned you are not ready for nirvana—you
have too many births to experience. There will always be another
birth, another kalpa. Practice what must be practiced, otherwise out
of nothing will come nothing.

SAINTS

Sai Baba* is barely known outside India, but here he is one of the most popular of all saints. He was born in 1856 and died in 1918. The name Sai means saint in Persian, and Baba, of course, is the Indian term of endearment meaning father. His first appearance was in 1872—he was then about sixteen—when he turned up as a wandering holy man in a small town called Shirdi, in western India. He lived under a neem tree, sleeping on the ground at night and eating whatever he could beg. Then he disappeared, but eventually came back to Shirdi. He tried to make his abode in a small Hindu temple in the town but was chased away by the caretaker, who thought he was a Muslim. Then he went to the town mosque, a tiny mud-walled building, and this remained his home for almost half a century. The people thought he was a little bit crazy, a little crazier than most wandering holy men. He scarcely spoke; occasionally he said the five-times-a-day Muslim prayers, the namas, recited the Qur'an, and maintained a small fire as did the Parsis. However, he also said the Hindu prayers. "All that is, is Allah," he had been heard to remark.

Although almost nothing is known about Sai Baba's early years, it is certain that he was born into a middle-class Brahmin family in Hyderabad state. About the age of eight he left home to follow a wandering muslim faqir (the supposition is that his parents had died by then), and then when the faqir died Sai Baba joined a Hindu guru, whom he later referred to as Venkusa. He told the story of his meeting with Venkusa a number of times:

Once I was discussing the Puranas and other works we were reading with four friends and arguing how to attain realization.

One said we should depend on ourselves and not on a guru, because the Gita says, "Raise yourself."

The second said that the main thing is to control the mind and keep it free from thoughts and doubts.

The third said that forms are always changing and only the Formless is unchanging, so we must constantly make a distinction between the Eternal and the transistory.

The fourth disliked theory. He said: "Let us simply do our duty and surrender our whole life and body and speech to a guru who is all-pervading. Faith in him is all that is needed."

As we roamed the forest we met a laborer, who asked us where we were going in the heat of the day and warned us that we would get lost in the trackless thickets, and for no purpose. He invited us to stay and share his food, but we rejected his offer and advice and walked on. And in fact we did lose our way in that vast, dense forest.

He met us a second time and said that we had got lost through trusting to our own skill and that we needed a guide. Again he invited us to share his food, telling us that such an offer was auspicious and should not be spurned; however, we again declined his invitation and continued on our way. Only I felt hungry and went back and accepted a piece of bread from him and drank some water.

Later the guru appeared again and asked what we were arguing over, and I told him all about it. The others left, showing him no respect, but I bowed down to him reverently. Then he took me to a well, tied my legs with a rope and suspended me head downward from a tree that was growing beside it. My head was about three feet above the water, so that I could not reach it. My guru left me there and went away, I knew not where. He returned four or five hours later and asked me how I was getting on. I replied that I had passed my time in great bliss. He was delighted with me and embraced me, passing his hand over my head and body. He spoke to me with great love and made me his disciple, whereupon I entirely forgot my mother and father and all my desires.

I loved to gaze upon him. I had no eyes except for him, I did not want to go back. I forgot everything but the guru. My whole life was concentrated in my sight, and my sight on him. He was the object of my meditation. In silence I bowed down.

This story is not to be taken literally: it is an example of Sai Baba's method of teaching. The forest symbolizes the jungle of the mind. In it a search for Truth takes place; the four young men are four different methods of seeking Truth. The laborer is the guru, and the food he offers is grace. "The guru appeared" means that this was the Divine Guru, whose authority Sai Baba accepts. When the guru ties him upside down, this means that his ego was overturned and that he was held close to the cooling waters of Peace. Thus the ordeal was blissful. And when Sai Baba says "In silence I bowed down," he meant that his ego had been extinguished in Realization.

Sai Baba kept with him a brick given by his guru. It dropped and broke in 1918, shortly before his death. Sai Baba remarked at the time, "It is not the brick that is broken but my karma. I will not survive its breaking." A few months later he was dead. However, as far back as 1886 he had experienced a kind of rehearsal for death. He told a disciple, "I am going to Allah. Take care of this body for three days. If I return I will look after it myself, if not, bury it in that open land over there and put up two posts to mark the spot."

He stretched out on the ground; his breathing ceased and his heart stopped beating; there was no pulse. The civil authorities held an inquest, pronounced him officially dead, and ordered the disciple either to bury him or burn the body, since the law stipulates that a corpse is not to be kept longer than twenty-four hours. The disciple refused. On the third day the crowd which had been watching the body saw that breathing had begun and the abdomen was rising and falling. Sai Baba opened his eyes and sat up.

About 1900 his fame spread. In 1908 Hindus began to revere him as a saint. A four-year-old child had been putting flowers on his head and worshiping him every morning. Soon adults were doing the same, though up to that year he had forbidden any kind of adulation. Like certain other Indian saints (and avatars) he was virtually unlettered. He did not read, nor did he encourage other people to read the scriptures, yet he was thoroughly knowledgeable in the sacred books of several religions. He used miracles like healing and foresight sparingly, yet when necessary he could restore people's health or appear in several places at the same time. A disciple, G. G. Narke (professor of geology at the Deccan Gymkhana College), wrote: "Baba frequently spoke of his travels with an invisible body over great distances of space (and time). Sitting near his fire in the morning with several devotees, he would say to what distant place he had been overnight and what he had done there. Those who slept beside him all night at the mosque and rest-house knew that his physical body had remained at Shirdi the whole night. But his statements were literally true and were sometimes verified and proved true." The professor adds: "This power to travel in an invisible body to distant parts of this world, to traverse other realms than the earth-life and control what takes place there and to see the past and future alike revealed one great fact about his nature. Some of his own observations also demonstrated it. I have heard him say: 'Where am I? Where is this world?' I have seen him point to his body and say: 'This is my house. I am not here. My guru has taken me away.' As even in the flesh, in this earthly life, he was not confined to his physical body, it may be truly said of him that he is alive. He is where he was then: even then he was where he is now.'"

Sai Baba refused to initiate some people on the ground that they were looking for occult powers and not spiritual development. He deprecated yogic practices (such as pranayama, or breath control) and told his disciples to continue in a normal manner of life, with their wives and children if they were married. A number of his disciples have stated that he did not give mantras or esoteric spiritual guidance. One of them remarked: "The peculiar feature stressed by Sai Baba's example and words is the vast importance of developing this devotion on the basis of devotion to one's guru. It is seeing God in, through and as the guru, identifying guru with God." However, Sai Baba is also recorded as having said (apparently for certain people only), "It is not necessary to have a guru. Everything is within us. What you sow you reap. What you give you get. It is all within you. Try to listen inwardly and follow the directions you get."

Sai Baba often said to disciples, "Stay with me and keep quiet. I will do the rest." This concept has been explained by Professor Narke: "According to the tradition of Sai Baba, the disciple or devotee who comes to the feet of a guru in complete surrender has, no doubt, to be pure, chaste and upright, but he does not need to continue any active practice of japa or meditation. On the contrary, any such practice or any intellectual process which involves the postulate, 'I am doing this,' is a handicap. All sense of ahankara or ego in the devotee has to be wiped out, swept out of the memory and mind, as it is an obstruction to the guru's task. The guru does not teach, he radiates influence. This influence is poured in and is absorbed with full benefit by the soul which has completely surrendered itself, blotting out the self, but it is obstructed by mental activity, by reliance on one's own exertions and by every kind of self-consciousness and self-assertion." The devotee must go a step at a time. "He need not trouble to decide about complicated metaphysical and philosophical problems about ultimate destiny. He is as yet ill-prepared to solve them. The guru will lift him up, endow him with higher powers, vaster knowledge and increasing realization of Truth. And the end is safe in guru's hands." In essence, the devotee not only should remain a householder, but should practice simplicity and invisibility in the path he follows.

Sai Baba's devotees came from all over India. He sometimes appeared to people in dreams or visions in order to bring them to him He said: "I draw my people to me from long distances in many ways. It is I who seek them out and bring them to me, like a bird with a string tied to its foot." One of his earliest disciples has described that invisible string: "I first heard of Sai Baba in 1909. I went to him with no worldly motives, though I was poor and an orphan. I was always desirous of associating with sadhus and felt drawn to him because I had heard that he was a saint. He appeared to me in a dream and summoned me to Shirdi. At the time my daughter (aged about six months) was very ill, so my mother objected to my going. Nevertheless, I persisted and took my mother and wife and the child with me. I stayed there for thirteen days and on the third day the child recovered from her sickness. Baba did not allow me to go back until the thirteenth day. I did not ask him about anything, but he told my mother that he had been connected with me for seven centuries and would never forget me however far away I was and would not eat a morsel of food without me.

With Baba's permission I left for Nasik and from there returned to our home at Dadar. On arrival there my wife got an attack of cholera and the doctor gave her up as hopeless. Then I saw Sai Baba standing beside the little temple opposite my house and he told me to give her the udhi (sacred ashes) that I had brought back from Shirdi. I did so and within half an hour she recovered sufficient warmth for the doctor to be hopeful. Soon she was all right."

The devotees gave Sai Baba all sorts of presents of money and jewelry, held processions in his honor with horses, an elephant, a chariot, treated him like a maharaja, but everything he received was given away. From time to time he would insult the devotees, abuse them, and turn them out. Sometimes he would demand money, either as a symbol (like asking for two rupees, which would represent faith and patience) or larger sums which he knew had been dishonestly obtained, which he would then give to the poor.

He lived in complete simplicity. He normally slept on a plank five feet long by fifteen inches wide, which was hung six feet above the floor from the roof on strips of old cloth. A biographer expresses the opinion that levitation was needed to get up on the plank and to stay there without falling off.

A Mrs. Manager, identified as a Parsi lady, said, "One's first impression of Sai Baba was of his eyes. There was such power and penetration in his gaze that no one could long look him in the eyes. One felt that he was reading one through and through. Soon one lowered one's eyes and bowed down. One felt that he was not only in one's heart but in every atom of one's body. A few words or a gesture would reveal to one that Sai Baba knew all about the past and present and even the future and about everything else. There was nothing else to do but to submit gracefully and surrender oneself to him. And he was there to look after every minute detail and guide one through every vicissitude of life." She says that in his presence "we felt safe, that nothing could harm us. When I went and sat in his presence I always forgot my pain, and indeed the body itself and all mundane cares and anxieties. Hours would pass while I sat blissfully unaware of their passage. It was an extraordinary experience shared, I believe, by all his real devotees. He was all in all and the All for us." She found his spiritual presence extraordinary: "One noticeable difference between Sai Baba and other saints struck me. I have visited other notable saints also and have seen them in a state of trance or samadhi in which they were entirely oblivious of their body. Then I have seen them recovering consciousness of their surroundings, knowing what is in our hearts and replying to our questions. But with Sai Baba there was this peculiar difference: he did not need to go into samadhi in order to achieve anything or to attain any higher status or knowledge. He was every moment exercising a dual consciousness, one actively utilizing the ego called Sri Sai Baba and dealing with other egos in temporal or spiritual affairs and the other transcending all ego and abiding in the state of Universal Soul. He was constantly exercising and mani-

festing the powers and features proper to both states of consciousness. Other saints would forget their body and surroundings and
then return to them, but Sai Baba was constantly both inside and
outside the material world. Others seemed to take pains and make
efforts to read the contents of people's minds and tell them their past
history, but with Sai Baba no effort was needed. He was always in
the all-knowing state."

A devotee named Y. J. Galwankar, who had visited Sai Baba in
1911 and several times after that, and had been visited by him in a
dream, described an incident in 1917. "He put his hand over my
head and this had a strange effect on me. I forgot myself and my
surroundings and fell into a state of ecstasy. I learned afterwards
that while I was in that state Sai Baba was telling those present that
I was characterized by integrity and purity. He described to them
various forms and conditions that I had passed through in previous
lives and said that he had placed me in my mother's womb in this
birth and I had still retained my integrity and purity."

In October 1918 Sai Baba sent away all but two of his disciples
with cryptic remarks (telling one, for example, "Go on ahead and
you can follow me. My tomb will speak. My clay will give you
replies"). His death a few days later, on the fifteenth, in effect meant
nothing. He had said to a woman devotee, "Wherever and whenever
you think of me I shall be with you."

I shall remain active and vigorous even after leaving this earthly
body.

My shrine will bless my devotees and fulfill their needs.

My relics will speak from the tomb.

I am ever living to help those who come to me and surrender
and seek refuge in me.

If you cast your burden on me I will bear it.

If you seek my help and guidance I will immediately give it to
you.

There shall be no want in the house of my devotee.

I give people what they want in the hope that they will begin
to want what I want to give them.

Sai Baba's death was irrelevant, as we will see shortly.

Glory to
Sree Sree Radharaman
and
all victory to
the feet of the Preceptor
IN QUEST OF LOVE*

First of all I offer myself unto the feet of my Preceptor who is savior
of the wicked and the redeemer of the fallen. I surrender myself
completely into the feet of all the Preceptors of our line. I pray to
Sree Sree Nitai Chand and Lord Sree Sree Gaura Kishore, the giver
of love and the redeemer of the fallen, and I bow down to them and
take shelter into their lotus feet. I know they make no distinction
between merit and demerit, the worthy and the unworthy; so throwing myself and putting my head on their feet, I pray to them along
with their devotees to be kind to me. Again I offer my homage to
my Preceptor, salute him falling flat on his two lotus feet and beg of
him to be merciful to me. I know that by his kindness a dumb may
get the power of speech, so I take shelter unto his feet. Thinking of
the endless mercy of my Grand Preceptor, Sree Sree Radharaman
Charandas Deb, I offer myself unto his feet. And completely devoted
to the maid Lalita Dasi, I bow down to her feet decked with twinkling anklets and pray to her that the "Quest of love" may cheer up
and enlighten my mind.

Nabadwip, a place of hallowed memory, is the birth place of
Gauranga Mahaprabhu. When I think of him how kind-hearted was
he who gave away all earthly bliss for the redemption of mankind
and when I remember of his incomparable and ineffable beauty and
virtuous play, tears roll down from my eyes. Krishna Chandra, God
Himself has taken Incarnation in this dark age holding the appear-

ance of Sree Gauranga. This is known to all and there are numerous examples to prove this truth. Many saints, holy and virtuous men took shelter into the feet of Mahaprabhu and after leaving this mortal coil obtained eternal blissful life. How much do I know of his beauty and quality of heart and mind that I shall make an attempt to narrate it. When we want to speak or write anything about him, it seems to be an attempt to catch the moon being a dwarf and pen stops to proceed further.

Before making an attempt to write anything, first of all I must mention the name of Sree Sree Radharaman Charandas Deb. Many used to call him "The great Babaji of Sreedham Puri." Fifty-three years before he left this world to meet with the Lord of his love. His burial tomb can be seen at Nabadwip. There are very few pilgrims who will not go to see Samajbari, also called Sree Radharaman Bag according to the name of the holy saint. His exact brass image is placed upon his burial ground in the midst of a temple and he is daily worshipped by the devotees. His life has been published by the name "Charit Sudha" in six volumes. He had innumerable disciples and among them are two great saints. One is Sree Lalita Dasi and the other is the illustrious saint Sree Sree Ramdas Babaji Maharaj of hallowed memory.

The object of my adoration is my Preceptor 108 Sree Sreemat Ramdas Babaji Maharaj* who was very kind to me and gave shelter unto his feet to a person who was the lowliest of the low. He initiated me into his holy order and the name that he is the redeemer of the fallen has been fulfilled. What can I say of his mercy which was showered upon his disciples, it fell like the flowers falling from heaven. His holy life is now known to all and I am not fit to describe it. Many had heard his songs which melted even the stony heart of the devils. Many a fallen man, the devil, the drunkard and the vilest of the viles, hearing his songs became purified, took shelter in his feet and were blessed. When he used to sing, tears rolled down from his eyes and all the holy symptoms of purity appeared in his body and there are eight in number.

Those who have seen his weeping face, inspired by love, were moved and their heart melted however fallen men they might have been. Their whole nature turned and they were ushered into a new life. They then spent their lives in joy immersed in devotion. Its examples are not rare. It is our sad lot that he is out of the picture for these six years. After his departure from this mundane world his holy body was buried in the hermitage of Sree Bhagabat Acharya at Barahanagar. At the time of his passing away, he uttered the name of the Lord with this hymn, "Vaja Nitai Gaur Radhe Shyam, Japa Hare Krishna Hare Ram," and also ordered us to do the same. So the name of the Lord in this hymn is still being chanted for all time day and night without any stoppage at Patbari. His holy life has been published in two volumes by the name "Charit Madhuri" and more is expected to come out in future. What he gave us and what has been left by him, if it is possible to count in figures it will surpass billions and trillions.

Sree Lalita Dasi, the maid, is the disciple of our grand preceptor. She completely surrendered herself unto the will of her spiritual guide. She never did anything in her life after her initiation into the order that would go against the will of her Preceptor. She thoroughly identified herself with her master's will, hence she could not do anything that would give unpleasantness to her spiritual guide. She always covered herself under a veil. Many have heard her name and seen her. She was born in a village, Harishena by name in the district of Barishal. Her former family name was Sree Gopal Krishna Bhattacharjee. Gopal acquired mastery over many scriptures in his young age and then left these worldly affairs for good. He traveled through the whole of India as an ascetic and at last reached Nilachaldham, the most sacred place in Orissa. There he met with the great saint Sree Radharaman Charandas Deb. Keeping company with his sweet association he thought that the object of his life would be fulfilled by the help of his guidance, so he surrendered himself unto his feet and accepted his discipleship. He then lived in the Jajpitha monastery and spent most of the time in the service of his master and worshipping the deities of the temple. The devotion to his master was unparalleled. His life, youth, body and soul, all were sacrificed in the service of his master, as if he knew nothing but the feet of his Preceptor. One day he was listening to the songs sung by his master about the love affairs of Sree Radha and Gobinda. He was completely absorbed in the idea of a maid of the Lord that he could not get out of his room for some days. After that ecstatic mood when he came to his senses he began to dress himself in the garb of a woman using scarf, jacket and petticoat and worship Lord following the love of the Gopies in Brindaban. From that time he took the name Sree Lalita Dasi, the maid, and lived in Jajpitha monastery. Her Preceptor Sree Radharaman Charandas Deb then came to Nabadwip and gave up his mortal coil. Hearing this heart-rending news she ran to Nabadwip almost maddened with grief. Fifty-three years rolled away since then. She spent there forty-one years of her life till she was carried away by death. A temple was constructed by her on the burial ground of her master and his brass image was enshrined within. The long years of her life were spent in worshipping the image of her master and doing the duties of the temple. In the monastery of Samajbari, which is also called Radhara-man Bag, at Nabadwipdham, the images of Nitai and Gaur, Radha and Gobinda, also called "Jugal Kishore" meaning "United Young Couple," were also established by her. She made necessary arrange-ments for their worship eight times a day according to eight Prahars which constitute a single day and night. She herself was blessed in this service of the Lord and made others happy by setting an exam-ple how to worship God. It was she who introduced this process of worship and it is still going on and the devotees think it to be the result of her infinite mercy upon men at large. Some addressed her by the name "sister" and many called her "Sakhi ma," meaning mother maid. But all had intense love for her. It has been said before that she was vastly learned and as such many learned men and saints, the rich and the respectable came to see her and thought themselves blessed being allowed to see her and her advice. But we called her "Sakhi ma" as often as we felt that she had showered blessings on our head. He who had the good fortune to be ac-quainted with her sweet association, realised how merciful she was and how she loved all irrespective of caste and creed. Her holy and pious life has been published in two volumes named "Sree Sree Lalita Sakhi" by Sree Diniseh Chandra Bhattacharjee.

"Sakhi Dasi" literally means maid servant, but she was our mother maid. She lost and hid herself in her Preceptor at Radhara-man Bag and that also took place some twelve years ago. We always remember her elegant and beautiful appearance and the sweet words which she often spoke to us in the midst of all her engrossing duties. We feel her absence with a painful heart, we lived by the side of a great mountain but we could not appreciate her greatness.

I pray to the lotus feet of Sreeman Mahaprabhu and the merci-ful feet of my Preceptor that they would bless us and their objects of life and the world will learn to love one another.

❖ ❖

It is virtually an article of faith that a holy man cannot be photographed without his permission, otherwise the negative will appear blank. The following is cited as proof of this phenomenon; from Sri Paramahansa Yogananda's *Autobiography of a Yogi,* it concerns an attempt to photograph a yogi named Lahiri Mahasaya:

It appears that the master had an aversion to being photographed. Over his protest, a group picture was once taken of him and a cluster of devotees, including Kali Kumar Roy [the man who told the anecdote to Yogananda]. It was an amazed photographer who discovered that the plate, which had clear images of all the disciples, revealed nothing more than a blank space in the center where he had reasonably expected to find the outlines of Lahiri Mahasaya. The phenomenon was widely discussed.

A student who was an expert photographer, Ganga Dhar Babu, boasted that the fugitive figure would not escape him. The next morning, as the guru sat in lotus position on a wooden bench with a screen behind him, Ganga Dhar Babu arrived with his equipment. Taking every precaution for success, he greedily exposed twelve plates. On each one he soon found the imprint of the wooden bench and screen, but once again the master's form was missing. [To cut a long story short, the yogi tells the babu, "I am Spirit. Can your camera reflect the Omnipresent Invisible?" and gives his permission for a photograph.] Again the photographer focused his camera. This time the sacred figure, not cloaked with mysterious imperceptibility, was sharp on the plate.

[When he was still a child, Yogananda was given a copy of the photograph.] In meditation I would often see his photographic image emerge from its small frame and, taking a living form, sit before me. When I attempted to touch the feet of his luminous body, it would change and again become the picture. [At the age of eight, Yogananda was stricken with cholera and his life was despaired of.] The doctors could do nothing. At my bedside, Mother frantically motioned to me to look at Lahiri Mahasaya's picture on the wall above my head. I gazed at his photograph and saw there a blinding light, enveloping my body and the entire room. My nausea and other uncontrollable symptoms disappeared; I was well.

❧

I have before me a little book, *The Saints of India,** by Swami Tattwananda, published in Calcutta sometime within the past ten or
fifteen years, judging by various references to recent events. The
book contains the lives of forty saints—forty men—which tells us
something about the role of women in Indian religious life, by which
we infer either that women don't attain sainthood or that, if they
do, swamis are not interested in them. I won't discuss the first saint
the swami mentions, though he was a founder of the sect of the Jains
and was a contemporary of Buddha; he is Tirthankar Mahabir, who
was born in 599 B.C. Let's stay largely with those who lived in the
nineteenth and twentieth centuries. Here's Trailanga Swami, who,
the author says, "attained Mahasamadhi [which is the act of passing
out of the body permanently] on the eleventh day of the bright
moon in the month of Poush in the year 1887." What seems rather
run of the mill is that Trailanga Swami was born "in the first half
of the seventeenth century." There is something wrong with the
author's figures, as we shall soon see, but on the side of conservatism.
When Trailanga was a child his mother "noticed to her astonishment
[her son was sleeping] that a ray of light entered the boy's body."
Later, as a young man, he refused to marry and so lived as a celibate.
When he was forty his father died, and twelve years later his
mother. "In this way all bonds which tied him to the world were
snapped." Trailanga went into seclusion as a hermit, practicing
"austere" yoga until he was eighty. However, "there was no sign whatever of old age in his boby," by which, I assume, the author means
body. He performed the usual set of miracles, like raising the dead
and floating on water, along with one that is peculiarly Indian, making a pet of a ferocious tiger which had fled to him for shelter from
a hunting party. After various wanderings and pilgrimages in the
Himalayas and Nepal, he spent some time in different holy retreats.

128

Then: "after some time Trailanga came to Benares and there he stayed for a long period of one hundred and fifty years." What made Trailanga something out of the ordinary is that he not only was "fat-bodied" (Yogananda, who also writes about him, says, "His weight exceeded three hundred pounds: a pound for every year of his life!" even though he "ate very seldom"), but he wandered about "clad only in nature's garb. He was arrested for this but each time he was handcuffed he miraculously disappeared." What happened next is worth a full quotation as an example of what impresses the public in my country.

"The bewildered European [that is, British] officer realised that the swami was no ordinary man. By that time a pleader who knew the swami well appeared on the scene. He spoke praise of the swami and said that as he was a spiritually advanced soul, to him sandal paste and excreta were the same and that there was no necessity for the swami to wear clothes like ordinary people. The magistrate wished to verify it. He asked if the swami should take forbidden food. The swami agreed on condition that the magistrate also should partake of it. Thereupon in the open court he answered nature's call [note the Western euphemism] and he offered the stool that he passed for anyone to take it. It is said that all present in the court including the magistrate noticed that the swami partook it. It turned into nectar and a pleasant taste. He thereupon ordered that the swami might be released so that he might wander at free will. Another magistrate who came afterwards was very strict, he had the swami confined in the jail but found that on the next morning he was at his usual place. Hearing from him that behind matter lies the spirit and that he who is tuned with the infinite spirit and has become one with the same can not be confined within the bonds of matter, the magistrate came to realise the power of Indian yogi."

Naturally a holy man like the swami attracted a lot of curiosity seekers as well as valid truth seekers and disciples. To avoid being bugged unnecessarily, "the swami had a number of holy verses written on the wall of his room and whenever people put any question he avoided all conversation by pointing out to one of the verses." (A most sensible act, I must admit.) Later he met the great Bengali saint, Sri Ramakrishna. "In reply to Sri Ramakrishna's question as to whether God is one or many Trailanga swami answered by means of signs that in the stage of Samadhi God is one but the moment the body consciousness comes with it also comes the sense of plurality." I won't detail the numerous events in his life that give proof of the swami's saintliness (there was the usual attempt at poisoning him, this being de rigueur for the average holy man; the poison of course went down harmlessly), except to give an unusual example of how the God-centered man sees himself. "One day he (another holy man) saw the swami passing urine in some Kali temple and sprinkling it on the image. The Brahma preacher was taken aback and he asked the swami why he desecrated the image. The yogi wrote on the earth that what was being sprinkled on the image was Ganges water for to a yogi of his calibre both the Ganges water and urine are the same." Yogananda adds a footnote to this enchanting fellow in his own account. "The only known living disciple of the great yogi is a woman, Shankari Mai Jiew . . . The *brahmacharini* (woman ascetic), born in 1826, is now well over the century mark [he was writing in 1946]. Not aged in appearance, however, she has retained her black hair, sparkling teeth, and amazing energy. She comes out of her seclusion every few years to attend the periodical melas or religious fairs."

The next saint, Charandas Babaji, deserves but a passing mention. He is a Bengali, of undetermined date. He was once traveling with a group of devotees when he came upon "an old Vaisnava of the name of Gadhadhar das. He was bitten by a snake and he fell down unconscious. Charandas Babaji who was in exalted mood kicked him mercilessly and miraculously enough the snake bitten patient regained consciousness."

Some saints experienced temptations rivaling Saint Anthony's, a common problem in any culture. Ramdas Katiababa, an East Punjabi of the nineteenth century, had just signed up with a guru when "a young woman who used to meet him at odd hours tried to tempt him. He pelted stones at her and drove her out. Later he thought that discretion was the better part of valour and he left the village for good." He went to another state, but "the beautiful widow of the dead king of the state who served him with great care began to feel attracted towards him. Thanks to the grace of God and the guru he escaped unassailed from this new temptation also." Ramdas now found another guru, Devadasji. This yogi had "a special attraction for Ganja and Charas [pot and hash], the most intoxicating substances, but he was capable of remaining absorbed in meditation for months together before his Dhuni [a sacred fire]." There are innumerable incidents involving charas and ganji, which Ramdas took to with great enjoyment, and another escape from "a beautiful young widow [sent] to tempt Babaji." Swami Tattwananda laments Ramdas's "fondness for Ganja" as he records the old saint's death, which came in 1909 after a cook poisoned him to the point of mortal weakness.

Vamakshepa, a tantric yogi born in 1837, also had trouble with temptations. He was not only tempted by a beautiful young woman attached to a temple (Vamakshepa drove her off with his sadhu's trident), but "on another occasion the officer in charge of the Tarapith temple engaged a public woman in order to tempt him. When she approached Vamakshepa with evil intention she found no male sign in him." Most of the remainder of his life is unspeakably dull, at least from my point of view. He had a run-in with a man called Nimai, who suffered from a hernia. "One day Nimai wished to smoke Ganja and he took some fire from the Dhuni of Vamakshepa. This enraged the saint and he kicked the hernia patient in the lower part of his abdomen. Although he fell down unconscious he got up cured of his hernia and he returned home to serve his wife and children."

Ramprasad, a tantric poet who worshiped "God as Mother"— that is, as Shakti or Kali—gives an interesting insight into how this worship was accomplished. Selecting a place to worship, under certain sacred trees, he built an asana "by placing underneath heads of five dead bodies, e.g., of man, monkey, jackal, mongoose and snake, four on different corners and one in the middle." He had several visions of the Mother—encounters in person would be more accurate —during an increasingly difficult series of sadhanas. "He also practiced the most difficult Sava Sadhana by sitting on a dead body on a new moon night . . . on a cremation ground—a place of terror to others. Thus by the grace of Mother he succeeded in all the tests of Sadhana and realised Mother inside and outside and in everything, his life overflowed with Divine Bliss." Finally, "As he advanced in his Sadhana Ramprasad realised that it is the Mother Herself who has become Krishna, the adored of the Vaisnavas, that the Mother is the Absolute concretised for the devotees and that She is the all-pervading Being. In this way he attained the synthesis of religion." Then, "His work was over. It was high time for him to lay his head on the lap of the eternal Mother. He had come to be eighty years old and he knew that his hour had come. When the time came he entered the Ganges breast deep and chanted the glory of the Mother. The vital breath passed away by way of the spinal column which the Kundalini takes in its upward ascent, for such was his last wish. His life became one with the Universal."

Krishnananda Agambagis (fifteenth century) was also a Mother worshiper, which he did on "a lonely cremation ground on the bank of the Ganges." Worship of the Mother takes place at midnight. One morning, on his way to the Ganges for his bath after a night of worship, Krishnananda "saw before him a beautiful little girl. She had three lotus-petaled eyes having a gracious and pitiful look, bright teeth, long black curling hairs hanging down to Her knees, tongue half out as if She felt shame at the sight of a stranger, dark complexion, radiant face in a symbolic divine pose," and so on, for the full vision of Kali even to the garland of skulls and her foot on the breast of her husband. This led Krishnananda to construct an asana according to the Tantra, "by placing underneath five heads of dead bodies, e.g., of man, monkey, jackal, mongoose and snake." This kind of vision and this sort of practice are the usual among the worshipers of Kali, and there is no reason to enumerate them.

Gambhirnath, who died in 1917, is called "a highly advanced yogi." He tamed a tiger, a common event. What seems to have impressed the swami more, however (and me too, I might add), is the following account about another yogi who has crept into the story. "When Goraknath was requested by one of his devotees to demonstrate his yogic power he vomited the milk and food which were served for him and kept separate although they had been served to him long ago, and that the very sight of it frightened the Brahmin who pressed for the display of yogic power at the beginning, then besought his pardon." "Strange are the ways of the yogis," Tattwananda adds.

By way of an aside, the publisher of the book, one Nirmalendu Bikash Sen Gupta of Calcutta, says in his foreword, "This valuable book will have a great appeal to the readers who may herein get some food for thought and may wish to satisfy their spiritual quest by pouring over the glorious lives of saints serving as tonic for vitalising the heart of society." The author himself adds that his book "supplies material for an aspirant to become optimistic about the life eternal by following the path chalked out by the seers. Thorough study of their lives is beneficial for the individual and the people at large."

Sometimes moments of simple truth shine through in Tattwananda's chronicles. There is one touching account of a low-caste man named Tiruppan,* who stood outside and below all castes and consequently was denied admission even to the temples. To a caste Hindu who locked him out of a temple to prevent him from worshiping and was about to beat him for arrogance, Tiruppan said: "Reverend sir, please do not defile your body, I have committed an offence by being born in a low caste. I deserve punishment, please punish me by pelting stones at me from a distance." In the book all is resolved. In real life this was (and is said to be now) a common practice.

One more to go, and then we will all retire and meditate upon yogis, "strange are their ways." This man is Ramana Maharshi, born in 1879, and mentioned in Paul Brunton's A Search in Secret India, which brings him within the range of reality and credibility, we may hope. Maharshi, sometimes known as the Brahman swami, experienced the standard pious boyhood. Then, says Tattwananda: "One day when he was sitting in his room he felt all of a sudden the spectre of death, his very existences were blotted out, doctors failed and it looked as though all was over; he experienced psychologically the whole process of death as though his body had been carried to the cremation ground and as though it were burned to ashes. And yet strangely enough some things remained and that was the witnessing consciousness for he remained as the witness of his death. It was that experience of death which opened before the young man the gate of immortality. His mind drifted towards meditation on God. He became indifferent to health, food and study. He went to the nearby Shiva temple and there he prayed while tears rolled down from his eyes." Soon he left home, wandering about, settling down for brief periods in various shrines and then moving on. "Brahman swami was indifferent to everything including food and water. His hairs grew long and became matted. He grew so emaciated and weak that he could not move about without help. The control of food and the observance of silence were not part of the vow he had taken. The fact is that his body needed very little and he had very little to say."

His mother (poor woman) tried to get her son to tell her what he was doing. Writing on a scrap of paper, "he informed his mother that God guides the destiny of every individual according to one's previous action. That which is to happen is bound to happen and that which is not to happen can never happen. Therefore the best course is to keep silent." To a questioner, a theological nugget: "If anyone searches sincerely the source of the I-consciousness and focusses one's attention upon that, one can obtain peace." He showed the usual miracles, including bilocation. The end is mildly interesting: The saint was suffering from cancer. "He used to compare the body to a plaintain leaf on which various dishes are served—when the feast is over the leaf is thrown away without any compunction." Later, the saint said, "It is useless to mourn for the body. All say, 'I am going to die.' Really speaking I am not going anywhere—where shall I go? 'I shall be there where I am always.'"

On April 14, 1950, at a quarter of nine, while sitting in the lotus position, he uttered the word AUM and "passed away exactly in the manner described in the Gita." (That is, with his soul exiting through the Third Eye.) "And then a strange phenomenon happened. A French photographer wished to take the last photograph of the saint and all that he saw was a flash of light shooting like a bright star and circling the sky before it vanished. Thus it was that the saint gave his last darshan to his numerous devotees who were scattered far and wide."

THE SONG
OF THE PHALLIC KING

The lingam is I myself, Shiva.
I ordain that henceforth men shall offer it
    their sacrifices and worship.
Those who honor me
under the symbol of the linga
shall, without fail, obtain
the object of all their desires
and a place
    in the Pleasure Mountain
      Kailasa.

I am the Supreme Being
    and so is my
      linga.

If you desire to become virtuous
learn what benefits are to be derived from honour
rendered to my linga.
Those who make an image of it with earth or cow dung
or do puja to it under this form
shall be rewarded.
Those who make it in stone shall be seven times rewarded
and never shall behold the Prince of Darkness.
Those who make it in silver shall receive
even seven times more
and those who make it
    in gold
shall be seven times more meritorious still.

Shiva temple

The linga, or lingam, an object of deep veneration in India, is the symbol of the god Shiva and it is under this form primarily that He is worshiped. The Linga Purana reports the origin of the cult. Brahma, Vishnu, and other gods and a numerous following of illustrious penitents went one day to Kailasa, the paradise of Shiva, and found him in the act of intercourse with his wife, Durga (that is, Kali). Shiva was not the least bit disconcerted by their presence, and in fact, went on enjoying himself at great length. Vishnu and some of the other gods began to laugh; a few became indignant and loaded him with insults and curses. Eventually everyone left, realizing that Shiva was too far into the joys of sexual bliss to be able to receive them properly. After Shiva had finished and was somewhat down to earth, he asked his servants who had been in the room with him and his wife. When they learned who his illustrious visitors had been, the news fell on the couple "like a clap of thunder" and they both "died of grief" in the position in which they had been discovered. "My shame," Shiva said, "has killed me and it has given me a new life, and a new shape, which is that of the lingam. Regard it as my double self!"

Needless to say, Indian reverence for and worship of the lingam (and the yoni, or vulva) caused no end of embarrassment for Europeans when they occupied the land and began to subdue and rob the inhabitants in the name of civilization and progress. Disgusting, degrading, vile superstition, brute sensuality, and so on, were some of the adjectives used to describe this very ancient practice of phallic worship. However, as with virtually all puritans, the linga had an endless fascination for Europeans, and they collected numerous examples, in stone, rare and common metals, wood, clay, to bring home as examples of the brute sensuality of the Hindu. Sir Edward Moor (*The Hindu Pantheon*, 1810), who had a magnificent collection of these "disgusting . . . generative organs," lamented at length throughout his work about their use and popularity, saying, "I continue of opinion, that such objects of depravity, continually offered to juvenile contemplation, cannot fail of exciting in such untutored, especially female minds, ideas obnoxious to the innocence we love to think innate there."

The lingam can be seen all over India: in temples, along the roads, in the bazaars, in homes, and as a personal adornment in the form of necklaces, belts, pendants, and bracelets. The city of Benares, which is Shiva's city, is the city of the lingam. Throughout Benares are thousands of lingam shrines, covered with red powder, flowers, oil, and the wax of lakhs of burned-out candles. We cannot understand why anyone should take offense at this symbol of creation and its feminine counterpart, the yoni or vulva. Is not the union of male and female participation in the divine act of creation? And are not all children marked with the sign of the Divine, the male with the sign of Hara, Giver of Wonders, and the female with the sign of Devi, the Great Goddess and the Resplendent One?

Space is the linga,
the earth the altar.
In it dwell
        all the gods.
It is called the "sign," linga,
because all dissolve in it.

The lingam is Shiva himself.
        It is white,
        it has three eyes and five faces,
        it is arrayed in a tiger's skin,
        it existed before the world,
and is the origin of all things.
        It disperses our terrors and our fears
and grants us the object of all our desires.

Let my priests go and teach these truths
and compel them to embrace the worship
        of my lingam.
In their union of Shakti, energy,
        and Shiva, Lord of Sleep,
the world is created
in a shower of seed
and thus all men, and all other creatures,
seek happiness
in the bliss
        of sexual union.

[Karapatri]* Manifest nature, the universal energy, is shown as the yoni, or female organ, embracing the linga. Only under the shape of a linga, giver of seed, can Shiva be enveloped by the yoni and become manifest.

The symbol of the Supreme Man, the formless, the changeless, the all-seeing eye, is the symbol of masculinity, the phallus or linga. The symbol of the power that is Nature, generatrix of all that exists, is the female organ, the yoni.

The linga stands in the yoni, which is the power of manifestation, the womb of the real and the unreal. The universal womb, in which all that is individual ripens. The linga fecundates the womb.

Pleasure dwells in the sex organ, in the cosmic linga and yoni whose union is the essence of enjoyment. The enjoyer is Shiva, He is the giver of enjoyment. There is no other giver. In the world also all love, all lust, all desire is a search for enjoyment. Things are desired for the pleasure they contain. Divinity is the object of love because it is enjoyment. Other things are objects of temporary love since they bring us only a temporary satisfaction.

All enjoyment, all pleasure, is the experience of divinity. The whole universe springs forth from that enjoyment; pleasure is found at the root of everything. But perfect love is love whose object is not limited, love without attributes, the pure love of love itself, of the transcendent being-of-joy.

From the relation of linga and yoni the whole world arises. Everything therefore bears the signature of the linga and the yoni. It is divinity under the form of all individual lingas which enters into every womb and procreates all beings.

It is He alone who dwells in every womb.

The seed of both Shiva and Sati (Kali) fell back on the earth and filled the world. From this seed all the Shiva-lingas are seen in the underworld, on earth, and in heaven become manifest. From these are made all Shiva-lingas of the past and those of the future.

Like a mother and a father, principal Nature and the Supreme Person give birth to all forms. In the world men desirous of progeny fecundate women, and likewise the Supreme Being, desirous of progeny, of multiplicity, fecundates Nature.

Those who do not recognize the divine nature of the phallus, who do not measure the importance of the sex ritual, who consider the act of love as low or contemptible or as a mere physical function, are bound to fail in their attempts at physical as well as spiritual achievement. To ignore the sacredness of the linga is dangerous, whereas through its worship the joy of life and the joy of liberation are obtained.

The man who spends his life without honoring the phallus is truly unfortunate, sinful and ill-fated. If we put in balance the worship of the linga as against charities, fasts, pilgrimages, sacrifice, and even virtue, it is the worship of the giver of pleasure and liberation, the remover of adversity, that prevails.

Just as we worship the Sun as the giver of light, the sum of all individual eyes, so also in the linga we worship Shiva, who pervades all generative powers. It is not a particular eye we worship and of which we make images, but the Sun, the eye-totality, the giver of sight, the source of visibility. Similarly it is the Shiva-totality which is worshiped and of which images are made. Shiva: "He who worships the linga knowing it to be the First Cause, the source of consciousness, the substance of the universe, is nearer to me than any other being."

PRAHALAYA,
OR
A BREATHING SPACE

[In a letter from a woman in America] "A friend of mine spent a fortnight at the Shivananda Yoga Centre (Valmorine, Que.). Terribly disorganized chaotic place. The swami, himself, absent most of the time—on a hunger strike at the local courthouse because insurance co. took away his private plane, decorated from end to end by Peter Max, on the pretext that his plans for a peace flight would endanger the plane. Large colony of ducks in the swimming pool—swami wouldn't permit their eviction—so pool unusable. Meals terrible. In spite of all the confusion and inconvenience (daily meditation at 5:30 A.M.) friend said she'd never had such a feeling of peace and calm before."

Random thoughts from Westerners . . .

Why is everything covered with a quarter inch of water? . . . Floors, temples, streets, courtyards, steps. All so wet—water, ghee, oil, spit, urine, like one great big seminal emission. They revel in it.

[An American] India is like trying to walk on quicksand, except that you shouldn't, and while you can explain quicksand scientifically, you can't explain India.

[A Canadian hippie] To me India is like a great big mother's breast very nourishing but
sometimes
malignant.

GOD THE MOTHER

&

GOD THE SON

Mother, Mataji, Anandamayee Ma,* the Most Blissful Mother.

Here we have a problem which I am unable to solve. One is led to Mother, or Mataji, almost mysteriously, in fact, quite mysteriously. The echoes of Mother reverberate throughout our lives. As children we have heard about Mother, have been brought to her darshan by parents or aunts or cousins. Mother's identity is an enigma in our land of enigmas, a land which is all enigma. Her devotees call her divine, God in human form. One of the earliest, J. C. Roy, who was better known as Bhaiji, was the first to tell the world that Mother was an incarnation of Shakti, the manifest energy of the Divine, the source of all, the universal creator, the all-embracing absolute divinity. Later she was to be identified as Parabrahma, the Transcendental Immensity which supports the trinity of Nature, Person, and Time, and the THOU ART THAT of the Vedas, a phrase which represents the fundamental unity of the macrocosm and the microcosm. She has also been called "a perfect vehicle," "the limitless ocean," "Lord Krishna in the personality of Mother," and so on. Yogi Bhai says firmly that Mother Kali and Mother Anandamayee "both are one and the same," that Mother "has appeared in the present form for the salvation of all of us." Another man, who says "to me she is divine," also states: "She is looked upon by about seven lakhs of devotees all over India [a lakh is one hundred thousand] as the Incarnation of the Great Power which is nursing and sustaining the entire creation—the Divine Mother." I might multiply such examples indefinitely, but the reader will now understand that for her devotees Mother is God or a form of God. To what seems like the majority of devotees, she is God in the form of the goddess Kali. Outwardly Mother is a trim, small figure, with flowing black hair only slightly grayed, a beautiful gypsy face, and willful, wistful eyes. She is now in her late seventies but gives the appearance of being a much younger person. If she is God, she is God in human form. So, the question of her identity remains to tease and to puzzle us. Who are you, Mataji? Tell us.

You want to know who I am. Well, I am what you consider me to be—not more, not less. All that I can say is that in the midst of all apparent changes of state in body and mind, I feel, I am aware, that I am always the same. I feel that in me there is no change of states. Call it by any name you like. Who or what I am will probably come out of my mouth someday. Now it is not so happening. If there were aham jnana, I-consciousness, in me I could express who I am. As it is not there, I am what you choose to say about me.

This entire universe is my house. I am in my own house even when seeming to be roaming from place to place. I am conditioned as well as unconditioned. I am neither infinite nor finite. I am both at the same time, I am with everybody, whether twenty, fifty, or a hundred years old. I exist before there is any creation, duration, or dissolution of the world. People have various visions of gods and goddesses in me according to their own conditioning. What I was before, I am now and shall be hereafter. I am also whatever you or anybody may think I am. Why don't you look at it this way: that the yearnings of seekers after Truth have brought about this body. You all have wanted it and you have found it. That is all you need to know.

❖

Mataji—Nirmala Sundari Devi (Immaculate Beautiful Devi)—was born in 1896 in a village in what is now Bangladesh. Her parents were Brahmins and were moderately well off. When she was two months short of her thirteenth birthday she was married to a young man named Ranani Mohan Chakravarty. In India young couples do not normally live together until several years after the wedding ceremony; this gives them a chance to come to know each other, so Nirmala stayed with her family until she was eighteen. The husband, whom Nirmala called Bholonath, was a simple villager, though he had some education and could write. One of the many people who have written about Mataji says: "When the time came for them to make their home together, the young husband found a spiritual aura round his wife which precluded all worldly thoughts from his mind." The marriage was never consummated. Mataji later talked about the relationship. "There was never any shadow of a worldly thought in Bholonath's mind when we [she speaks of herself in the plural] lay near him at night. He was never troubled by any self-consciousness. He guarded and looked after this body [a phrase she likes to use about herself] most confidently and unselfconsciously. Once or twice, when there was an inkling of a worldly thought in him, which was so unformed as not to be on the level of his consciousness, this body would assume all the symptoms of death. He would feel frightened and do japa, knowing that he could establish contact with me by that method alone. He led an extraordinary life of self-denial and rigorous asceticism." Such was the state of affairs until Bholonath's death in 1938.

During the first days in her own home with Bholonath, Mataji began to exhibit the signs of holiness that led people to prostrate themselves before her and to call her Devi Durga and Mother. The signs were not so much literal as intangible: there was something in her appearance, in her being, that impressed people. Nirmala herself remarked much later that "in the dark I sometimes perceived a strange effulgence enveloping my body and that light seemed to move about with me." She began spiritual practices called sadhana, which, she said, are for "the purpose of preparing one-self for self-realization." Then, "One day I went to bathe in a pond near the house where we lived. While I was pouring water over my body, the kheyala suddenly came to me, 'How would it be to play the role of a sadhaka?' And so the lila began." The Sanskrit phrases Mataji uses are important and cannot be simply translated in a word but must be explained. In ordinary usage "kheyala" has been explained as "a sudden and unexpected psychic emergence" such as desire, will, attention, memory, or knowledge. Mataji, giving the word a wider meaning, described as kheyala the incomprehensible acts of the Supreme, as for instance, His showing Himself in creation. In using "kheyala" in reference to herself, it denotes "a spontaneous upsurge of Will, which is divine and therefore free." A sadhaka is a person who practices a certain kind of preparation to attain self-realization, and "lila" means, literally, "play" or playfulness—in Mataji's case, "movements and activities of the Supreme Being that are free by nature and not subject to ordinary laws." (Creation of the universe is lila of God.)

Yet despite the signs of holiness, certain neighbors thought she was possessed by demons, and so an exorcist was brought in to chase them away. What happened was that the exorcist went into spasms and rolled on the floor. Bholonath failed to bring the man to his senses and appealed to Nirmala, who restored the man to consciousness. The exorcist prostrated himself before her, saying, "She is the Devi. It was a mistake to have tried my powers against her."

Mother has talked quite simply about her spiritual development:

After the lila of initiation, for five months there was hardly any time for me to take food. My body was like an automaton. I went through the motions of my daily routine of housework like a machine. I would light the fire not thinking about what I could want it for—then like an onlooker I would go through the actions of cooking and serving.

Once this body lived on three grains of rice daily for four or five months. Nobody can live for so long a time on such a meager diet. It looks like a miracle. But it has been so with this body. It has been so because it can be so. The reason for this is that what we eat is not at all necessary for us. It may also happen that the body is not taking in anything at all, yet it is being maintained unimpaired as in a state of samadhi. Thus you will find that as a consequence of sadhana it is quite possible to live without what we call food.

Lack of food did not have an adverse effect on my body. As a matter of fact, at that time the necessity for food itself vanished. You are told that people have to abstain from the pleasures of life, but in this case everything was the other way round—I saw that I had to partake of food—sometimes less than a mouthful, so that I did not get the kheyala of doing without it.

Sometimes this body would be affected by the reading of religious books, just as it used to be by the strains of devotional music. Then again, there was a time when the words of the book were not important at all—they would appear to be of little significance—whatever had to be known was already there. After this came a time when it was realized that everything is that only. Just like sparks of fire, where each itself has all the characteristics of the whole.

The variety of experience at the time of the sadhana can hardly be enumerated exhaustively. A time comes when everything becomes clear to the vision, for example, you light a lamp—the house, trees, bushes, people around you, everything becomes visible at the same time. There may be another way of looking at things, namely what is there to visualize? After all, there is nothing to be known further—whatever is, is always so.

One afternoon I sat in an asana and measured with my fingers the distance from the centre of the head to the middle of the eyebrows, then to the neck and down to the centre of the spine. I have a kheyala that there are centres [chakras] at specific spots within the body. From the lowest to the highest they range from gross to refined. These centres are formations of nerves only. The aptitudes and propensities of the human being, being determined by the experiences of his sense organs, are located in these centres. The stream of vitality flows through them slowly or fast, determining the emotions and actions of the individual. Just as the world has different strata, such as earth, water, the void, and so on, the human body also has different levels. The vital force lies as if somnolent at the base of the spine. By perseverance and faith, thought and action are purified. The vibrations engendered by the action of inner and outer purity shake this sleeping power into motion. When this power [Kundalini] moves upwards, penetrating level after level, the sadhaka feels free from any ties.

I had the kheyal to be like a sadhaka, so it was only natural that the characteristics attending intense sadhana should occur spontaneously. The earnest sadhaka does not attach any importance to these powers which develop in him. He may not make any deliberate use of them. But all the same, people may derive great benefit from the abundance which overflows his efforts.

In August 1922, Nirmala, without a guru, went through the rite of diksha, spiritual initiation, a rite that is normally given after a long training under a guru and with his permission and direction. Mataji later explained what had happened:

"You want to call somebody you can see, but you don't know his name, so you somehow or other try to attract his attention by beckoning or calling out, using any words which occur to you. He comes over and says, 'Why are you calling me? My name is such and such.' Similarly, God Himself in the role of the guru discloses His Name to the pilgrim wandering in search of a guide. After initiation random efforts are over for the pupil. He has touched the lifeline which will lead him to the goal. In the ultimate analysis, the disciple realizes that he is One with the Name and the Guru. And how can it be otherwise? He alone can impart the gift of this Name and none but He Himself can sustain the knowledge of His Name."

She began to undergo intense spiritual experiences, openly. During these experiences the normal functions of her body were suspended for hours and even days. She often did not require food or sleep. In December of the year in which she received diksha she spontaneously became silent, a condition described by Hindus as mauna. Disciples began to come (there are now hundreds of families in the second and third generations who are her devotees), and her fame spread. On the occasion of a solar eclipse—the date was 26 January, 1926—Nirmala experienced a mystical state which was typical of many more to come. Her family and friends were holding kirtan, or mystical singing of the names of God, when, without warning, Mataji went into a mystical state of ecstasy.

"At one moment Mataji was sitting like one of us," said her sister Didi, "the next moment she had changed completely. Her body started swaying rhythmically. Her sari fell back from her head. Her eyes were closed and the entire body swayed to the rhythm of the kirtan. With her body still swaying she stood up, or rather was as if drawn upwards on her toes. It looked as if Mataji had left her body which had become an instrument in the hands of an invisible power. It was obvious to all of us that there was no will motivating her actions. Mataji was quite oblivious of her surroundings. She circled round the room as if wafted along by the wind. Occasionally, her body would start falling to the ground—but before it completed the movement it would regain its upright position, just like a wind-blown leaf which flutters toward the ground and then is uplifted and blown forward by a gust of wind. It seemed her body had no weight or substance. Moving in this manner, Mataji crossed the verandah and entered the kirtan hall, her gaze unblinkingly fixed in an upward direction, her face glowing with a wonderful light. Before the crowd had time to realize that she was in their midst, she fell to the ground from an upright position but did not appear to be hurt at all. Like a leaf in a whirlwind, her body started rolling at a tremendous speed while she was lying prostrate. Some of the women tried to hold her, but it was beyond their power to check even a little of that force.

"After a few moments her body, of its own accord, stopped moving and Mataji sat up. Now she was still like a statue. Just as the tremendous motion of the body had been awe-inspiring, now the utter quiescence was likewise wondrous to behold. Her face was flushed and radiant, and there was an effulgence all around her." Mataji Nirmala then began to sing a few lines of kirtan:

Hare Murare, Mudhukaitabhare,
Gopala, Govinda, Mukunda, Shaure.

She again slumped to the floor as if she were dead, lying in that position for a long time. Bholonath roused her with difficulty, and Nirmala sat up, her limbs apparently out of control. She spoke a few blurred words. All the while her face was gently radiant with an enigmatic, ineffable smile. Kirtan lasted for hours, and Nirmala now sat in a corner while the singing continued and sugar cakes and fruit were served. Eventually she got up and moved into the midst of the singers. Then a strange event occurred. "A variety of bhavas (spiritual ecstasies) manifested themselves on her body," reported one of her biographers, "all marvellous to behold. Now it seemed that she was engaged in a great battle—the expression on her face was fierce and even her complexion had darkened—then it appeared that she was performing arati (a devotional ceremony with the waving of lighted candles) with her entire body. The fierce expression of a moment ago changed into a beautiful gesture of supplication. The bhavas were too numerous and were changing too rapidly to permit more than a glimpse of them." Eventually she ceased experiencing bhavas and sat on the floor, speaking mantra-like verses that resembled Sanskrit, though no one knew what she was saying. She collapsed again, but later was able to rise and leave the kirtan as if nothing had happened. This was the first of a long series of bhavas, which occurred almost daily. Mataji was more often in an exalted than a normal state, though the two states seemed to flow into each other. Witnesses were constantly present. Her devotees claim that Mataji's bhavas cannot be described in words, but "the shape and substance of her body, the color of her skin, and the expressions on her face underwent incredible changes. Her countenance would be flushed and glowing. At times her body would move at a tremendous speed and then again be immovable like a rock. Actions, gestures and facial expressions would change so rapidly as to defy observation." The sight of these bhavas is said to have lifted the onlookers out of themselves. After a bhava Mataji would sometimes lie in a heap for hours. It was supposed that she was in samadhi. Sometimes in the midst of a conversation or while she was at household chores her eyes would become fixed and her body rigid and immobile. Or her eyes would close and she would sink to the floor. Bodily functions stopped "as if being drawn inwards." Breathing would slow down and cease. Her limbs would become either rigid or limp as cloth. "Her entire body would become luminous and on her face there would be an expression of indescribable peace." These states lasted ten to twelve hours, and sometimes as long as twenty-four.

There were various theories about Mataji among her devotees and neighbors in the late 1920s. She was sometimes seen in the posture of various gods and goddesses. Simpler people accepted her as an incarnation of Kali and called her Manusa Kali, Kali in human form. More sophisticated devotees saw her as a sadhaka of great spiritual powers or as a person who had attained self-realization and, instead of accepting final release, had decided to remain in the world to help other pilgrims. One of her most astounding bhavas happened in the presence of a devotee who had accepted her as Kali and then began to have doubts. Along with Bholonath and the devotee and his servant, Mataji went to visit a nearby temple. Everyone was sitting on the verandah in meditation when "suddenly Mataji stood up. She was in a state of bhava and the men gazed at her with folded hands. They were not perturbed because whatever be Mataji's physical condition, she never evoked anything but reverence in the onlookers. There was always beauty and grace in the most startling of her states of bhava. Now her complexion appeared very dark, her black hair fell all around her in a cloud; her eyes were huge and unblinking like those of a statue; her tongue hung out over her chin. In an instant, her head bent completely back to rest between the shoulder blades. The body appeared to be headless." A moment later she sat down and appeared to be her normal self. She had gone through the various appearances of Kali, culminating in Kali as Sati, who is headless when carried by Shiva in his grief and sorrow.

Mataji finally explained—or dismissed—these ecstatic states one day. "All of you want to see these manifestations and therefore they occur now and then of their own accord. For me, the states of bhava, as you call them, are not different from what you call a normal state." On another occasion she said: "The consummation of action and feeling may be called samadhi. It is a state where the question of knowledge and ignorance does not arise. A stage comes where the sadhaka realizes that he is one with his object of contemplation. From that plane he may again come back to ordinary levels of self-consciousness. This type of samadhi also must be transcended. The ultimate state, being unparalleled, cannot be explained or expressed in any language. It is solely a matter of direct experience."

As more and more devotees were attracted to Mataji, a large number of ashrams were established for her use. There are now about two dozen scattered throughout India. Mother travels from one to another, staying a few days or weeks, depending on her mood. News of her arrival spreads rapidly, and in a matter of minutes an ashram is filled with devotees in darshan, coming to see her, to offer gifts, to ask for advice, or merely to sit mutely in her presence. On rare occasions she has exhibited various siddhis (powers), but sparingly, unlike many other well-known holy people who will heal, foretell the future, stop or call down the rain, levitate or bilocate, produce scents or gifts mysteriously. Mother has been known to foretell future happenings, sometimes from the mere sight of a photograph of a person; she has also taken upon herself other people's illnesses so that the invalid suddenly became well while Mother suffered.

The one sign of unusual powers or other worldliness is that she apparently went for a long period with almost no food, and today she requires feeding by someone else, being unable to lift her hands to her mouth. She eats only when food is given her, but eats everything placed before her, on one occasion consuming seventy puris (a kind of fried bread) before her host ran out of flour. Her teeth must also be brushed for her. Her inability to raise her hand to her mouth is a puzzle to me. When I saw her she was a very active woman; even though she was in her middle seventies, she walked briskly and without any sign of her age, at the head of her disciples, who seemed winded. She sat straight, her back firm, and her motions—she was accepting fruit and other gifts and passing them on —were those of a young woman.

Mother has become not only the object of a widespread cult (among, it seems to me, primarily middle- and upper-class people), but the object of a lot of serious adulation, much of it quite uncritical. One reporter says: "People flock around Her from early morning till late at night. Some are painting Her forehead with vermilion drops, other are dressing Her hair, yet others offering to give Her a bath, or to wash Her face and mouth, or to clean Her teeth with toothpaste. Some may request Her permission to change her sari, others express a desire to put some sweets or a slice of fruit into Her mouth, some whisper their secret requests into Her ear." What impresses the reporter is that "She sits up, hour after hour, day after day, in Her exquisitely peaceful manner in the midst of all this noise and bustle, rush and tussle. She remains steady and firm with a face brimming over with cheerfulness." Her first disciple, Bhaiji, left an interesting account of the effect of Mother on himself:

On one occasion Mother came to our house. In the course of our talk I said casually, "It appears, Ma, that to you hot and cold are the same. If a piece of burning coal fell on your foot, would you not feel the pain?" She replied, "Just test it." I did not press the point further.

After a few days, taking up the thread of our previous conversation, Mother placed a piece of burning coal on Her foot. There was a deep burning sore. For one month it did not heal. I felt very upset about that silly suggestion of mine. One day I found Her sitting on the veranda with Her legs stretched out and Her gaze fixed on the sky. Some pus had gathered on the sore. I bowed down at Her feet and licked the pus up with my tongue and lips. From the following day the sore began to heal up.

[Perhaps we should conclude from this account that it was Bhaiji who was the saint. At any rate, one of Mataji's official biographers rewrites the facts by saying, "Bhaiji was mortified to find a bad sore on Mataji's foot due to this experiment. Through his ministrations the sore healed up gradually."]

On another occasion I observed Mother striking the ground with a bamboo chip when a fly was accidentally killed by a stroke. With great care and concern Mother picked it up and kept it in Her closed fist. Many persons were present. Four to five hours passed in conversation. Mother then opened Her fist and said to me, "Can you do anything for the good of this fly which has passed on to the other world?" I said, "I have heard people say, there is heaven inside the body of man." So saying, I swallowed the fly.

[Bhaiji lost his mother when he was a child and would weep over his loss, lying on the floor. When he was ten he was given a mantra by a guru and told to worship the Mother Divine, which he did, saying over and over again, Ma, Ma, Ma. He had a tremendous desire to find a living mother like her. At the age of twenty-eight his wish was fulfilled. He heard of Nirmala and went to see her.]

One morning I went there in a prayerful spirit, and was fortunate enough to see Mother. It sent a thrill into my heart to see her serene yogic posture along with all the modesty and grace to be met only in a newly married lady. It at once flashed upon my mind that the Person for whom my heart had yearned for so many years, and in whose search I had traveled to so many sacred places, stood revealed before me.

My whole being was flooded with joy and every fiber of my body danced with ecstasy. There was an impulse to throw myself prostrate at Her feet and to cry out in tears—"Mother, why have you kept me away from you all these long, long years?" I had come with a load of thoughts struggling for expression, but all were hushed into silence under the spell of Her soothing grace. I sat there speechless and dumb. Mother, too, spoke not a word. After a little while, I bowed to Her and left the place. I could not touch Her feet though I had a strong desire to do so. It was not through fear or delicacy; some mysterious power pushed me away from Her presence.

[Bhaiji eventually demanded that Mother state her identity, with the following result.]

Immediately a dazzling flood of heavenly light shone forth from Her face. I was struck dumb with awe and wonder. All my doubts were laid at rest. About fifteen days later I went to Shah-bag [her home] one morning and found the door of Mother's bedroom closed. I sat down in front of it some 25 to 30 cubits away. The door opened all at once. I found to my bewilderment, the figure of a divinely beautiful goddess as genially bright as the sun at dawn, illumining the whole interior of the room. In the twinkling of an eye She withdrew all the radiance within Her body and Mother was there, standing and smiling in the usual manner. I realized that Mother had revealed Herself in response to what I had said a few days back. I began to recite a hymn and prayed to Her.

After a while Mother advanced toward me. She picked up a flower and a few blades of durba grass and placed them on my head, as I fell at Her feet. I was beside myself with joy and rolled on the ground at Her feet. From that moment a deep conviction began to take root in my mind that She was not only my mother but *the Mother* of this universe.

Adultation continues from this point. Mother is called "Lord Krishna in the person of Mother," "the human incarnation of Divine Bliss or Ananda," and so on, without end. Her devotees have told us that "She has indicated in clear language that birth and death do not touch her"; that "there were rays of powerful blue light emanating from Mother's eyes"; that "She is practically illiterate and yet she is the repository of all wisdom." One devotee told the world that he left "family, friends, country, profession, wealth" to follow Mother. Another writes, "It is not an exaggeration to say that even Divine Personages come near to Mother for her darshan." Her devotees number some Westerners who speak in the same terms. A Frenchman writes that Mother has "become one with Sri Krishna Himself" and calls her "that source of Life Eternal which is Ma Anandamayi." A German woman said, "In Mataji, God allowed me to see him with the closeness of intimacy." Some of these foreigners have given up their Western identities and have taken Indian names, like Vijayananda and Premananda. However, Arthur Koestler, who spent a year in India examining Eastern spirituality, had a different reaction. He included Mataji (he refers to her as Ananada) in a chapter called "Four Contemporary Saints" in *The Lotus and the Robot*. During the darshan he attended he found that "I was the only one left out in the cold" and that he had "a feeling of acute distress." He began to tiptoe toward the door of the ashram hall, but "I was intercepted by several indignant devotees and made to pick up the two tangerines I had left behind. They were sticky and dirty, but sanctified by Mother's touch, and I gave them to some urchins in the street, hoping they would derive a darshan that, for one reason or another, was denied me."

Some various facets of Mother's personality and thought might be mentioned. Her ashrams are tightly run: "The sexes are not allowed to mix in a way that may spell danger. Women are taught by women, and the monks warned against women visitors. Mother is meticulous in the observance of pujas, which are performed according to the rituals laid down in the shastras." The same devotee adds: "Nor is she in favor of abolition of the caste system, which, she says, came by the will of God for the maintenance of order in society. If caste goes, it will do so by His will only. Until then it should be conformed to." Another devotee, who approached her in concern over the frightful poverty of the masses and the mounting social tensions in India, was told: "Baba, don't lose heart; these are all His forms, in which He has chosen to appear in these distressful times before man.

Don't be afraid: such birth throes are inevitable for the coming New Social Order, which He is planning." What is important, rather than social consciousness and charity for the poor, is to "attune one's self to the Supreme Reality which is the goal of human life and the only way of attaining to a state of natural and everlasting poise, union and harmony." She advocates self-control—that is, sexual abstinence —and repetition of the Divine Name. Much of what she says is incomprehensible. A devotee says, "It makes no difference if they understand her words or not." Another: "Sometimes Mother speaks in a tongue that is not of this world."

The night of 11 November. In the car, on the way to see Mataji, Mr. and Mrs. Bahadur, relatives of some close friends (also named Bahadur), tell me that Mother is God incarnate in human form. The Bahadurs have been devotees for eleven years. His sister was the first to become a disciple. Mr. Bahadur informs me. "My sister brought home two photographs of Mother and gave me one. From the moment I saw that photograph I knew she was God. I worshipped her through the photograph." Mrs. Bahadur was not impressed at first, but is now a fully dedicated devotee. They want to tell me more—I have been asking questions—but Mr. Bahadur says it's best to wait until after I have seen Mother. The Bahadurs are very pleasant, elderly people, and quite well off. Their sincerity and devotion are impressive. I must see for myself, they say again, and then we will talk.

Mother's ashram is far out in the environs of New Delhi. The area was once actual countryside, but the city is developing at a ferocious rate and swallowing up the tiny villages and settlements on the plain. The night is very dark and foggy and the driver has trouble in finding the way, but then we see a landmark, a mosque with a huge minaret set off in electric lights, and turn off the road and go up to another smaller street and then into a dirt track and arrive at the ashram, a large, clean-looking building with no special characteristics. We enter the courtyard and remove our shoes and go inside the ashram. There is a large central hall with a raised platform at one end and straw mats on the floor. We sit down. Several dozen quite well-off people are scattered about; the majority are women wrapped in expensive-looking shawls (it is now winter in this part of northern India). The shawls give the women a timeless effect, graceful and eternal, and it occurs to me that we Hindus are better off existing in uncharted, unclocked lives than following the rigid measurements of time and space imposed upon us by the Islamic-Christian world, which brought us hourglasses and clocks and railway schedules. However, I have been so conditioned by Western influences not to waste time that I quickly become tired of sitting with nothing to do and begin to read a letter.

Then: conch shells begin to sound, a great, deep, hoarse call to the eternal regions. Mother is coming. Everyone stands and forms a double line up to the door. Mother enters in quick strides. A small woman, black hair, small round granny glasses, bundled up in a white smock and looking like Gandhi in drag. A man prostrates himself before her but is quickly pulled aside by some monks from the ashram, and Mother walks swiftly to the platform and sits with her feet tucked under her (to avoid people's touches, perhaps, or is it the cold?). Two large white bolsters are propped against her back. She has a pleasant, relaxed face, smiling slightly, is missing two or three teeth on the right front of her mouth. No wrinkles, though she is in her seventies.

Devotees come up, prostrate themselves or bow in the usual crouch, offer fruits and flowers, try to put garlands on her neck. Mother takes off each garland and places it on the neck of the devotee. Apples, bananas: offered in bags made of old magazine pages (nothing is wasted in India). Mother returns an apple to the donor, turns the rest of the bag over to a monk, who then distributes the contents. This is prasad, the offering one makes to God which God returns sanctified. All this handing of garlands and fruit is done very quickly and efficiently. Long years of practice. Some people want a few words. Mother talks very softly, directly to the person, so that each one seems to feel specially favored. Each devotee knows her role: give and receive. It is a prescribed ritual. One woman puts a yellow bath towel across Mother's shoulders, like a dupatta, and another on her lap, then a thin blue-green chiffon shawl over the towel. Mother won't return them. This woman is persistent: she refuses to retire as the other women have done. She offers bags of fruit, lights a small oil candle. Other people come and go, and meanwhile Mother ignores the woman. The woman is fat, unattractive. Mother seems to resent her but says nothing. I sense a latent air of hostility. Some monks in saffron robes are given bags of fruit. A few bags break and there is gentle laughter among the devotees. Suddenly Mother gets up and goes; she enters a small room next to the hall and someone closes the door. She has been traveling for five hours and is tired. The devotees, about forty in all, break into small clusters and talk for a few minutes, aimlessly, and when everyone has accepted the fact that Mother is through with them for the evening, they get into their cars with a lot of little good-byes (the drivers have been waiting outside) and roll off into the fog.

Mr. and Mrs. Bahadur tell me again that Mother is God in human form. What does Mother say about herself? I ask. "That she is God—so I have heard." I try to nail down this idea, but it is not clear whether she actually says she is God or whether people merely assume it. The Bahadurs are unable to explain it to me. Mother appears to give the impression that she is. "Her devotees say she is, and she has not denied it." When people ask point-blank, "Who are you?" Mother answers, "I am what you think I am."

The Bahadurs tell me what is common knowledge and what I already know: that when people go to Mother with questions she gives an answer in a few words that always seem to be precise and pertinent. "She may not know who you are, but she knows enough about you so whatever she says is to the point. People go with problems intending to speak to her, but often merely being in her presence is sufficient. The answers come to them, unsaid."

Is she ever angry? I ask. "No, but she may be stern with the young women who live with her."

Anandamaya Ma is an unlettered village woman, a Bengali. She can read but has had no higher education. Bengali is her mother tongue but she has learned Hindi. The Bahadurs say she does not know English, but Maya, their cousin, with whom I am staying, says she is sure Mother speaks some English. Mother "knows" the Vedas and other scriptures without any training in them. Sometimes she doesn't speak but just sits. The devotees sit too. That is darshan.

There is motion in rest and rest in motion.

Everything is contained in everything.

Whatever a man thinks, feels, or realizes about the Supreme is true from his particular standpoint and has full significance for him.

An eternal friendship exists between God and man, but in His play it is sometimes there and sometimes severed, or rather it appears to be severed. It is not really so, for the relation is eternal. As such, we may begin from anywhere.

Belief means to believe in one's own Self; disbelief means to mistake the non-Self for one's Self.

Melt by devotion the sense of separateness, or burn it by knowledge —then you will come to know your Self.

By virtue of the guru's power, everything becomes possible; therefore seek a guru. Meanwhile, since all names are His Name, all forms His Form, select one of them and keep it with you as your constant companion. At the same time, He is also nameless and formless; for the Supreme it is possible to be everything and yet nothing. So long as you have not found a guru, adhere to that name or form of Him that appeals to you most, and ceaselessly pray that He may reveal himself to you as the Sadguru. In every truth, the Guru dwells within and unless you discover the inner Guru, nothing can be achieved. If you feel no desire to turn to a guru, bind yourself by a daily routine of sadhana, as school children do, whose duty it is to follow a fixed timetable.

If you hanker after anything such as name, fame, or position, God will bestow it on you, but you will not feel satisfied. The kingdom of God is a whole, and unless you inherit it in its entirety, you cannot remain content.

The supreme duty of man is to undertake the quest for his true Being. Whether one takes the path of devotion, where the "I" is lost in the "Thou," or the path of self-inquiry, in search of the true "I," it is He alone who is found in the "thou" as well as in the "I."

❖

Though many disciples see Mataji as Kali, or Kali in the form of Durga, a leading Indian philosopher (perhaps India's most outstanding philosopher of the present) dismisses this view. He is Mahamahopadyaya Dr. Gopinath Kaviraj, M.A., D. Litt., Late Principal, Government Sanskrit College, Benares (India's most prestigious theological university). One fall morning I went to see Gopinath Kaviraj at his home, in a part of Benares quite remote from the tourist and pilgrim areas. His name is engraved on a marble plaque outside a large rambling mansion in a state of disrepair, but the servants told me that he was no longer there, having moved into Mataji's ashram about a mile away. At the ashram, which stands high on the north bank of the Ganges, with a splendid view of the river and the sandy plain on the other side, I waited in a corridor with several other people because Dr. Kaviraj was sleeping. He sees people only from 10:30 to 11:00 A.M. because his time is limited (he is an old man) and he still has much work to do. At 10:30 we were allowed into his room, and seated ourselves on mats on the floor. The professor was stretched on his side on a cot, with several pillows under his head, still sleeping. A desk was covered with vials and jars and tubes of medicine. I felt very eerie, watching this sleeping, aged, ill man, as if I were intruding on some sacred ritual. Finally he opened his eyes, vaguely, a few times, and once or twice tried to raise his head but fell back on the pillows, exhausted. "He is dying," a Mr. Sen Gupta whispered to me. Mr. Sen Gupta seemed like a wily little sparrow waiting to steal some crumbs. We sat and watched the professor for the allotted half hour, and then it was eleven o'clock and time to leave.

Gopinath Kaviraj has spent a major portion of his life studying Mataji and serving as one of her devotees. He has written about her at length, in rather dense philosophical terms loaded with Sanskrit

170

terms which require a classical background (Indian, of course) to comprehend—"We have to recognize four ultimate types, *viz.*, anupaya, sambhavopaya, saktopaya and anavopaya" would be a fair example, so I won't burden the reader with unnecessary excerpts. What Gopinath Kaviraj thinks about Mataji, discarding a lot of scholastic ramblings and false trails (of which he is a master), goes as follows.

I sympathize with those people to whom Mother is a riddle. She is so unlike ordinary or even extraordinary persons known to us that it is extremely hard to make any positive statement about her with any degree of confidence.

The possibility of an antenatal existence [a basic tenet of Hinduism] is ruled out by Mother's definite assurance that her life is not subject to the laws of natural causation and that she has no prior life to account for her present existence. Mother has had no experience of darkness in her life, either of the soul or of the spirit [as is commonly experienced by mystics], nor has she any experience of the descent of Light except as a matter of play. It is said that from her very birth she was aware of what she had ever been and what she would always continue to be and that there was no possibility of a deviation from her self-conscious stature for a single moment. Mother's self-knowledge, we are assured, did not arise under the impact of an extrinsic element outside herself—it was always with her, being a state of her nature. It was already there in its fullness, requiring no effort on her part, nor any grace from above, to bring it into greater perfection. This self-knowledge is not easily explicable. It cannot be interpreted in terms of saints and sages. We cannot ignore the fact that she was never subject to ignorance and that the question of saving grace even in its highest degree can never arise in her case.

Mother herself has confessed to some that she never loses her supreme self-consciousness. Samadhi or no samadhi, she is where she has always been: she knows no change, no modification, no alteration; she is always poised in the self-same awareness as a Supreme Being and Integral Universal, transcending all limitations of time, space, and personality and yet comprehending them all in a great harmony.

She has said times without number that her body is not like that of an ordinary person through prarabdha karma [past karma fructifying in the present] under the dominating influence of ignorance and that she has no previous life to account for her present existence. Nor will she have a future life in continuation of and for the adjustment of her activities in the present life.

Now then, how are we to account for what appears to be Mother's body and mind? May they not be due to an act of the Supreme Will playing in its freedom or to the same Will in response to the cumulative karma of humanity crying out for ages for a Divine Appearance? It comes to this, then: Mother's body is no body and her mind is no mind in the ordinary connotation of the terms. They are only apparent and exist for the ignorant who are under maya and unable to see behind the veil. This is a docetic view to be sure, but there seems to be no escape from it. Mother herself has said: "For a Self-Realized Being neither the world with its pairs of opposites exists, nor does the body. If there is no world there can obviously be no body either. Since there is no world and no body there can be no action either: this stands to reason. After Self-Realization there is no body, no world, and no action—not even the faintest possibility of these—nor is there such an idea as 'there is not.' To use these words is exactly the same as not to speak: to keep silent or not is identical—all is That alone."

We hear a general complaint that Mother's language is not intelligible. It seems to me that what appears to the average reader, with his logical bent of thought structure, as a riddle is a plain truth on a higher level of consciousness. Mother often says "Ya ta," which may be rendered as "It is what it is." These words are often said by Mother when she speaks of the Absolute. It is difficult to say exactly what they stand for. One may equate them with the conception of Pure Being, Non-Being, Self, the Infinite, the Ineffable, the Universal, the Immaculate, the Immutable, etc., according to one's point of view. It is the Nameless referred to under different names and the Formless under different forms.

As for the implications of the enigmatical *Ya ta* we may compare the following sayings of Mother herself:

Whether you say it exists or does not exist,
or that it is beyond existence and non-existence,
or even beyond that—whatever you like.
Whether you call it the One,
   the Two,
or the Infinite,
whatever anyone may say
    is well.

When this is possible, the wall is not there,
although it exists
  and even if no wall exists,
   yet it is there.

For the Supreme it is possible to be everything and yet nothing.

A state of being exists where it is immaterial whether He assumes a form or not—what is, is He.

In this state of complete poise nothing at all
is any longer apart from Him,
what is,
  is the Thing itself.

These statements [says Dr. Kaviraj] show that there is no difference at all—not even between Being and non-Being, between Light and Darkness, between Good and Evil, between Motion and Rest, and between Personal and Impersonal. All is one—one is all. Even the equation is not possible, for True One is where there is no sense of the one. All this sounds paradoxical, but it is the highest truth. Whatever is expressed in language is only a thought and appeals only to the thought level of human consciousness.

  Mother says that all her activities are really spontaneous and not prompted by will or purpose, nor influenced or coloured by desires. Will power is not the spring of her actions. The untrained will of the layman and the trained will of the yogi are equally absent in her, and what appears as the will is only an expression of the Great Power beyond the will working from within.

That Mother is untouched by karma of any kind need not therefore be an enigma. There being no previous karma, the origin of her body is to be explained in part by the play of the Supreme Power, either in itself or as reacting to the collective aspirations of humanity. As to why the Supreme Power should have expressed itself in a particular human body is a question which the ordinary man is not in a position to answer.

It is a very difficult task to try to describe Mother as she really is. She has appeared differently to different persons, and even if these differences are contradictory we can quietly accept them, knowing full well that in a higher synthesis even contradictories may meet together. She is too near us to be seen in her proper perspective, and as for ourselves we too shall have to rise up to the height and attain to the broad outlook in which an attempt may be made to study her properly.

What is really needed is to feel that she is Mother and we are her children and that as mere children we cannot be expected to know her as she is, but only as she shows herself to us in response to our cravings. It really becomes us to behave as infants crying out in the night and to invoke Mother with an inarticulate language for her actual descent and benediction.

"Mother, who are you?"
"I am what you say I am, not more, not less."

Salutations at the Lotus feet of
Satgurudev Shri Sant Ji Maharaj

Divine Light Mission*
offers an
Antidote to Atom Bomb
by inventing
PEACE-BOMB
which explodes in Delhi
at India Gate, 8, 9, 10 November

Air cups its hands to hold eulogical voices proclaiming—
to learn the Truth and vizualize the divinity within.
Millions from all corners gather at India Gate
to hear the Satguru of the Space Age
BALYOGESHWAR SHRI SANT JI MAHARAJ

WE ARE SPIRITUAL REVOLUTIONARIES—OUR WEAPON IS PEACE

Salutations at the lotus feet of
Satgurudev Shri Sant Ji Maharaj

God is born in the knowledge and
lives in the devotion, dies in the nes-
cience.

Satguru bestows grace
                    Which is the embrace
Of love and spirituality
                    Which brings equality.

God expects but one thing of you,
and that is that you should come out
of yourself insofar as you are a created
being and let God be God in you.

Param Sant Satgurudev Shri Hans Ji Maharaj was born into a Suryawansh, or sun, dynasty and was descendant from the lineage of Lord Rama's family, Rama being the incarnation of the solar aspect of Vishnu. In childhood he was extremely spiritual and had mystic experiences which could not be rationally explained. As a young man he was influenced by various reform movements and rejected the idea of guru, until he met one who influenced him profoundly, largely through a miracle. Maharaj Ji was on his way to meet the guru; in attempting to cross a stream which was swollen after a heavy rain, he almost drowned. A mysterious hand pulled him from the waters, but on the shore Maharaj Ji could see no one. The guru was waiting for him and bestowed updesh, or initiation.

Back home again (and dried out), Maharaj Ji began to browse through the Bhagavad Gita and found that suddenly all its secrets and its full meaning had become crystal clear and what had been a mystery before was now revealed to him. The next morning he went into samadhi, and in this state of bliss where all body consciousness is lost and man dives deep into the Absolute, he realized the divinity. He began to attract devotees, mainly poor factory workers and farmers, by preaching that "the kingdom of heaven is within." His appeal went directly to the underprivileged, being against caste distinctions —his devotees were largely members of the lowest caste, the Sudras —and opposing the outer (that is, Brahminical) forms of worship, such as the counting of prayer beads, penances, and fasting. His argument was that it is actions, not caste, that make a man superior, and if God is polluted by worship by a low-caste person, how can He be God? "No one asks about caste in the court of the Lord. The man who remembers God in his heart attains God."

The kingdom of heaven within man, said Maharaj Ji, is to be gained by the practice of yoga, which according to the Bhagavad

Gita was "first imparted to the sun, who then passed it on to Manu," the great Hindu sage and lawgiver. The knowledge of yoga that Maharaj Ji was giving to the world was, he said, the same that Lord Krishna had given Arjuna five thousand years ago, enabling him to comprehend the universe as an integral whole. This universal consciousness (Vishwa Rupa is the technical term) seen by Arjuna through the Third Eye can be seen and comprehended today by everyone, provided he is told where the Third Eye is located and how to open it.

With the Third Eye opened and in use, one can see the dazzling Light brighter than a thousand suns within oneself and can merge the self into God while still living in the physical body upon the earth. "What is the Divine Eye?" said Maharaj Ji. "The only true Guru is he who can open this Divine Eye by showing the disciple the self-effulgent Light within. By focusing the mind upon the self-effulgent Light again and again we will reach the abode of the Lord from where there is no return. This is the state of moksha. Lord Krishna describes this supreme abode by saying, "Having reached that from which men do not return, that is, My Supreme State, neither the sun nor the moon can illumine it." Light merges with the Light. The Divine Light cannot be visualized with our outer, gross eyes. It can only be seen with the Third Eye, the Divine Eye which is opened by the grace of the spiritual master. We are all in possession of our Divine Eye, but most of us are ignorant of its existence and its power. Divine Light is simply the radiance of the life essence, of our own true inner essence." To gain this inner vision, the mind is directed uninterruptedly through japa to a particular object. Japa practice purifies the mind and brings it under subjugation. Ordinary japa consists of counting prayers and mantras mechanically (by a rosary or on the fingers), but Shri Hans Maharaj taught ajapa japa, or repetitionless repetition. The aspirant is instructed to concentrate the mind on the "Flight of Hansa" within the tip of the nose merely as a conscious subject. "Hansa is a mysterious sound movement, a mantra which is the Thought-Form of the Swan of Knowledge." This ajapa japa "could kindle the Divine Light within, which dispels the ignorance of man as to the reality of his own self."

As his teaching, with its emphasis on castelessness, attracted more and more devotees, Orthodox Hinduism began to attack Shri Sant Ji Maharaj. It was usually the most conservative among the

Brahmins who denounced him, though in a strange twist of karma, his most virulent enemies were the Arya Samaj, the reform sect which had appealed to him when he was a young man because of its denunciation of the evils of the caste system and its emphasis on a clear-cut contemporary approach to life in preference to the ritualism with which Hinduism was encrusted. The Arya Samaj attacks became so fanatical that Maharaj Ji was forced to go to court to obtain a public apology from the society. In 1950 Maharaj Ji organized the Divine Light Mission; some of his first devotees from among the factory workers and farmers were given the title of mahatmas (great souls) and sent out into the world to preach. The Mission spread across northern India, appealing in general to the urban proletariat, the farm workers, and the lower middle class in both cities and the countryside. "The world is for the wealthy," said Maharaj Ji, "but God is for the poor." His teaching, his disciples said, "transcended caste, color, and creed." Maharaj Ji himself said: "Who are the Sudras? Only those people are Sudras who lack faith in the Lord God, no matter what their caste may be." He added: "Religion does not mean surrender to dogmas and religious scriptures or conformity to ritual. The religion I teach, my religion, constitutes an abiding faith in the perfect values of truth and the ceaseless attempt to realize it in the innermost core of our nature."

A basic tenet of his teaching was the need for guru. He saw himself as the satguru, the truth teacher, the great guru: "It is a spiritual law that there can be no divine knowledge without the grace of the living Satguru. The Satguru is the living embodiment of grace, and the very ocean of mercy. Guru is the dispeller of the darkness of ignorance and the bestower of the Divine Light. Search for the guru [that is, himself] who reveals the true Name of God. All other gurus are false. What was told to the sun at the very beginning of creation, which was what Krishna imparted to Arjuna, is what I am offering to you today. The Name and the 'form' of God referred to in the sacred books cannot be found in the Scriptures. The texts speak of the self-effulgent light of God, but this Light can only be seen within man. The words Ram, Ram, Hari Krishna, or Om Namo Shivai are not the True Names of God. The True Name of God is beyond the alphabets and is unmanifest. It is the primordial sound, the breath of life. Light merges in the Light."

There is a fine dividing line in our holy men between mere

sanctity and the divine. There comes a time when the man who is filled with the divine is suddenly realized to be the Divine. Was Maharaj Ji, the Satguru, God? His followers seemed to think so, some of them, and it appeared that he did too. Early in 1966 Maharaj Ji told a huge gathering in Bombay: "You know not the greatness of the Guru [again, himself]. Lord Rama was an incarnation of God, enjoying fourteen types of divine powers. Lord Krishna was an incarnation of God, having sixteen types of divine powers. But I am all-perfect, and am the master of all sixty-four divine powers. None can match the greatness of the Guru." The people were said to have been bewildered by these revelations.

A man named C. L. Tandon (M.A. History and Pol. Sc), who serves as secretary of the Divine Light Mission and seems to be a buffer between the extremists on one side who see Maharaj Ji as God and those who view him as just another holy man, has written: "In the last two to three years of his life, Maharaj Ji was all dance and bliss. Taking the tamboura in his hands, he would sing and dance on the platform, giving peace and bliss to the devotees who delighted in these lilas. He was in a state of divine ecstacy. He said, 'O mortal men of the world, I announce, I proclaim, none but Guru can save mortals from the clutches of death and maya.'"

On 16 July, 1966, Shri Maharaj Ji died ("shed his mortal coil," as Tandon expresses it). "The people were in a state of extreme despair, losing themselves in an anguish of misery over the loss of their beloved Guru. To thousands on that day, the grief of the child left parentless was experienced. His followers felt adrift and anchorless without his presence amongst them."

The story should end there, but to admit a conclusion at this point is not to know eternal India. The reader whose memory is as fallible as mine will have to try to keep in mind Shri Sant Maharaj Ji, more formally known as Param Sant Satgurudev Shri Hans Ji Maharaj, and Sant Ji Maharaj, fully entitled Balyogeshwar Param Hans Satgurudev Shri Sant Ji Maharaj, the satguru. They are father and son, and so we move to another generation. Mr. Tandon: "Just as we discard our garments when they are worn out and old and replace them with new ones, so did Maharaj Ji reject his aging body to change his outer form, passing into the frame of Sant Ji Maharaj. For Guru is the Holy Name, and this name is immortal. Death does not touch it, nor time destroy it. The body is the home of the Divine and He simply left his old body to take up a new one. Guru never dies, He is immortal, all-permeating, divine. He lived, and lives, and will live forever in the hearts of all. For the Guru always lives in the present." Tandon makes it somewhat clearer in another passage: "Shri Hans Ji Maharaj aroused millions from the slumber of ignorance by his magic wand of spiritual knowledge. Balyogeshwar Shri Sant Ji Maharaj was acclaimed a born saint by Shri Hans Ji Maharaj. Yogiraj Shri Hans Ji Maharaj left his mortal frame on 19 July, 1966, transmitting His power potential of the secret Yoga to his Holiness Shri Sant Ji Maharaj." (Tandon gives two different dates for the transference.)

What the situation comes to, as I heard it from other sources, is that shortly before Maharaj Ji died, he had a presentiment of his coming death and called his sons together. There are four, and they stood before him while he looked them over. Then he placed his hands on the shoulders of the youngest, who was then about nine, indicating that the boy was to receive the father's spirit and would carry on the work. "Others also saw the Divinity manifested in him," writes Tandon of the son, "and were constantly in awe of his unusual behaviour from his very childhood. He was destined to fulfil the mission of uniting all religions with the silken bond of love."

Salutations at the lotus feet of
Satguru Shri Sant Ji Maharaj*

Millions gathered in Delhi yesterday to take His Holiness Satguru Balyogeshwar Shri Sant Ji Maharaj on a mammoth procession, proclaiming him as the Lord Incarnate of the Space Age (Kalki Avatar).

The procession, which is part of the Hans Joyoti Celebrations held in honour of the founder of the Divine Light Mission, was the largest Delhi has ever seen. Indian and foreign devotees walked together on an eighteen-mile route which ended at India Gate.

The thirteen-year-old child yogi addressed a gathering of some 300,000 people in the evening at India Gate, and declared that this year will go down as the year of Spiritual revolution.

He said that there were two great forces arraigned against each other, that of good and evil. The clue for victory is to be found in the Real Name of God which will bring about the spiritual revolution.

The clash, he continued, will culminate this year in the establishment of "Ram Rajya," the Kingdom of Heaven, here on earth.

He asked the people to regard the procession and events of the Shri Hans Jayanti celebrations as but writing on the wall for the tide of future events.

Spiritual insight is made possible through the Name, and Maharaj Ji stressed that all nations and intellectuals should know the secret of the Name, which amounts to knowing the Vedas or all other Holy Scriptures.

The scriptures can only give theoretical knowledge of inner peace, while the knowledge of the Name makes this knowledge practical. The knowledge of Name is beyond Mind and intellect, it is a constant process which can only be known through the grace of the Satguru.

Shri Sant Ji Maharaj said that the mind must be attached to the real Name which alone can cleanse the mind of all its evil tendencies, thus transforming the individual and his world.

The Spiritual Revolution will take place within the individual through the knowledge of the real Name of God, and will have its effect this very year.

Shri Sant Ji Maharaj will deliver spiritual discourses at India Gate at 7 P.M. on the evenings of the 8th and 9th November.

In a mammoth assembly at India Gate, Paramhansa Shri Sant Ji Maharaj announced here today that he possessed a knowledge which would bring about a spiritual and cultural revolution in the world.

Shri Sant Ji Maharaj, who has been acclaimed by lakhs [hundreds of thousands] of people from all over the world as the Lord Incarnate of the Space Age (Kalki Avatar), gave an electrically charged discourse on the only way to bring about peace and obliviate the use of armaments and wars in the world.

He said, "I have that mysterious knowledge with which I will bring about a peaceful spiritual revolution. All hatred and fear will be completely uprooted without the use of any type of armament. The time has come when the lion and the goat will work and live together in peace."

Lord Krishna's prophecy has come true, continued the child yogi, for God has again incarnated himself in this world to relieve the sorrows and miseries which beset the globe, and replace them with knowledge of the spirit.

Reminding the audience of the slogan of Shri Subash Chandar Bose, "Give me blood and I will give you freedom," Shri Sant Ji Maharaj said, "Surrender the reins of your life to me and I shall bestow on you peace and the eternal."

His emotion-packed discourse was marked by his revelation of the nature of Guru, and of the great opportunity of spiritual peace which man does not avail himself of that is now being freely offered to the world.

The thirteen-year-old Balyogeshwar remarked that some think he is too young to transmit spiritual knowledge. He pointed out that spiritual knowledge has nothing to do with the age of a man. It is transmitted power which transcends all barriers.

Shedding tears, he reminisced over the late Shri Ji Maharaj, who devoted his life selflessly for the enlightenment of the people, and urged all to take advantage of the love and knowledge which only the Satguru can bestow.

The Spiritual Academy Exhibition being held on the occasion of Shri Hans Jayanti Celebrations was inaugurated on November 5 at 7:00 P.M. For the first time in the history of Delhi, representatives of the poor and down-trodden section of the people opened the doors of a spiritual exhibition to the public.

The exhibition employs multi-media to demonstrate its message. Charts, paintings, and photographs are combined with film and electronic devices. Especially to be mentioned are the use of stroboscope and liquid projector displaying the science of genesis.

The ten avatars of Vishnu are strikingly depicted in their relation to Darwin's theory of evolution, giving evidence of the continual progressive change in man's nature.

Concluding, the 13-year-old Satguru said that man can never know the ultimate Truth through intellectual effort alone, for the sense organs are finite and naturally they cannot by themselves realize the Infinite. That is the reason why the aspirant should seek the grace of Satguru who is the human expression of Divine Grace and who alone can enable one to transcend the sense limitations and realize the Supreme.

Shedding tears . . .

Salutations at the lotus feet
of Sadguru

QUESTION: What is Peace Bomb?
ANSWER: Peace Bomb is the Brahma Vidya, otherwise known as Raja Vidya or Divine Knowledge, added with the Divine Spark of the Satguru. The theoretical knowledge of Brahma Vidya is given in the Vedas, but it is only the Satguru that can give it life and destroy the evils and warring tendencies which exist within man. Peace Bomb is manifested as the highest stage of evolutionary development yet attained by man.

Q: What is Brahma Vidya?
A: There are four essential constitutents which make up Brahma Vidya. These are separately discussed in each Veda.

Q. What are the subjects discussed in the four Vedas?
A: In the Rig Veda the Sabda Brahma, or Holy Name, is discussed. In the Yajur Veda we are told of Divya Jyoti, or the Divine Light. The Sama Veda is concerned with Nada Brahma, or Divine Harmony. Lastly, the Athaiva Veda deals with Amrit Tattva, or Holy Nectar. The Vedas are concerned only with the theoretical knowledge but are not complete until they are made practical. These four "elements" provide the raw materials for Peace Bomb.

Q: What occurs when Peace Bomb is detonated?
A: Whereas before we have dealt only with theoretical knowledge, with the coming of Peace Bomb we are concerned only with its practical aspects. The practical aspects of an atom bomb are (1) intense vibrational waves which draw all matter into its pull, (2) intense light, (3) high volume of sound, and (4) residue or fallout.

In the detonation of Peace Bomb we experience exactly the same phenomena but the results are just the reverse as those with the atom bomb. Whereas the atom bomb causes by its vibrations total destruction of the environment it explodes in, Peace Bomb brings the immediate effect of spiritual stability in its vibrations, otherwise known as Sabda Brahma.

The overwhelming sight of the atom bomb blinds man and signals his death, while the Divine Light of Peace Bomb opens the eyes to the secrets of nature, leading men to self-realization.

The fearful sound of the atom bomb exploding causes great consternation and unease, while the Divine Harmony of Peace Bomb brings calm and tranquility to the life of man.

The deadly fallout from the atom bomb causes death and poisons the land and air, while the Divine Nectar of Peace Bomb falls like sweet rain, alleviating all mental and bodily ailments, rejuvenating the whole being.

The combined result of these four manifestations of Peace Bomb is one of total transformation. Love radiates within the heart of the individual and all warring tendencies are destroyed. On the personal level Peace Bomb works upon the evils within the heart and brings peace. It is only when this individual peace becomes widespread reality that worldwide harmony can be established. Working first upon the inner nature of the individual, Peace Bomb spreads to the society, the nation, and finally the world. This is the only way to establish peace on an international scale.

Q: How can this Peace Bomb be detonated?

A: The only way that Peace Bomb can be detonated is that we find a master who is able to impart to us the practical knowledge of Brahma Vidya, or Divine Knowledge. But it is to be remembered that Peace Bomb is latently within us, and it is the only personification of this knowledge, or the Realized Soul, that can give us the spark needed to activate our inner self.

Q: Does such a spiritual master exist?

A: Yes, Peace Bomb is Balyogeshwar Param Sant Satgurudev Shri Sant Ji Maharaj himself, who will "explode" upon Delhi to bestow his divine radiation to all those who avail themselves just like the atom bomb directly affecting only that area where it explodes, only those who are receptively open to the Bomb of Peace will profit from it. But just as the radiations from the atom bomb spread through the atmosphere to surrounding areas, the spark of truth once ignited will spread throughout the world like wild fire, affecting all by its influence.

꩜

A lot of rumors and gossip. Seems that the father was the incarnation of the "inner man," also of Vishnu through being a descendant of Rama, one of Vishnu's forms on earth. The movement seems to go on two levels: (1) A mass, popular "religion of the people," a religion of the oppressed (that is, the very poor, the peasants, the lowest castes, the people who are not twice-born as are the three higher castes). The movement is anti-caste, anti-intellectual, anti-Brahmin (the priests, who have a stranglehold on everything), developing spontaneously as the masses find their own strengths through the boy-god. (2) A cynical level: the boy is being used by people behind the scenes for their own purposes. The mother is said to be very powerful, as is the oldest brother, who is also an incarnation of Vishnu. But the emphasis is on the boy, who is only thirteen but is God. Obviously both levels coexist. It is impressive, seeing these peasants come to worship their God. They are terribly poor. They're camped out in a huge park called the Delhi Gate. It's part of a mall leading up to the government complex, the huge mass of Parliament House in cream and red sandstone, the secretariats and Rashtrapati Bhavan, another gigantic British-built edifice. The Delhi papers (that is, the Establishment) have been complaining like hell about the peasants, what a mess they're making, but no one has given them sanitary facilities and they're doing their best, washing in the limpid pools, cooking on tiny fires or eating cold rice and vegetables they've brought in little brass or clay pots. Mostly they're in family groups, with all the babies and children and in-laws and friends. They've been sleeping on mats on the ground, rather cold, because winter is coming. I've been hanging around all afternoon, looking at people and trying to get some information. The Mission has set up a number of tents, some selling large gawdy calendars of the boy and the father and of various gods. Finally found a tent with printed literature, a few pieces in English. Now it is dark. At the far end of the encampment is a stage, too far away to see, and impossible to get to, as the ground is full of people sitting patiently, waiting for His Holiness to appear. I get into a conversation with a thin, rather poor-looking man. There is a continual blare of Indian devotional music on the loudspeakers, so I have trouble hearing the man. He says he is a homeopathic doctor. I want to know why this man is a devotee of the boy's. "I receive a special light from him, not the light of the sun, not the light of the moon, but a special light. If I close my eyes now I will see that light." And what else do you get from him? "Solace."

The next day. Miss Joan. The Mission has been given the use of a very large mansion near India Gate where the boy-god and his entourage may stay. It serves as a kind of nerve center for the celebration. I am sitting on the floor (naturally) with a large number of people in a big antechamber awaiting the arrival of His Holiness, the Satguru Balyogeshwar Shri Sant Ji Maharaj, the thirteen-year-old avatar. There's a lot of milling about, total confusion; people come up and walk away after asking me a question, or half a question, as there is also curiosity about someone who is better dressed than the ragged farmers outside and the crowds in the hallway trying to break into the antechamber.

Miss Joan is brought to me, perhaps as an expression of a highly vocal, dedicated member of God's entourage. She is an American, about twenty-five, slim, red-haired, pale-skinned and slightly freckled, and wears a white sari and a golden yellow scarf. Says she is a former music and drama student, spent two years at a university (where, she wouldn't say), left three years ago to take the drug trail (Turkey, Afghanistan, Pakistan, Nepal, etc.). Came to India eight months ago, has been clean for the last five, ever since she found God, that is, the Satguru. "Satguru is God, but he is also greater than God, because he can show you God. He is God in human form, an avatar of Krishna, the last of the ten avatars according to Hindu belief." What she is telling me is that Vishnu has ten avatars in all, the first nine, among them Krishna, having already ap-

Followers of Sant Ji Maharaj, founder of the Light Mission, point out his portrait, which had miraculously appeared in the leaves of trees at the great meeting at the Delhi gate.

peared; the tenth, whom Hindus have been awaiting and who is expected to usher in a new age, is, according to Miss Joan, the thirteen-year-old kid the peasants are so excited about. To get down to the facts, I want to know what God does for you and how you get plugged into the Divine Light they're all talking about. "One receives the Light after initiation—about two and a half hours with a mahatma, followed by a session with Guru [that is, the boy], who bestows Light." Guru goes to Dehra Dun School, which is on the edge of the Himalayas and is our version of Harrow or Eton or Choate or Andover. Miss Joan says he has the "normal" teen-age interests—plays with toy trains and likes cars (I forgot to ask about girls, pot, and rock). His devotees want the best for him—an American boarding school someday, and so on. Seven thousand devotees in Bihar—they're very poor farmers, in one of the most miserable godforsaken parts of India—collected some money so he could come visit them. No fool, Guru bought himself a nice new Chevvy station wagon—a white one (why not?). I ask a pointed question. Miss Joan: "Why can't God take the train? For the simple reason that his devotees want Him to have a car." Jesus walked. "Jesus made a lot of mistakes." She adds that Jesus should not have performed the miracles because people then look for signs and not the Truth. "What's wrong with a car? His devotees would like to see Him live in a palace."

[Mr. Tandon] This is a human religion. You cannot call it Hindu, Muslim, or Sikh. Nor Christian. None of these in the traditional sense. Shri Maharaj Ji was a saint above caste, color, and creed; and there is no financial bar. His message was for everyone. It is just an accident of history that the Mission began in India. Its true meaning is world-wide, and someday we will have branches everywhere. We've already started in the U.K. and South Africa, and soon we hope to be able to send mahatmas to the States.

This is a people's religion. The priestly class, the Brahmins, regarded Maharaj Ji with supercilious indifference since he had no knowledge of Sanskrit and showed no sign of formal erudition. The Westernized, educated, sophisticated class also has not been attracted because they are devotees of the pursuit of material gain and too full of self-pride. It is the poor in their poverty who have arisen to the inner fountain of bliss which make them immune to the outward sufferings of life. Maharaj Ji was a support to the faltering, tottering, shattered section of mankind. That the ordinary people of India should be forced to live in a manner hardly better than animals is an affront to human dignity. Maharaj Ji demanded that all men should have ready access to at least the bare necessities of life.

The intellectual classes of India have made religion a very complex affair. Instead of having a desire for an intuitive realization of the ultimate reality, they prefer to give a fine exposition of religious scriptures and ritual: They have fallen into the clutches of maya and are being swallowed by death. The intellectuals may talk about the spiritual path at great length, but their minds and lives are still entrenched in the world. All their theory is valueless because they are bound to maya. They can never be free. Real spirituality is freedom, and the man who practices it earns the true reward.

In the wake of Western materialism the mind of the average Indian has weakened and become captured by the lure of material progress. As a result of this he has been separated from his ancient heritage and culture. Now the dead soul and the live soul are awakened. Is there not a difference between a sleeping man and an awakened one? The awakened man will trod the path—he will "realize." He will be led to the saints. When a child is born, when he is in the womb of the mother, he remembers something of God. After birth, when he comes into the world, he forgets, because of his surroundings.

Today people are doing less for the betterment of their own souls. When they are doing something it is just a show. It is all senseless ritual and pretension. This is what Maharaj Ji opposed. "The mess that has been made of religion," he said, "is more because of educated scholars who merely recited the scriptures like parrots. They may make wonderful expositions and arguments, but they have no direct experience of the truth."

How to open the Third Eye in man—that was Maharaj Ji's task. How to see the dazzling Light brighter than a thousand suns that exists within the self, how to merge oneself into God while remaining on the earth. This is obtained through the knowledge of the secret Name. It is only by the practice of Raj Vidya that a seeker of Truth attains a balanced frame of mind and becomes a non-doer. The extrovert mind is changed into an introvert mind. A realized soul, while touching, smelling, eating, and speaking, is not involved in the perception of the sense objects. Only the senses play in the sense objects. The devotee remains as spectator. The yogi while sitting in "the frame with nine gates" is merged with God and sees the world as a mere spectator. Neither good nor bad actions bind him.

The powers of Maharaj Ji have passed on to his son, Sant Ji Maharaj. His Holiness speaks in the language of parables and disdains all intellectual conceptions of God. His glittering personality and beatific appearance shed a halo of divinity around him. He is the manifestation of the supreme power and gives the knowledge of the Holy Name and Divine Light to all who ask for it. He promises the gift of the knowledge of the soul to everyone who comes to him, irrespective of caste, color, or creed. Balyogeshwar Shri Sant Ji Maharaj has incarnated himself to reveal the truth and to complete the destiny of man. He has come to give man the sharp sword of the Holy Name with which to cut down the snares of the world, to kill all desires and to find victory in truth and everlasting life. He has come to speak to us. It is for us to listen. He is a living Satguru. He has delegated some powers to his mahatmas, to his devotees, his power works through them—they are the medium, not the givers. He is the giver.

The Peace Bomb is the antidote to the atom bomb. It is for all mankind. Orthodox Hindus are part of mankind, which is why Ji Maharaj has started here. When His Holiness the Satguru goes to the United Kingdom, America, China, people will get knowledge. He wants to establish peace throughout the world.

[Yes, but is he God? Does he think he is God?] The people say he is God. And if you tell a man long enough that he is God, will he not believe you?

Someone calls a meeting of the mahatmas. They crowd into the anteroom and sit on the floor, all facing in the same direction. Then someone gives them an order, and they shift around to face in another direction, toward the speaker, who begins to brief them in Hindi. There are little jokes and slight ripples of gentle laughter. They look like people who know what they are doing: clear-eyed, clear-skinned, alert. Some are round and plump, like a good Hindu holy man, some are bone-thin, gaunt, like a good Hindu holy man. There are a few women among the crowd, also wearing saffron robes. I go into the adjoining hall, where the peasants are crowding together in anticipation of seeing His Holiness. Wandering around in the background are six or eight American hippie types, who have given up drugs and have found religion. They wear saris or Indian pajama trousers and kurtas (shirts). They have made themselves part of the inside circle, the self-elect, the self-select. Important people. They know *all*.

Another brief flurry with Miss Joan while the mahatmas are in their meeting. She makes several references to suicidal wishes in the past; the current runs through her thought even now, I suspect. She was miserable, just miserable. Now God has given her happiness. Balyogeshwar Param Hans Satgurudev Shri Sant Ji Maharaj is God. Miss Joan has gone all out for God. You really believe that boy is

God? I ask somewhat incredulously (or naïvely). Yes, he is God. "Whatever God wants I will do. The Satguru can destroy you completely if he wants. He sees right through you, and then he can destroy you. It might take ten minutes, it might take ten weeks—whatever he wants. He does what is best. Then he fills you with the Divine Light." So he is God? "Yes." And how do the devotees see him? "As Satguru." And the Satguru, what is his view? "As Satguru. Satguru is God."

God is sleeping. He will be out in thirty or forty minutes. Meanwhile the mahatmas continue with their meeting, getting ready to go out into the world in their saffron robes and shaved heads to spread the Divine Light. They seem rather saintly to me. Suddenly they disperse like people disappearing before an unexpected rain. God has appeared, and takes a chair against the wall. He is wearing a white kurta and full white pajamas. His black hair is slicked down with pomade. Hundreds and hundreds of devotees push into the room in an ecstatic state. The Mission's guards, in khaki military uniforms, try to keep order, ruthlessly, while the devotees in their ecstasy and their poverty and their gauntness throw themselves at God's feet, passionately kissing his lotus feet. On the floor, kneeling and sprawling, kissing his lotus feet with the rapture of divine love, God's lotus feet. God is plump, wise, in complete control, a little bored. My God, what a sharp kid, I think, he knows everything! On they come, in their cheap saris and worn-out dhotis, in plastic sandals or barefoot, offering paper bags of fruit, prostrating themselves on the dusty carpet before God. The guards keep the crowd moving. In the background is Mr. Tandon, subtly directing the scene. Sometimes people break into tears. The guards move them on. God hands me an orange via an aide. God and I look each other straight in the eye as the farmers slobber on His lotus feet and the odor of peeled oranges and ripe bananas perfumes the room. He knows and I know. Both of us know.

Sant Ji Maharaj accepting salutations

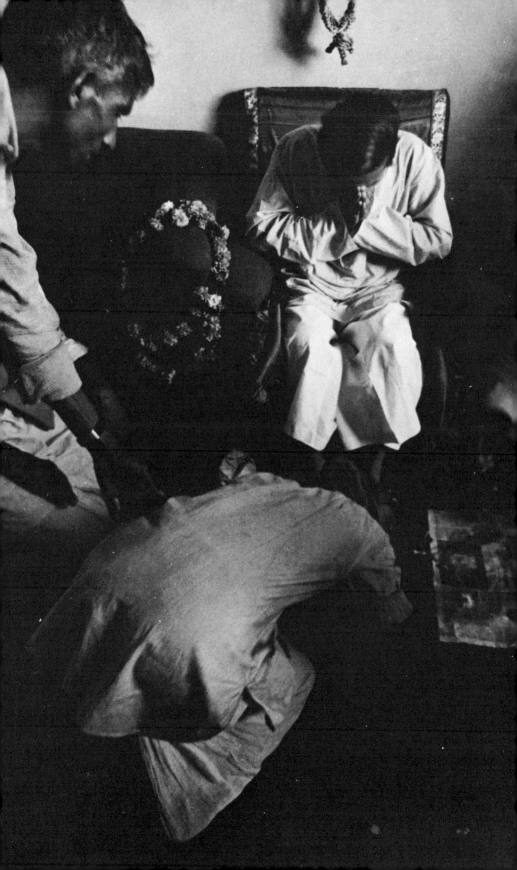

SADHANAS
NEW DELHI, CALCUTTA

❖

Here's another one of those Babajis. This one is B. F. L. Bedi, Master of the Occult Circle of India, Grand Master of the Celestial Order of the White Lion, Sag-i-Astana-i-Hazoori-Hazrat Mehboob-i-Ilahi. He is also M.A. (Pb) B. A. Hons. (Oxon), Alexander Von Humboldt Research Scholar (Berlin), Director, Institute for Inquiry into the Unknown, Director, World Centre for Conscience, and a sixteenth-generation descendant of Sat Guru Baba Nanak, the founder of the Sikhs, the movement that tried to steer a central path between warring Hindus and Muslims in India four hundred and fifty years ago and resulted in still another religion. Baba, as he likes to be called, describes himself as having "led the life of a revolutionary freedom fighter for the liberation of his motherland. After Independence, he withdrew from political life and now leads the mystic life of the occult." He adds: "His publications, large in number, include a volume on Sat Guru Nanak, entitled *The Prophet of the Full Moon,* and *Mystic India* in three volumes, which is a research report on the Nature of Nature and the Anatomy of the Inner Man." He has also written a book on the teachings of Nanak ("The author with his mystic vision has furnished the explanations to many mysteries and miracles associated with the life of the Great founder of the Sikh faith").

Baba now lives in a new house in a new "colony" on the outskirts of New Delhi. The house is rather hard to find, and though I made the trip there many times I invariably got lost on the way. Babaji specializes in American hippies, or hippie types. On my first visit he had four surrounding him: none of that darshan B.S. for them—instead of sitting respectfully at his feet they swarmed all over his cot. They sit anywhere, the girls snuggling up to him and being kittenish; he looks both confused and pleased (one of his self-written biographies mentions an English wife, but she seems to have disappeared). One of the girls, a tall slim freak in a purple velvet suit, big floppy hat, large yellow sunglasses, and endless beads, strokes his hand; she has just arrived from the States, flying all night and all day. The Americans are talking, in hippie argot, about whether or not violence against the Establishment is justified and what to do when it is used against them. I recall that they all decided it was OK to trash the FNCB. They have big plans for a magazine or newsletter for other Americans in India to keep them informed of the alternate culture(s) and to let them know how the Establishment is ripping off the world. For a moment I wondered about translating for Baba (he was having trouble following the conversation) but then I decided, what the hell, let Baba get darshan from *them*. Only once did I find an Indian at Baba's house; he was an older man, apparently someone in business. Otherwise it was the Americans, with the girls on either side of Baba, drinking coffee or Scotch.

It wasn't until several visits that I realized Baba was crippled almost to the point of incapacity. I had come for a talk, but the housekeeper's niece told me he was out. After an hour's wait I was about to leave, when Baba arrived in a taxi with some disciples. He came into the house slowly, painfully, on massive crutches, an excruciating walk of about twenty feet. Standing, he is a huge man, over six feet tall and weighing, at a guess, about two hundred and fifty pounds. He has a big head, a massive head, a big chest and belly, and great gentle brown eyes that show understanding, pain, and love all at once. He had been described to me as a Sufi, but I found that he had been born a Sikh. Now, like other Indian mystics and would-be mystics, he has made his way through all paths to the One, though he has not forgotten the Sikhs and Guru Baba Nanak.

My friend (he says to me, obviously impressed, or at least puzzled by my numerous visits) total maturity points have been touched on all sides. We must arrive at the inner sense of things, the in-ness, the in-scape of our psychic geography. The dynamics of the psychic are becoming an operative force in a more recognizable way than ever before in directing man's footsteps into the future. It is in the psychic forces as the fountain of light that we discover the source for the dynamics behind conscience, as an organ of the spirit which belongs to every human being as the birthright of the species.

What makes a rose a rose and not a dahlia or a chrysanthemum? Why does it have a certain shape that identifies it as a rose no matter what its color? Why does a man stand on two legs, while animals walk on four and reptiles creep? This question brings us face to face with the grand majesty of Nature, its vast differences, its enormity of size. What keeps it all in a certain order? We are in the bonds of relationship in the One-ness of the Almighty Creator. This bond is a common one, regulated, tightened or loosened as we come nearer or retreat further from the Divine. We human beings were created erect and given the self to determine our own future, through Divine Grace. We were given all the faculties which enable us to choose. Having been granted self-determination, it was left for us to brighten or blacken the scroll of our destiny. Thus good and evil as the two inseparables of the Pair of Opposites are the equally inseparable qualities of the Almighty.

The reality of the unknown is like an open book for those who are in the know of what lies in the depths of the Inner Heart. The joke of the situation is that in the past, saints and seers and prophets all preached the totality of one-ness and could cut but very little ice with the human mind. But their failure was not the fault of the human mind. The human consciousness was delineated on both sides with two brackets. Looking downward on the scale of evolution, down to the scale of a grain of sand, there was a point where the frontiers of life were reached and the boundaries of lifelessness began. Looking upward, the second bracket was located at the frontiers of the visible and beyond that lay the vast realms of the invisible.

Now see how the change has come: modern science has established the base for everything as energy and perpetual movement, and transformation is the language of existence. So the terms lifeless and inanimate go out of the vocabulary, so much that this very sinful prohibition, the word It, has no meaning left. On the other side, with awakened psychic perception, the barrier of the invisible is breaking fast. In fact, it has already crumbled. Psychic vision enables you to see the colors, hear the sounds, smell the odors, and sense the wave length of all the vitalities functioning in the field of creation. Psychoperception is not limited to just a few—mankind has entered the democratization of Light. There are millions of people all over the world who have this capacity. And like the snow-flakes of grace descending, psychic vision is spreading. The most infectious thing of all in this age is psychic perception. It is the "epidemic" of the age. The banners of the invisible have been raised. The stage is set for true freedom, for everything in creation and with every object in creation.

Everything in creation has its own aura.

Ecstatic experience emits blue light.

Ecstasy is a perfection: since there are flashes of cool blue Light in all aspects of consciousness.

The phenomenon of the beatniks and the hippies and their counterparts in the West and in the East, and the volcanic unrest gripping youth all over the world, only reflect the new temper of the new generation, demanding a new way of life and a new social order. Very few understand the urges of inner seeking expressed by these young people. Most adults look at their unshaven faces and take them for drug addicts. (May they be forgiven for their error of non-understanding.) I know the depths of the search. I feel the agony of their seeking. They are experiencing the manifestation of the invisible, in the form of visions, in sound, color, and transparency. I know that what they seek and feel escapes their understanding. It is their effort to grasp the mystery and meaning of what they see and experience which urges them to take to the way of search. Among them are artists, writers, painters, and musicians searching for new values.

What has happened in this century? Ever since the First World War there has been increased emphasis on the part of all men of good will in organizing and searching for peace, and yet the result, as we all have seen, was increased armaments and bloodshed. But this generation will not pick up the musket. Ten years from now this generation will furnish the legislators, the cabinet ministers, the leaders . . . Not one of them would give the order to press the button that destroys the world. Out of them will spring the Light, the blessing of psychic wisdom. We have reached a new stage of evolution and are beginning to live in the age of Light. The ecstatic lives I see people leading: they eventually, like rose petals, open up toward the inner heart of the invisible. If the old would only see the phenomenal blossoming of their young people, and could only envision what they attain in their intimacy with the invisible!

What these young people are looking for is what we are already doing in the Circle of the Occult. We are concerned with aiding those who are the pilgrims of the spirit to evolve to a higher voltage in functioning as human beings. What they seek in their understanding of experiences of the invisible, in the form of visions or seeing color or hearing sounds, is phenomena that are interlinked—and which is what we are doing ourselves.

Esoterically viewed, Sat Guru Baba Nanak was the embodiment of Total Light. It is this light celestial that he spread in words and actions. When one goes into the spectrum of light celestial, five colors appear, each one of them representing a vitality of the celestial. Splitting up the light celestial, they are the five esoteric qualities which became functional with the earthly existence of Sat Guru Baba Nanak. Looking at the spectrum, the inner eye sees these vitalities as the Vitality of Humility, the Vitality of Service, the Vitality of Evolvement, and above all, the mother of all vitalities, the Vitality of Compassion.

It is this esoteric appraisal of the dynamics of light which the great Sat Guru incarnated which explains the most astounding phenomenon: that in the ecstatic state, if one attempts to visualize the human form of the great Sat Guru before one's eyes, it is just not possible to bear the dazzle of light in the normal human eye. All and the utmost the eye can see is the halo of light around the sacred feet of the great Sat Guru. Above the feet, up to the ankles and no more, is all the human vision can stand, so lustrous is the blue light celestial which emanates through the fifth vitality, the Vitality of the Occult.

In his wanderings about the world, from Arabia to Tibet, Ceylon, the borders of Burma, and all across India, the Sat Guru had to converse with peoples having over two hundred languages and dialects. What language did the Sat Guru use for so universal a following? The mystery of this perfection of communication can be understood only by recognizing the strangest of happenings, that every time Sat Guru Baba Nanak spoke it was a miracle he performed, though he always used his own tongue, Panjabi. If, for example, he spoke in the Telegu area, he spoke in Panjabi yet was heard in Telegu. The explanation of this form of language trans-formation lies in the vibrational Vitality of the Occult, which func-tioned through the divine will of the great Sat Guru, transcending all linguistic barriers. It was the dynamics of light operating for the purpose of dispelling the darkness of ignorance.

Now let me speak about JAP JI SAHIB, the Holy Mool Mantra, which is among the holiest of the holy texts not only for the Sikhs but for all God-loving men. Through some five centuries, ever since Guru Baba Nanak, the founder of the Sikh faith, praised the Lord with such soul-entrancing sublime words recounting the qualities of the Almighty, only those devotees and disciples understood the inner and true meaning who were blessed with the ecstatic experience, through the overwhelming vibration of oneness with the Great One-ness. JAP JI SAHIB is not a prayer to the Almighty but a hymn of praise, reflecting the unimaginable greatness of the Almighty. The vibrations of prayer by the very essence of its content of human wants are at a very much lower level than the vibrations of holy praise of the attributes of the Almighty, which are absolutes in their formless form and ethereal in their conception. Therefore the vibra-tions of praise are pure shafts of light projected from the illumined inner self leaping in oneness toward the source eternal and infinite.

JAP

EK

ONKAR

SATNAM

KARTAPURKHA

NIRBHAU

NIRVAIR

AKAL MOORAT

AJOONI

SEH BHANG

—GUR PRASAD

JAP

AAD SACH

JUGAAD SACH

HAE BHIA SACH

NANAK

HOSI BHI SACH.

I translate the Jap Ji Sahib as follows:*

Praise
the One
the Parent of soundless sound
Truth is thy name
Creator of the cosmos
to a beginning and an end unattached
independent of the pair of opposites
the image of immortality
free of the cycle of birth and death
self-created
Thy knowing is the gift of Thy self, the Guru.

Praise be to you
From beginningless beginning Truth is Thy name
from the beginning of time Truth is Thy name.
in the present, indeed, Truth is Thy name
O, Nanak!
till endless end of time, Truth shall be Thy name.

From this point of the Infinite and the Eternal the wings of ecstasy start closing. Thus I have presented this holy rendering of the Praise Divine as confirmed by the mechanics of ecstasy and the totality of experiential data.

Reihana Amani, better known as Reihana Behun or Sister Reihana, is a Sufi woman who lives in a desolate section of New Delhi near the banks of the Jumuna River. She is old, ill, and virtually bedridden, spending most of her time in a high posted bed in a closed, cluttered room, with the windows blocked off and light coming from a single naked bulb near her head. She receives visitors at limited hours (open house on Sundays from three to five and nights at about nine or ten or later). Normally a disciple or two lives in the room with her; it is an eerie awakening to be in the midst of a conversation with Reihana Behun and suddenly become aware of the presence of another person lying motionless and silent in a mound of old blankets in a dark corner behind one. Reihana Behun suffers from leukodermia, an incurable disease in which the pigment fades away, leaving the skin a pinkish gray-white. She is also toothless and partially blind, but nevertheless she sits up in bed cheerfully giving darshan to disciples. She wears layers of loose clothing, with a hood over her head and tied beneath her chin, and blankets spread over her knees. Visitors—many of them young Americans—come by at odd hours after dark, through the fog that flows in from the river and envelops the house in a gloomy, unearthly mist.

I've always been a very sick person, from childhood on. Eventually one comes to live with illness, as with everything else.

My own path has been pathless. I go wherever I have found the landscape interesting. I've taken the path without let or hindrance.

That's the thing in my spiritual development. Mentally we are very free. We must make the most of it.

In the beginning stages we are faced with all those disciplines, Islam, Hinduism, Buddhism, Christianity. The ultimate attitude is what counts. This is called Sufism, no matter what religion you were born into.

But you have to practice, to discipline yourself.

My own discipline is a very stern one, and rigid, but with no detours. No sect.

I have no "don'ts" about food except for meat, which would be harmful to me. My body can't endure fasts.

There are as many ways to the Lord as there are people. Each person to his own discipline.

I was born unorthodox (in a Muslim family). My family was unorthodox, but it would have made no difference if we had been orthodox. By nature I would have been unorthodox. I had very wonderful parents who didn't stop me from doing anything.

Nobody ever kicked me out of the Islamic brotherhood, for as long as I conform to the five basic daily prayers no one has anything to say.

Actually, when people talk about religion, what they mean is the *mechanics* of religion. Formalism of behavior and dogma become a way of life, an attitude.

Certain practices are necessary too, but if you can attain the proper attitude, so much the better. Then there is no compulsion.

Allah is One, everywhere. He is in you and you are in Him. You are responsive to Him and the whole universe follows Him.

If any laws are broken, then there is complete catastrophe.

You must realize that life is everywhere. There are no such things as inanimate objects. Even a stone is animate.

This acceptance of all-pervading life means that there is no such thing as death, that man is infinite, vast, universal.

Everything that happens in the universe affects every man. This creates a deep sense of responsibility.

In order to get to the ultimate goal of the merging of human consciousness into the divine consciousness, these attitudes have to be practiced, not merely professed.

This means the acceptance of extra-human beings as being entities, the acceptance of many worlds. For example, in Islam, Allah is called Lord of the Universe, not merely of one unit of it. He functions in all.

The yogi Knows—he's conscious.

The Sufi path is really yoga. It is identical with yoga or Vedanta. That is why Islam has flourished in this country more than in the "Islamic" countries.

Sufism is identical with the Vedas.

The great Sufis are both Islamic and Vedantic. There are mystic Sufi saints who have any number of Hindu followers. They practice their own techniques but don't convert to Hinduism. It is very strictly forbidden to convert. It is not necessary.

As an example of what I mean, I have Hindu sons, Christian sons, Sikh sons. What I am doing is not only nondenominational but antidenominational.

If you can't feel equal love, then you cannot have equal faith.

So, the Sufi is the inheritor of the universe, as every man is, as every creature is, but the Sufi is the man who knows it, who is aware of his own wealth.

If you have a vast world and cut off only a little corner, then you have deprived yourself.

Actually, I think that if one gets down to the core of the matter, religion is the vanquishing of the ego.

Egoism in the sense of I-ness and me-ness—that is the great sin, the great heresy.

In the Gita, Krishna disposes of the whole matter when Arjuna asks Him, "Lord, what is the compulsion to sin?" The Lord Krishna says, very briefly, "Desire and anger."

Anger is nothing but frustrated desire.

If you really get down to the root of every negative action, the root is desire or the frustration of desire.

My religion, *my* country, is superior. Such egoism, pride of possession, the desire to dominate—these are what lead to suffering, to pain.

In our experience there are no such things as punishment or reward.

What is called punishment is merely suffering as the negative result of wrong actions, wrong desire.

The Lord in His own sweet will has made a law, and that law is called the Law of karma.

Thus man is very free: if man didn't have a choice, he wouldn't suffer or enjoy life.

There are reasons for everything one does, and what happens as a consequence.

This is a very great freedom.

Both the Gita and the Qur'an are the scriptures I live by. But they are exactly like all other scriptures.

It is stated implicitly in all that we have shown you the right path and the wrong path. We have given you knowledge and power. This should be clear in the most eloquent details. You know the results of right actions and wrong actions.

Now it is *your* choice. So as you act you will enjoy life or suffer. The authority, responsibility, the choice is *yours*.

Each man is in reach of his own destiny. We needn't sit and blame the government and the age and Allah for what has happened to us.

If we know the laws of karma we know the *why* of what has happened to us.

Fate and destiny and circumstance, all of these are merely the external results of one's own basic nature. I am a certain kind of person and in my living I act and react. So life is made up of actions and reactions—the things we do and the things that are done to us in home life, by parents, environment, the country, the world.

We may think we are the slaves of circumstances, but we are not. We are the masters. It isn't circumstances that are important but how we react to them. My reaction depends on the kind of person I am—what I am and what I have made of myself throughout my life.

By changing my own psychology—my samskara—though the circumstances might be the same, I might react quite differently. This is growth—the mastery to control one's own actions and reactions.

I was in prison for a year. This was during the 1942 freedom movement against the British. I had a sick body, a difficult, sick body, I was a sick woman. But even with prison food, prison conditions, it was the happiest year of my life. I was in notable company—musicians, social workers, doctors, teachers. I then realized that external circumstances don't matter at all. A doctor who came to see us remarked on how happy we all were, not neurotic, not miserable. We had an object, we were there by choice, not compulsion. Then I realized that externals don't matter. I liked the murderers very much among the nonpolitical prisoners we were thrown in with. There was something big about them. I didn't like the sneak thieves. The prisoners finally accepted us—the politicals —on our own merits. They gave us names showing us what they thought of us.

I never tasted freedom until I went to prison.

When I came out, I was in a vast prison: do this, do that. In prison there was no social pressure, no domination of one person over another, no careers. Each prisoner was equal with the others. Factually we were prisoners, actually we were free.

Happiness doesn't rely on circumstances. You create your own happiness. You are completely responsible. This makes one master of life. [So far she has been talking into the distance, as if to no one, or to a million people; now she turns to me.] Life is very exciting, isn't it?

There is no synonym for despair. Karma disposes of it. There is no full stop in the book of karma. You may come to the colon which people call death, but you go on after that. Life and more life, and more life!

Incarceration in a body is mistakenly confused with life. Life is eternal and so is living. When you realize this you are a Sufi.

SUFI!

Vedanta or Sufi—whatever you chose, they are identical.

She takes some snuff, and sneezes. A Hindu couple, in their thirties. I'd say, come in with a paper bag of sweets. There is a lot of bowing and touching her feet under the blankets. She puts her hand on their heads and tells them to get up; they don't seem to know what to say but stand smiling and looking as if they are about to fall on the floor again. She gives each a single sweet, and when they leave she gives me one. "If you are not going to eat it now, be sure to burn the wrapper, as once I have touched it, it is sacred. Otherwise give me the wrapper and I will dispose of it." I assure her I will burn the wrapper.

In rebirth and in freedom, there is one indispensable: to forget the past. Otherwise one is still bound. With freedom, habits change, everything changes.

The beats and the hippies . . . I have a great affinity with them. They are the pioneers of a new age of consciousness. (A man I hadn't been aware of, lying on a bed in back of me, suddenly protests. He is a Hindu. Reihana says, "No, no, no!" to him. He slides back into obscurity.)

They have been coming for ten years now. They may be rotten with drugs and bad habits, but there is in them a core of yoga. They are experiencing a state of consciousness which I find to be a kind of yoga. I have come to know them intimately, then they go to the guru they want. When they first come to me they don't know what they want to do, but by Allah's grace we learn where they should go and to whom.

Through these young people I have made a series of discoveries. A very serious discovery is that tantric techniques are very harmful, particularly to Americans, but the Vedantas are good.

A second discovery is that when consciousness is opened, it is opened to Christians as to others.

My third discovery is that mantras on the correct wave can be an antidote to the effects of drugs. A young man called Gabriel—very dear to me, a dear son of mine with quite a capacity for mystical growth—was given mescaline by a well-meaning but misguided friend. He came to me looking like death. I said, "My son, what is the matter?" "So and so gave me mescaline and for eight hours I vomited blood." The massive nerve centers were affected, so I gave him some mantras to say. The mantras worked on the neurons, on the drugs, on his physical condition, and finally he was saved, cured.

Another thing the West should become aware of, besides the danger of Tibetan tantric yoga, is black magic, which is so much practiced here. In India we have our antidotal techniques, which the West has flung away as superstition. Western asylums hold many patients under the guise of insanity who are actually victims of black magic. We must return to the old knowledge.

A French lady I know was terribly agitated over her son, who was pursued by a demonic force—in the streets vehicles attacked him, things fell upon him. My guru said to get a priest. The sign that you have the right priest will be that when you enter his house you will see a most beautiful picture of the Holy Mother. We found a priest, though there was no picture of the Holy Mother in his house—and the result was that instead of exorcising the boy, the priest was almost killed by demons. A friend gave me the name of a priest-exorcist. He had a picture of the Holy Mother, and he was able to exorcise the boy and save him. But what about the thousands of others who don't know they are being pursued?

The difference between the West and us is that the West lacks discrimination. They don't know what to leave alone. There are many things that are highly dangerous, but they have inquiring minds and go after black masses and black magic. Americans are such inquirers and seekers!

Millions upon millions of those who are called Red Indians in the Mahabharata have been reborn as Americans. They have brought the old knowledge back with them. This explains their drug taking: because of their mystical practices they take drugs. This is also an explanation of the deep confusion between child and parent —it's all karma. Parents are those who victimize, and the children are the victims.

This is a new age, a new state of consciousness. The children are demanding gurus. In their early marriages it is old India asserting herself. If this goes on, it may lead, hopefully, to joint families. The communes, in fact, are a kind of joint family, something deeper than blood, a common outlook—what we call samskara or samskara families.

The young people ask me about yoga. I give them the name of an ashram. They go to the ashram, but they can't stand the discipline and run away. But they will come back, in this life or the next.

The hippies, all of them, tell me they want a permanent life, permanent marriage. I do feel this urge for permanence, this desire. There is complete impermanence today. Human freedom means a great responsibility to others. Without traditions you have a house without a foundation. What the young people are seeking is a well-structured, solidly based house, a mansion.

Consciousness is changing with breathtaking rapidity. People like me work in the field of consciousness. The young people come and ask questions—they come because they are in trouble. I teach them mystical and spiritual techniques, the saying of OM and other mantras, forms of worship. I tell them about pilgrimages, and most important of all, about guru. It's a very great part of my sadhana to know about guru. It's human nature to be confused and to seek. They try everything and then they come here, on the way to faith. Family after family come to be transformed—husband, wife, relatives, the entire family.

OM: at first there was the Word. "The Word was God" is very difficult to understand, but the word is a very perfect way. The vibrations of the word take the consciousness up and up until by practice it enables the human consciousness to merge with the divine. The vibrations are divine, divine in the form of sound, divine in the form of shabda, sound with meaning. Then the mantra has form and color. Those who have developed inner sensibility can see color in mantra. It's not my own experience, but from what I have heard it seems that certain mantras have the same color for everyone. Some mantras might share the same color. The divine mantra OM is seen by some as a blinding light, others as a glow according to their nature. As far as I can remember the color is golden.

The Third Eye is a fact. It is the eye of knowledge. When the yogi reaches a certain state the eye opens and you can actually see the indentation here. [She touches her forehead. I am aware that she herself has the indentation.] It's quite clearly marked. I've seen it on the forehead of those who have reached very high in yoga. [So she has it! She sits in silence.]
     It is rare.

The silver cord is the name given to the nonmaterial cord that binds the individual who is out of his body to the material body in samadhi. Whether it is a mystical umbilical cord or not I do not know. There is certainly some connection between the person out of his body and the body which draws him back. As far as I recall the Egyptians also called this force the silver cord. It is very clearly mentioned in that remarkable Joan Grant book, *Ringed Dharashi*. The Egyptian experience is very similar to our own. I think the Grant book was written in the early thirties—time is rushing by so fast for me that each year is like several centuries or a day. It was written under inspiration from first to last. She was inspired by an old man, an ancient Egyptian who wrote the book through her. It created a tremendous sensation. Egyptian scholars said this is what they had been seeking, this message from the past. Miss Grant wrote some other books but they were a mistake: she had that one book, only one, the true one. The sequel had no value, the voice was lost, gone. You must read Ron Landau, a Californian, and Manly Hall— he's still in the body and lecturing. People are returning to the very ancient faiths.

Sai Baba appears even now. He is even more active . . . which is why Sai Baba #2 is not authentic. Sai Baba #2 is what is called a siddha, a miracle man who does tricks. Many people believe in him, but many have been harmed by his powers. Objectively they regard him as the Almighty, which he isn't. When a man claims to be the Almighty, then I suspect him.

There are many kinds of avatars—the prophets as in ancient Israel, the messengers like the nabis, the sadgurus. They have reached the stage where they are one with the divine, so to speak, the messengers of the Lord. Anandamayee Ma is definitely an avatar. Each avatar has a ration of his beloved, of Krishna, of Christ, whomever. Mother is both the receptacle and the channel. Mother is more than a saint: she has all the hallmarks of an avatar.

I have had a personal experience of Sai Baba, of the original. As I say, he is still with us, as he said he would be. A very personal experience; I cannot talk about it.

Why the war in Vietnam? . . . They were growing. They were a nice, placid, happy people, but definitely they had no challenges.

Suffering is very painful, but it doesn't make you grow. One isn't able to cope any more. What is happening to the Vietnamese is that they are paying off their karmic debts.

Once you accept the basic truth that life is for growth and not enjoyment, you accept everything that makes you grow, pleasurable or unpleasant. The Vietnamese are growing.

Tragedy comes upon those who impose tragedy upon others. This is America's future. The law of karma is that you get what you have earned. The law is infallible. I have learned from dire past experience. Victims and victimizers gather together: war is the only way to work out karma en masse. It makes the head reel to sit down and try to think; the blood escapes and one feels dizzy. The brain cannot stand this kind of inquiry. This is the cause of war everywhere, this working out of karma on a grand scale. Therefore it is very sensible not to allow anything inimical to remain in your consciousness because if you die with it, it is going to work out in a very unpleasant manner.

The earth that Allah has given to his people, if it is filched, will be returned in another way.

As far as I am concerned the only reality is here.

Once you realize that all are the same—all religions, all forms—then you are a Sufi.

It is a very great blessing if you leave the body at the right moment, because after that, life is an anticlimax.

Now I'm very happy to be in the body, because this is a most wonderful time.

Have you noticed how life has been speeded up? Thousands of years are condensed into a few. This applies to every country. The social fabric is in tatters, but man is coming back. But we need discipline, self-discipline.

[Have you ever been to Mecca? I ask.]
Yes, but not in this body.

✤

Bhaiyya was talking about his cousin, Colonel Lal, whose bad back was being cured by a healer, a woman named Mrs. Chakravarty, who lived in a place called Defense Colony. Colonel Lal, whom I had met, was a bluff extrovert who liked a good time, shooting, and the military life. He had pulled out his back while doing handstands at a party. After half a dozen sessions with Mrs. Chakravarty, his back was almost healed, and Bhaiyya, who also had a bad back, thought he'd go see Mrs. Chakravarty. Bhaiyya had to carry a cushion with him to prop up his spine; his face sometimes showed traces of pain. He went off to his first treatment saying he really didn't believe Mrs. Chakravarty could do anything, but since the doctors hadn't helped him, he was desperate and would try anyone, even a witch doctor.

"I don't know if she is actually doing me any good," reported Bhaiyya when he returned, looking somewhat less pained, "but she's an awfully attractive woman." His wife, Maya, snorted. "She acts as if nothing happens," continued Bhaiyya. "You lie down on a couch and she holds her hand over you without touching and then moves it ever so slowly, stopping every two or three inches, above your body. When she comes to a trouble spot her hand vibrates and some kind of energy flows from it. All the while she doesn't seem to be paying attention. She's making jokes and shooing the dog away with her foot and calling the servant for tea and talking to her husband in the next room. But something happens. I feel better already." We all had a drink, and another, and another, and Bhaiyya for once didn't seem to be sitting in his usual stiff, pained position. We discussed whether or not Mrs. Chakravarty's cures were merely psychosomatic or actual, but couldn't come to a decision. Surely, Bhaiyya really didn't believe she could do anything for his back, but against all the evidence there was a slight sign of relief. And the

Colonel showed remarkable progress and was talking about hand-stands again.

After Bhaiyya's second session he became very enthusiastic about the treatment, and I went along with him for the third. The Colonel was also to get another treatment.

Mrs. Chakravarty and her husband, also a colonel in the Indian Army but now retired, live in a pleasant second-floor flat in Defense Colony. They are childless. Mrs. Chakravarty seems to be about forty or so; the Colonel is a number of years her senior. She is a small, vibrant woman with flashing brown eyes, beautiful white teeth, and a tremendous amount of well-handled energy. Her long black hair, which has a few touches of gray, flows in gentle waves well below her shoulders. She wears a large orange bindi, the decorative spot that Hindu women paint on their foreheads between the eyes, at the approximate site of the ajna chakra. After we had talked for a few minutes all of us went into the room she reserves for treating her patients. It was furnished with the kind of Westernized modern furniture we Indians are so proud of, a pickled oak table and chairs with plastic seats, a few cabinets of knickknacks, two cots with Western mattresses, and an old Victorian-style cabinet on which was a small shrine to Sai Baba. The saint's picture—the standard photograph of him sitting on a rock looking somewhat hostile—was hung with garlands of small flowers. "I have a great devotion to Sai Baba," said Mrs. Chakravarty. "Do you know who he is?" I did, and was interested, but I knew that Bhaiyya thought such things a lot of nonsense.

Bhaiyya stretched out face down on one of the couches, and Mrs. Chakravarty crouched over him. She rested her hand gently on his head for a few moments, and then raised it and began to move it slowly a few inches above his neck. Suddenly the hand began to flutter wildly. "I have no control over it," she said to me. "It just goes by itself." The fluttering began to stop, and she moved to another spot. More fluttering. The treatment continued for about half an hour. Except for the initial touch on Bhaiyya's head, there was no physical contact between her hand and her patient. Bhaiyya got up a bit stiffly but said he felt a lot better; he was able to sit down in a chair without the usual moans. The Colonel stretched out with ease. He was almost completely cured, and this was his last session with Mrs. Chakravarty.

I had the urge to touch sick people. There was the compulsion to reach out to them physically, to be in contact with them, to lay my hands on them. Some of them showed signs of getting better, even a few who had been given up as hopeless by the doctors. I think I first had this urge about 1963—I'm a little hazy about dates, and names too. Three years later I began what you might call full-time "therapy" when my husband retired from the Army.

My powers were first "discovered" by a Dr. Ala-ud-Din S. Drooby, M.D., D.P. M. Beirut, a neuropsychiatrist at the American University at Beirut. He is also a famous Arab poet. Up to that time I had been healing on an irregular basis. I had been working on his wife, who had a spinal problem. She had been suffering for sixteen years with a slipped disc and was about to leave for Zurich for an operation when her husband overheard her talking about my treatment and wanted to know what was going on. He told me point blank that he didn't believe I could heal. He wasn't feeling well himself and hadn't been able to get well here, so he said I should try to cure him. He wouldn't tell me what he had, but as soon as he stretched out and I held my hand over him I realized he was suffering from colitis. He screamed with joy when I mentioned it. After I gave him some treatments he said, "I have changed my opinion." Dr. Drooby brought me to the Syrian ambassador to India—I can't recall his name, and he's since left—but he had a six-year history of a back ailment. He was also skeptical but he thought he'd let me work on him. When I was finished he could not only lift his arms but even move chairs about. He was so impressed by what I was doing that he opened a clinic for me to work in. Then I cured the wife of the Yugoslavian ambassador, who had "pains all over." I had a lot of diplomatic people among my early patients—the Tanzanian ambassador, the Yugoslavian ambassador to Japan, who flew in for treatment; he had spinal trouble—he had been damaged in the hospital when his spine was set after an accident. He came for a short time, got better but relapsed, since four sittings were not enough. I treated the Indian ambassador to the U.S.S.R. He had heart trouble. Then the Indian ambassador to Belgium. People came from Beirut. The Prince Maharaja of Chami Dhami. People came from all over for treatment, from as far away as the United States.

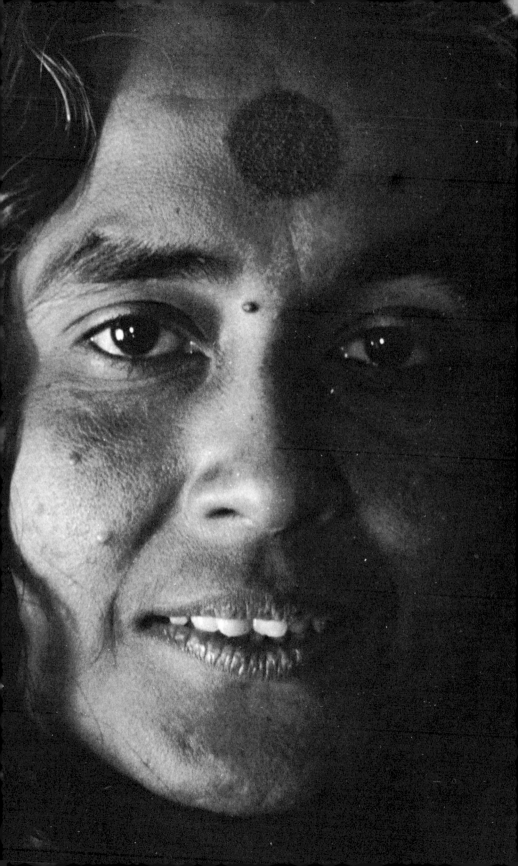

A man from Chicago came by; he was on a world tour. He too had spinal trouble but after a few treatments he was much better.

I try ten sessions with a patient. If there is no substantial progress by the tenth, I stop. I always insist on a medical check-up before and after treatment. Some cases respond very well, others not at all. I cannot promise a cure, and do not. What happens is beyond my control. I am merely the channel for healing. I treat virtually all but mental cases—blood clots, cancer, aches and pains, unhealed sores, heart trouble, spinal injuries. I love to treat slipped-disc cases. They show the best signs of improvement. I have just been working with a child who has nephritis. The doctors had given up, but after ten treatments he seems to be all right and is about to have a urine test to see if he is actually cured. A man came in recently with a spine so badly twisted that he was in the shape of a 7. I had to go to Beirut before I was finished with him, but I gave him some oils to use when I was gone and when I returned he was completely cured.

There was the case of a boy with double vision in one eye. The doctors suspected a brain tumor and were about to operate. The father—he was a big insurance man—insisted on bringing him here. After twelve sittings he was fully cured. Then there was a man from Air India, a brain case. He was in his early twenties. He had fainted while taking a bath. The doctors thought he had epilepsy. The young man complained of "some heaviness in my brain." He had hurt his spine and was very morose. He didn't want treatment, but his relatives insisted. The moment I touched him I found that my hand was dancing on the left side. One day I touched a spot on the spine and he said he felt some sort of current passing into his head. He started laughing and talking. He had been wearing an abdominal belt and was taking drugs to kill the pain. I told him to reduce the drugs.

An Air Force officer had an accident to his head and was in the hospital for eight months with a hole in the left side of his skull. Pus and blood were oozing out, and he had amnesia. My hand vibrated on top of his head. The trouble was deep inside. Eventually he was cured.

I don't know what it is that happens. There seems to be a transfer of some kind of energy. I begin the day by meditating. Nothing unusual, like the lotus posture. I merely sit in a position that is comfortable. I can feel the energy being pumped into me. It takes about half an hour. When I meditate I can sense the energy coming. Sometimes it rises in me like a spiral. It can be so strong that I have to get up to stop it. I have been meditating since 1968, when someone told me that it would help me with my work. Later I met a yogi, Babuji, who gave me transmission. Babuji said to sit with him for five minutes and I would be able to meditate. He told me, "Just imagine some sort of light in the region of your heart and focus your thoughts there." I had an immediate reaction. Transmission normally requires three sittings, but one seemed to be sufficient for me. Babuji told me to give up healing. He wanted me to become his disciple, but I told him I didn't want to. He said, "I will teach you how to give transmission to many people. Healing is a lower type of work." He thought I was throwing away my powers. But I told him, No, I have been given this gift. For a mother, looking after children is the most important type of work. For me it is the same: my patients are my children. Babuji teaches what is called Sahaj Marga, the Easiest Path. But my own path is what it is easiest for me. I cannot follow another person's path.

The beginning and the end of the day are the best for meditation. Something happens at sunrise and sunset. You have to be alone, to be with the Inner Self. In the morning I have my bath, do my puja, and meditate. Sometimes I go up to the roof at sunset because that seems to be a very auspicious hour. Since my father died in 1963, my life has changed. I was terribly upset over his death. I lost my son and also had several spontaneous abortions, so we have no living children. It was my father's death that upset me most, however. Now I am becoming more detached. The world doesn't interest me. When I go to a party, for a few minutes I am there and then I am not. The ordinary world seems so remote to me now. My life centers on meditation and on my work with the ill. I don't take any payment. How can I ask for money for what God does? I treat fifteen or sixteen patients a day, every second day. The sessions take a lot out of me and I must rest. I have the most energy in the morning, after meditation—that's when the Americans want to come. I lose weight during the day as the energy dissipates.

There is no explanation for what happens except that my powers come from God. I have nothing to do with them. I am merely the channel. One doctor came with a patient but said he didn't believe I could do anything. When I cured his patient he still wouldn't believe. But an English doctor who saw me said, "Anything can happen in the East." I was invited to Munich by some German doctors who had heard about me and wanted to study me and learn my "secrets." So I went there. First they gave me all the terminal cases, people they had given up on. I healed a few but failed with many of them. They were too far gone. I told the doctors they weren't being fair; I wanted a cross section of the new cases coming into the hospital. With them I had far greater success.

The German doctors were convinced that I had some secret, esoteric knowledge, from the Himalayas perhaps, and they wanted to be told. I said, it's nothing secret, it's a gift. But they became quite convinced that it was something special I had learned from some old yogis in the mountains, and they offered me all kinds of money. "It's a gift," I kept saying, "it can't be bought. God gave me a gift." But they wouldn't believe me and kept offering more money. The Germans think that with money they can buy anything. But the gift I have can't be bought. I was very distrustful of them, and they were very angry. They thought I was holding back for a higher price. But there's nothing to buy or sell. Then I went to the University of Zurich. The doctors didn't believe it. One finally said, "Fantastic therapy."

In Beirut the doctors were very open, and I did some more healing. Two newspapers published articles about me. [She has them but can't read what they say, since they're written in Arabic. Colonel Chakravarty remarks that the *Statesman,* a leading Indian daily, has wanted to write about his wife but he has refused them permission, since he thinks the publicity would be very bad for her; it would interfere with her work. Both the Colonel and Mrs. Chakravarty are against any exploitation of her powers.]

After I opened up the clinic which the Syrian ambassador gave me [it's now closed, as she prefers to work at home], an American psychiatrist brought his wife in to be treated for food poisoning. The American looked at my eyes and said, "You are very psychic." He and his wife had heard about me from the ambassador. The American had sciatica and also wanted to be treated, so when I was finished with his wife, he lay down on the bed. After a few minutes he asked me who was standing beside me. I said, Why do you ask? He said, "Someone is standing beside you. He is a famous saint in

India, but he is no longer living. His name is Sai or Sayed, something like that." Sai Baba? I said. The moment I spoke he started laughing. I was quite scared. I said, Why are you laughing? He said, "I didn't laugh, *he* did." Then the American said, "First finish the treatment and then I'll tell you a lot of things." I treated him but I was quite scared. When I was finished, he told me that when I touched him it was not my hand but a male hand. Then he said, "I have to give you some messages: 'Tell her not to worship me so much. And that I love her just like a daughter. And that she must not speak so much and she must not try to treat so many patients.'" The American said, "I can see an old man standing beside you." He gave a description: high cheekbones, blue eyes. It was Sai Baba. Sai Baba said through the American: "This is an order from me." He told me not to take life so seriously. The American kissed me on the cheek. I felt very strange. He said that this was just an American custom, but I felt I was getting some kind of sign from him. The American said, "This is not me but Him." [I wanted to know what the American looked like. Mrs. Chakravarty said he was a tall, handsome elderly man, very courteous but also quite sure of himself. Unfortunately, as she keeps almost no records, she has lost his name.] The American later told everything to the Syrian ambassador, remarking, "Her power is so strong that either she will become very spiritual and stop, or will become very proud. There's no in-between." [Colonel Chakravarty remarks, "That is my own way of thinking."] In Syria, the ambassador had a dream: Sai Baba came to him and said, "Tell her not to boast of her powers." When he returned to India he told me.

When I am in a holy place, a temple, a shrine, the river bank, even a church, I vibrate all over. Sometimes I have to leave. I don't know what I have. It just happens.

In meditation my mind becomes completely blank and then something comes to me. Focusing on the heart doesn't work for me. I must concentrate on the bindi area, the Third Eye. That is where I concentrate. Some different colors appear. I don't know if it is my imagination or not. Some purple, orange, different shades of blue. Sometimes it is just white. Pure light, I would say. When I get that, the light, I feel most peaceful. When I try to force it, it does not come. If I should put some effort into it, I fail. One has to be free of effort, of strain, in meditating.

I still remember the first time I was sitting, I saw an orange light. It may have been in my subconscious mind. I constantly think of Sai Baba; he is always within my mind, my thoughts. If I try to focus on something else, on some deity, I don't succeed. It doesn't lead anywhere. I am just going deeper into myself. I can't break out. I must bring myself down to this earth. With force, I should say. Bring myself back.

✦ ✦

Amiya Roychaudury, a Bengali otherwise known as Dadaji (Revered Older Brother) lives in a mansion in the southern section of Calcutta, where he attracts a substantial middle-class following. Dadaji is known for his miracles, some of which seem truly astounding, and others quite suspicious. Dadaji holds daily darshan in his house but, like many sadhus, moves frequently from one center to another. As in the case of Anandamayee Ma and other holy people, he does not say who he is—his disciples do. Dinabandhu Sahu, Advocate General of the State of Orissa, an ex-minister of the state government, and an advocate before the Supreme High Court of India, says: "I am of the view that he is beyond comprehension. He cannot be valued with the help of science or scientific laws and with the help of Sastras or knowledge received by study of Religious books." Sri Sahu adds a passage that is of interest in the light of what R reports later: "One sometimes feels that he is one of us because of his form, habits, dress and manner of talking, but suddenly one is made to feel that he is no longer with us and has gone much above the world of our understanding and how far he has gone and how high he has flown, one does not know. He is so much different from what I know that he remains unknown and perhaps unknowable for me. I bow down to Him and his spiritual Eminence."

Chandramadhab M. Misra, a leading Indian industrialist, speaks of Dadaji in the same awed terms one might speak of God: "Changes take place in this world as it is His [Dadaji's] wish and it is only His wish that creates and diminishes. Truth and Dharma which is eternal can never be forsaken by the humanity in spite of all the modern thinking based on the theory of science and technology that seems to guide the thought and action of ours at times. Truth and Dharma are nothing but 'His SELF,' which people like us, swimming in darkness, cannot perceive, surrounded with the misery of riches, power, personality, fad or vanity or whatever it may be. Nothing of these are real and lasting. I had once upon a time the same feeling that I am big, rich, powerful, strong and capable of doing anything that I wish, but since my meeting with my 'DADAJI,' whom I consider as the 'Lord Eternal,' I have been rid of these false vanities of life and then can you guess and believe how happy I am now, having surrendered to him completely."

Mahendra Narayan Shukla, who holds an M.A. in Sanskrit and philosophy, says that Dadaji has "become one with the Cosmic Soul or Ishwar Brahman. Though living physically in the world of empirical mundane values, he actually dwells in the realm of higher spiritual and metaphysical realities beyond the frontiers of Maya or ignorance. Dadaji is a great Saint and Maha Yogi. He has complete control over the force of nature and knows the mystery of creation. He has complete knowledge of the working of the Science of the Sun, the Science of Moon, the Science of Wind, the Science of Astronomy, the Science of Sound etc., and hence he can create anything, viz. Sweets, Spectacles, Flowers-Scents, Photographs etc., at any time by dint of his sheer will to do so. His will seems to be the predominant factor and the moment he wills to create anything that thing becomes created. He has encompassed the whole of the cosmos." Moreover, says Sri Shukla, in initiation, when the disciple is given a mantra, it is God who speaks through Dadaji, since "either an Omniscient Saint or only God can conduct the initiation and no human being with limited perfection and knowledge can give mantra." Dadaji has "realized God or Truth and his self or soul has become one with the cosmic soul and hence he is beyond the restriction of Time and Space and the Laws of gravitation. As the result of this highest state of Perfection he can create as many as he will and can assume the same body or different bodies at different places at the same moment for doing human welfare by his sheer will."

Dadaji's philosophy reflects standard Indian thought as expressed in the Vedas, the Upanishads, the Gita, the Vedanta, and so on. As follows:

[Dadaji speaks] Reality is one and that is Brahman or Cosmic Consciousness. Bliss and power and every individual soul on the metaphysical plane or in reality is nothing but Brahman. There is no difference whatsoever between the Individual Soul and the Cosmic Soul or Brahman. They are one and the same. It is only on account of ignorance or maya that we feel the difference, and with the dawn of wisdom through complete surrender to God the difference vanishes away and the enlightenment or self-realization is attained.

The aspirant of truth should not think that he is the doer of anything but that it is God to whom he has surrendered who does everything and the aspirant is only the instrument of God. The ego should be totally melted in the heat of Para Bhakti, only then does surrender become perfect, and as a result the self becomes unveiled to the aspirant and self-realization takes place.

And so on. Dadaji makes the important point that "the state of self-realization is beyond the grasp and reach of words and mind." Think about that.

Of more interest than Dadaji's standard, rather prosaic philosophical thoughts are the accounts of miracles experienced by Dadaji's disciples. I will give a few:

[Srimati Gita Dasgupta, a disciple] On the twenty-fourth of August, 1970, Dada arrived at Cuttack. It had been previously arranged that he would stay at the Chaoliaganj Circuit House for some particular reason. In the evening his wife informed him that she had seen a ghostly hand in the bathroom. It seemed that Dada had been prepared for this. He went and stood at the place where the spirit was waiting with outstretched hands for Dada's mercy to release it. At long last the spirit attained salvation. Everyone present received a distinct smell of incense.

[Biren Mitra, Member of the Legislative Assembly, Orissa] On the twenty-third of August, 1970, Dada arrived in Cuttack. The next morning I came to his bungalow and he asked me to pray for "mahanama" (that is, the name of God). As I sat there the divine grace was showered on me and I could clearly see the "mahanama" written on the small piece of paper in my hand. Dada put one hand on my heart and gave me a large sandesh [sacred ashes], saying, "Take it, this is God's grace. Don't you believe me?" As he said this, the letters "Satyanarayana" [a name of God] appeared in the sandesh [in Bengali characters]. I went home and distributed the sandesh, which was about one kilo in weight, to about 150 persons and still it did not appear to diminish. Dada next took hold of my hair and shook it and out came a king-size packet of 555 State Express cigarettes. He gave it to me, saying, "You like this brand, don't you?" I had no knowledge how he came to know that I smoked this brand. When leaving I took two books with me and, seeing them, Dada asked me what I was taking. When I told him he said, "All right, take them with you." When I opened the first page later, I saw written on it as if by magic, "To Biren Mitra from Dada." The same day I, who had been unable to sit down due to a pain in my back, climbed three stories of my house. On the evening of the twenty-fifth, satyanarayana puja was held at my house. As I bent to touch Dada's feet, he kept his hand on my back and brought out a packet of Benson and Hedges cigarettes.

[Besanti Misra] That Dada is omniscient I witnessed for myself in the case of my sister-in-law. No one had informed Dada that my sister-in-law was suffering from tuberculosis of the bone. But he smiled and told her, "I will be with you tonight. You must sleep in a separate bed." We were all elated with gratitude. After dinner Dada came to spend the night with us as previously arranged. Lying on my bed, I wondered how Dada would come to my sister-in-law. My mother, brother-in-law, and myself were sleeping in the same room with my sister-in-law. Sleep was beyond question. Then suddenly Dada appeared. I exercised all my strength to keep from announcing his entry. At the same time, my sister-in-law heard the tinkle of bells from the feet of Gopal [Lord Krishna]. Then she saw someone sprinkle water over her whole body and the three fingers of a small hand caressing the spot on the tubercular bone. The room was filled with that heavenly incense of Dada's presence. Another miracle happened the next morning when I heard that my brother-in-law's incurable heart condition had been completely healed. After puja Dada had called him and caressed him on the heart. My sister-in-law also became completely normal from the next morning.

[Dr. Manas Maitra, M.B., M.S.] About three or four months ago Dada informed me that my wife would be struck by paralysis and therefore he was feeling sad. I was stunned with worry and became silent. Dada continued to tell me that in such an eventuality I should inform him immediately, as otherwise a cure would not be possible.

For the past few days my wife had been suffering from pain in the legs and hips. As per Dada's advice I had consulted a doctor, who was not able to shed much light except to say that her disease originated from her mind. And then came that terrible day! I was out on an emergency when I was informed that my wife had lost the use of her legs. I was told that Dada was being informed also. At that moment my chauffeur arrived with my car, although he never comes in the morning.

So I went to Dada's house. Dada had just finished puja and when he heard the news he came straight to our house. Then the strange incident occurred! This too in front of me, a student of science and a surgeon by profession whose duty in life is to relieve others from pain! We pricked a needle into Madhuri's feet, but she had no sensation. She lay there motionless, unable to move or walk. Dada took a glass of water and anointed Madhuri's feet with it and said, "You will stay in bed and keep all the windows and doors closed." This was done and Dada and myself waited in the next room. After a few moments Dada said, "Come, let us go to Madhuri's room." As the door to the room was opened an inexplicably sweet and pleasant scent came to my nostrils and pervaded the whole room. Dada spoke: "Madhuri, how are you?" My wife replied, "Dada, you caressed my feet all the time, and now I have regained all the strength in my feet. There's no pain, either."

On Dada's lips quivered that mischievous but divine smile so characteristic of him. He said, "But I was sitting in the other room all the time, drinking tea. Ask Manas!" Madhuri was dumfounded. She took the dust of Dada's feet to her head and said, "Then God Himself must have visited me. He has made me well." And what about me?—I had lost all sense of consciousness and existence. Medical science stood by helpless and speechless. In the face of this great supernatural force all human knowledge seemed like a tiny blade of grass.

[Sachin Roychauduri, C.A. London, M.A., Ll.B.] There was a time when my wife and I were passing through a very difficult stage which brought us to the very extreme of our endurance. I was also feeling very disturbed as I had not told all my troubles to Dada. But one day at 1:20 in the afternoon, while I was working in my office, I clearly saw Dada come into my office. He came toward me, put his hand on my forehead, and said, "Don't worry. I am with you." After a little while he went away, leaving me deep in his thought. At 3:30 that afternoon my wife called up to say that Dada had been to see her at that very time. She had made him tea and had chatted with him for quite some time. When she had risen to telephone and let me know that Dada was with her, he had given some excuse of not feeling well and had left! I have heard later that it is not at all strange for Dada to be in more than one place at the same time.

[Dr. Saroj Bose, Head of the Department of Chemistry, City College, Calcutta] Dada was spending an evening with us in a light mood when he suddenly wanted to make a telephone call. He inquired of the lady at the other end as to how her daughter was and received a reply that she was running a fever of 104 degrees. Dada put the receiver down and in front of all of us seemed to go into a trance. His vision appeared to extend beyond the room through the walls and into distant space. Gradually his eyes became reddish, he coughed once or twice and after about fifteen minutes he relaxed once more. He again picked up the phone and called the lady and was told the fever had gone down to 99 degrees. Dada sighed with relief and continued his broken conversation with us.

Dadaji's disciples have an endless number of accounts of his making scents like sandalwood occur, of the fragrance of his body and feet, of bilocation—often to members of the same family—and of miracles of healing. A number of disciples think Dadaji is "Narayan

in person," that is, an incarnation of Vishnu. R's view of Dadaji
which follows is more objective—or is it more biased?

[R on Dadaji] Large, heavy-set man. He is (in appearance) like a Mafia *capo* or a Greek ship owner. Big, fleshy stomach. He wears an orange lungi and no kurta or shirt. The first time I saw him (on a Sunday morning) he was lying on a Western-type bed with about thirty people sitting on the floor before him. He would say a few words, almost into the air, and pause. Sometimes there would be questions. People come up, shyly, ask him something in a low voice. The answer might be given in a whisper or, if Dadaji thinks it has universal application, said aloud, but as if to no one in particular. From time to time he glances about the room with a catlike smile. Silence. He will address someone, not as an individual but as a focal point for a remark. His feet are being touched steadily, but he ignores the disciples. When his ankles are wet (after going to the lavatory—Indian toilets are a hole in the floor, and even men squat to urinate) women come up to him and, kneeling on the floor, wipe them with the end of their saris. Blue-green bedspread, mirrors on the wall (in one of them Dadaji can see himself), old photographs of Dadaji as a younger man, decorated with flowers and tinsel, garlanded. He has a lightly serious face, a kind of determined, controlled blandness. He never frowns, but never laughs, though he can show that pleased grin. There's a certain ferocity about him; he impresses me as a man who would be dangerous to antagonize. He drinks tea (dunking a Glaco biscuit into it) and smokes heavily. The floor of the room is waxed and polished, but there is dust under the bed; I can see it, as I am sitting on the floor along with the disciples. Everyone else sits neatly and compactly, with their legs tucked under their bodies, but I am forced to sit with my legs going out before me and my back against the wall. I am unable to sit in the tidy fashion of the Orient. Women approach Dadaji for advice; he puts his arm around their necks and lifts the sari (which covers their heads) to whisper in their ears. Some older women arrange and rearrange his clothes on the rack behind the bed.

On this particular Sunday, Gopal Chatterjee, a musician I had met in the Kalighat, plays the tabla and scat-sings, repeating the same vocal phrases on the drums. Then he suggests that I take a snap of the group. They arrange themselves on the floor, and Dadaji sits upright on the bed. Later several people inform me that if Dadaji hadn't wanted to be photographed, the film would be blank. This point is emphasized several times. But, having enough faith in Eastman Kodak and American technology and Japanese optical systems, I know that Dadaji, no matter what he wills, is an image on my film. After the picture taking, Dadaji lies down on the bed again and more people come up to him, touching his feet and prostrating themselves before him and saying a few words. Some squat to one side to hear his reply, while the other disciples press closer. A man who seems to be making a list of people present asks my name. He tells me: "When I touched Dada's feet, I could suddenly smell a rare perfume on his feet and breath. It is a miracle." Dada is known, it seems, for making scents appear. In the adjoining room is a small shrine, with photographs of saints decorated with flowers. On the floor are dozens of jars of ordinary tap water brought by the disciples; when the jars are taken home they are found to contain perfumed water. A miracle, obviously. A Mr. G. K. Bose, a retired businessman about fifty, tells me of others of Dadaji's miracles. He healed someone's driver of a fever; he predicted that a doctor's wife, who had a pain in her leg, would suffer a stroke. A few weeks later, while the doctor was in the operating room, word came that his wife had had the stroke. The doctor rushed her to Dada, who cured her. Bose also tells me that Dada had once warned him not to use his car on a certain day. Bose took a taxi instead; the next day, when he went out in his car, it broke down after half a mile. "You see, if I had used the car, I would have been in trouble because my appointment was three miles away and the car would have broken down in a very inconvenient place and I would have been late for a very important meeting."

Dadaji never says he does cures or performs miracles; the disciples say it. They tell me about his appearances in several places at the same time. He was seen carousing (as they put it) in Howrah, a suburb of Calcutta, with "bad companions" while he was also on vacation with disciples. He was in one room massaging the doctor's wife's leg at the same time he was in another room sitting and talking to the doctor. They all know of a famous miracle of Dada's: "Dada was driving in his car when it ran out of petrol, but he kept it going another five miles on an empty tank until he could reach the petrol station."

I return Tuesday. More of the same, but there are only about a dozen people present, since it is a work day. The majority are men. People ask about my snaps. I reply that I haven't received them back from the laboratory. Everyone is doubtful that I actually have succeeded in photographing Dadaji. "If Dada doesn't want to be photographed, the film will be blank." Mr. Bose tells me, "Twenty-five years ago if anyone had said I would bow before another man, I would have said he was crazy. Now I bow before Dadaji." A teen-ager says to me, "I didn't want to come. I had to be dragged by my mother. Now I come every day." Similar testimony from other people. The young disciple says, "Can you see God?" No. "How do you know God is here?—When Dada comes, you will get His fragrance." I am told about another example of Dada's special powers: on Sunday, after I left, Dada informed the disciples that he had just learned (that is, by occult means) that two men were about to arrive from Poona. Half an hour later two men came in, saying they had just come by train from Poona.

Dada enters and lies on the bed. The disciples become quiet and attentive. A woman brings Dada tea, Glaco biscuits, and cigarettes. His glance roves about the room; his eyes meet mine for a second and wander off. He never seems to rest on anyone's face for more than a moment. He speaks briefly, and when there is silence I ask if I may put some questions. Dada agrees, but then ignores me and says in adequate English: "There is no caste, there is only one humanity in the world. Human being is one, God is One. Everyone is God. Individual is looking. Part of everybody is full of God." Then he has a discussion with Gopal Chatterjee in Bengali. Gopal reports: "Dada says come tomorrow at eight-thirty and he will show you Hindu yog." I repeat the time, 8:30 tomorrow, Wednesday, and Dadaji says Yes.

Wednesday, 8:30. This is a tough area, and every time I enter it I am somewhat nervous. Dada lives at 188/10A Prince Anwar Shah Road, near Lord's Bakery, which is on the fringe of Naxalite territory. Recently there have been one or two murders a day by different revolutionary groups or by the police. Several bystanders have also been killed. There are political slogans scribbled on all the blank walls. Opposite Dadaji's house there are usually groups of young men in white stovepipe trousers and pomaded hair who always look menacing. This morning they shout at me, "Heepie, heepie!" I give them the V sign and go inside. Upstairs in his room, Dada is lying on the bed in his usual pose. There are about ten men seated on the floor, and five women. As usual, they are all middle-aged and middle-class; they seem to be business and professional men. So far I have never seen a really poor person at Dadaji's darshan. As I enter, Dada says "Oh, yes" in English, as if he were being reminded of something he didn't want to remember. He talks on and off with the disciples. I sit down to wait for the exhibition of Hindu yog, but Dada ignores me completely, even avoiding my eyes. At ten he says, "Come tomorrow at four and bring your flash." End of darshan. Where was the bilocation, the mysterious showers of flowers, the levitation? Dada had not become airborne.

Thursday. This is Kali Puja. I arrive at 188/10A and sit in the downstairs room with Gopal Chatterjee and another man. Precisely at four Dada enters, but doesn't acknowledge my presence. He is very brisk and businesslike. We get into a small car and go to another house about five minutes away. Dada takes up a kind of command post on a small bed, giving darshan and making telephone calls. We are in a small room, about ten by fourteen feet, and it is crowded with people sitting on the floor. The usual scene, with people touching Dada's feet and asking questions in whispers. Dada sips tea and dunks his Glaco biscuits, and smokes endlessly. A Dr. Mukerjee asks me about the snapshots. I tell him they have been developed and came out perfectly. "Did all of them come out?" Yes. "Even of Dadaji?" Yes, even of Dadaji. This seems to be a blow to Dr. Mukerjee and some of the other disciples, because they know that Dadaji rarely appears on photographic negatives. "And the snaps of Dadaji alone?" asks Dr. Mukerjee. I tell him that I didn't take any photographs of Dadaji alone, but he assures me that I did. Somehow Dada has regained his miraculous powers by this. A few minutes later Mr. Bose's daughter asks me the same questions, exactly, and I give the same answers. She, too, assures me that I took photographs of Dada alone. (Later that night I looked carefully through my proof sheets but could find no single pictures of Dadaji.)

Dada smokes, drinks more tea, dunks his Glaco biscuits like mad. He gives a whole biscuit to a young woman crouched at his feet and part of another to a second young woman, as if he were distributing Communion. They try to take the biscuits in their hands, but he deftly puts them between the girls' soft full lips. Dadaji likes young women.

It is getting dark outside and there seems to be a tension rising in the room. A man is pointed out to me as having written a big book on Dadaji and the cult of Dadaji. It is in Bengali. I ask if I can get a copy, saying I'll have it translated. Dr. Mukerjee says it cannot be translated—you have to *feel* with Dadaji. He adds: "A lot of what Dadaji says is meaningless and irrelevant. There are depths I do not understand." Dr. Mukerjee tells me he teaches English literature. Classical or contemporary? I ask. Confusion. Shakespeare or Philip Roth? "It is all the same," he explains. More people ask about the snaps and are surprised when I tell them, emphasize, that they have come out perfectly. Dada constantly ignores me. He has met his master, I think. He knows I see through his Indian nonsense. He is in danger of exposure. The hard light of the West confronts his Hindu irrationality.

The room empties and fills, as if a tide brought in people and floated them away. At one point I am alone with Dada and a woman. Dada is sitting up straight, rather rigid, with his eyes closed. I am slumped on a couch. I close my eyes, feel twenty seconds of—what? Spiritual empathy, peace, nirvana. Thought: "I am getting something from this wonderful man." Strange thought! I am succumbing to Indian bullshit. Dada is a fraud, not God. I am annoyed at myself, and remember how I have been warned that yogis enter one's mind and possess it. One must be careful. I open my eyes, return to normal. The room fills up again. Gopal Chatterjee plays drums, while a very plain woman in Gandhi glasses sings. Someone had given a harmonium to Dada. He plays a few notes absentmindedly. I thought he was about to sing—someone remarks that Dadaji had been a famous radio performer—and wanted to hear him, but the telephone is ringing. Tea and sugar cakes and raw cashew nuts are passed around.

Six o'clock. People begin to stand up. We are going somewhere else. A lot of milling about. Several people tell me that while we were sitting in this house with Dadaji he had also been in another part of Calcutta with his son. This has been confirmed by telephone, so there is no doubt that Dada has again bilocated and that we are witnesses to the miracle. To continue the miracle, Dada is going to stay in the house in meditation and at the same time will appear in another part of Calcutta to celebrate Kali Puja. We all get into cars and trucks. Dada says good-bye and returns to the house. I look at him carefully, try to memorize each line of his face, each wrinkle on his kurta and dhoti (which is bordered by a thin green line) so I can recognize an imposter at the puja.

The city is wild, brilliantly lit, and echoing with the explosions from firecrackers, like a great battle. Rockets shoot overhead in spasms of sparks. As we rattle through south Calcutta in our truck someone remarks from time to time, "That was a bomb." I feel that we are especially vulnerable in the open truck. There is a constant blare of sound systems and radios playing at cross purposes. The night is steaming: it has been an exceptionally hot and wet fall, with temperatures running at 97 degrees and humidity at 100 percent day after day. We plunge through Calcutta's baffling traffic, cars and trucks and trams and buses, rickshaws, oxcarts, cows, and pedestrians all going in different directions, and then we pass beyond the neon lights and sound systems and a gauntlet of firecrackers into a suburb where the houses are set far apart and sleek black water buffalo are standing up to their knees in swamps, and go down a dirt road between walled gardens to a great, rambling mansion which is brightly lit and noisy and full of people.

There is a tight crowd in a small room off the entrance, and through a doorway I can see a courtyard with a large group of women. They are singing the Hari Krishna chant with wild joy. Everyone is spaced out with religious fervor. It seems like the foreplay of a great celestial orgasm. Some of us squeeze into the already crowded room and sit doubled up on straw mats on the floor. There is a chair against the far wall under an Air India poster. In a few minutes Dadaji appears and sits in the chair. It is the same Dada I saw half an hour previously, with the same sleek black hair, faint Cheshire-cat smile, and green-edged dhoti. He has taken off his shirt. But at the same time Dada is also sitting in the other house in meditation. I know that because that is what I have been told, and this is the miracle: Dada is in two different houses at once, confirmed by his loyal disciples.

Dada sits in the chair, leaning forward, while people come up to him, kiss his feet, ask questions, whisper in his ear, but he seems to be losing contact. He is not with us, I realize. Then he gets up without a word and goes into the adjoining room and closes the door. We sit for a long time, and finally I become restless and go out into the courtyard to listen to the women sing. It is always the same song, the Hari Krishna, Hari Krishna, but from time to time they stop abruptly and begin again with a different melody, though the words are the same. The entire house seems to be drifting up and up into a higher plane. The tension is unbearable, yet agreeable, as if we are all about to be swept away and consumed in a cosmic explosion. Dada appears in the courtyard, on a small verandah, and enters the front room. I follow to see what is happening, but he leaves almost immediately. He looks remote and seems to fade away into the other room. Another hour goes by, with the endless, lilting, driving chant of the women and Gopal Chatterjee's hard-edged drumming which plays above and below and inside the rhythm of the singing, up and around and at cross currents, higher and higher to the edge of the universe. Suddenly everything stops. The rattle of firecrackers and bombs echoes away in the distance, and rockets light the sky. Dada stands for a moment on the edge of the verandah, as if he is barely touching the tiles, and then goes into the front room. I slip in and sit on the floor. He is awake for a moment, but then he drifts off, into a faraway world.

When he entered the room, Dada walked very straight and stiff, as if he were being transported by unseen beings. Now he is slumped in his chair, a strange, remote look on his face. He opens and closes his eyes. His head falls on his chest; his breasts bulge like a woman's. I begin to take some photographs. So, I think, Something has Happened. People begin to touch his feet, but he is unaware of them. The door to the other room is open and the crowd presses into it. Dada is floating. Unaware.

He is floated away to an
unknown land

whose account no one can give
even a glimpse of it.
The rooms of the palaces
are humming with the noise of the inmates.
Their heart is also lifted up in joy.
Numerous flowers
    the rose
    the jessamine
are blooming there.
Lotuses are blossoming in the lake
and the humming of the bees
is echoed with the chirping
    of birds of different tribes.
The giver is intoxicated and perplexed
    by love.
Every day we see the twilight dissolve
    into darkness.
The midnight of the universal night
will be the time of absolute silence
    over the universal power
    of destruction,
    the transcendent power
        of Time.
Mahakali rules unchallenged.

Great Mother
    sprung from the sacrificial hearth
    of the fire of the Grand Consciousness,
whose play is a world play, whose eyes flash
like fish in the beauteous waters of her Divine Face,
open and shut with the disappearance of countless worlds
now illuminated in terrible Light
now wrapped in her terrible Darkness.

Unsullied treasure-house of beauty
slender waist bending beneath the burden
    of the ripe fruit of her breasts
jewelled hips

heavy with the promise of infinite maternities.
Hers are forms without end. She is seen as One and as many,
one moon reflected on countless waters.
Existing in all animals and in all organic things
the universe in all its beauties is but part of her.
Infinite manifestation
    of all the flowering beauties of One Supreme Life.

There is but one Sun, one Light, one Spirit
whose manifestations are many.

Kali is the supreme night, which swallows all that exists.
With her four arms she stands as the symbol of fulfillment
of all and of the absoluteness of her dominion over all that exists.
All the powers and pleasures of the world
    are transient.
All human joy
    is but a momentary and feeble perception of our true nature
which is unbounded joy.
But such is temporary and hidden by pain.
True happiness exists only in the permanent.
Only Kali, the Power of Time, is permanent.
Kali alone,
    the giver of bliss
can grant happiness.
Kali is beyond all attachments.

In the meditation room there is a small black statue of Kali, covered
with flowers. The floor is wet, sopping wet, the walls are dripping
with water, the ceiling is beaded with water. Around the statue are
jars of water and bowls of cut-up fruit, candles, flowers, more
flowers. "It is a miracle," several people say to me, "a real miracle."
The room had been dry before Dada entered. "During Dada's meditation the room has become wet. It is Ganga water, sacred water
from the Ganga. Dada made it appear miraculously." People are
dipping their handkerchiefs and scarves into the water on the floor,
mopping it up, crying with joy. Mr. Bose takes a handkerchief from

a woman—she doesn't seem to mind—and gives it to me. It's wet, steaming. I decline it politely and return it to the woman. In the front room Dada is coming and going, opening his eyes and drifting off again. He has a cigarette in his right hand, but it is burning down without being smoked. His feet are being covered with kisses, with embraces, with love, love, love.

Love.

It is an hour later. Dada seems to be back to normal. He is carrying on conversations. He has refused to speak to me, to acknowledge me, though he was dimly conscious that I was taking photographs, that I have him imperishably captured on film, Dada with disciples, Dada is samadhi, Dada coming and going, Dada in the Cosmic, Dada enraptured with the Great Goddess Kali. Dada, who has been united with the One, who has spanned the universe, who though his body remained alive as an unconscious automaton for a period of time, is the attained, the perfected soul. But I held in my hand the powers of the West, the silver nitrate film, the perfected optical system, and beyond them I have at my disposal the electric blender, the electric carver, the electric shoe-polisher, the instant cake mix, the superhighway, napalm, the defoliant and the depilatory, the jet plane, the democratic vote (for two undifferentiated candidates).

He is floated away to an
    unknown land
whose account no one can give
even a glimpse of it.
Kali alone,
    the giver of bliss
can grant happiness.

MIRABAI

Krishna playing the flute for the gopis

I am in love with Mirabai (c. 1500–1550), Rajput princess, wife of the ruler of the ancient state of Mewar. Her devotion to the Lord Krishna led her to abandon her husband (he must have been a surly fellow, according to my ESP) and to spend her life in complete surrender to the praise of her God. About the only anecdote of her life that I know is of the time when the king, overhearing her talking behind closed doors to a man, drew his sword and broke in. But it was Krishna she had been talking to. Krishna turned Mirabai into countless multitudes of forms (you know how we Hindus multiply, all those arms and legs and heads and multitudinous figures), and the king was as confused as any Westerner and could not tell which was his wife and which was an illusion: thousands of eyes, thousands of arms and legs, even thousands of vulvas, so that he was surrounded (!) with forms so identical that each became as a reflection in rapidly shifting mirrors, the multiplicity of exuberance, the exuberance of multiplicity. Surrendering to Mira's constant pleading for a sign of His love for her, Krishna finally revealed himself in all His glory and absorbed her soul into His. Mirabai was known as a poetess and singer; her songs (haunting is the only description of them) are still popular throughout India.

Hers was a love of high passion. Her petticoats askew, her bare midriff sleek and lean, her blouse tattered, her shawl slipping from her head showing her long straight shining black hair falling in a cascade to her waist, great black eyes shining, white teeth sparkling, the diamond in her left nostril flashing like the North Star, feet bare and lined with red, silver anklets and silver bracelets and bells jangling and ringing the celestial harmonies, frenzied with the love of Krishna her celestial lover, dancing in the ecstatic joy of a woman loved, raped, seized, consumed, pierced, abandoned, and reclaimed, now singing and dancing like a woman distraught with passion before Lord Krishna's shrines, scandalizing her relatives, leaving home and the court (raised eyebrows, threats, warnings from the royal brothers and sisters-in-law)—leaving home and singing and dancing her way along the roads to Mathura, the Krishna-sacred land.

Krishna, who could make love to sixteen thousand (you heard me) gopis each of whom had thrown off her clothes in order to make herself worthy of the blissful embrace of the Divine Lover, each feeling as if only she enjoyed Him alone—Krishna found his greatest passion in Mirabai.

My garments I tore
I clad myself in a coarse wrapper
        merely a small piece of cloth
I threw away my jewelry
        and passed my time
        in the company of saints, saying good-bye
to all the affectations of society.
I reared the creeper of the Lord's love
with my tears.
That too I did fearlessly
ignoring the tyrant's tortures
the scoffers' hostile aspersions.
Courting the scorpions touch
the snake's embraces
and the bed of nails
I now stay in a haunted house.

O my lord I am insane with love for you
but whom can I tell of my suffering?
My bed is made of thorns
how can I sleep on it?
The bed of my beloved is the universe
and mine is the hard earth
so how can we be united?
One who has suffered knows the pangs
        of love
but not one who has not.

He who has drunk poison
knows its bitterness
others do not.
Wounded I wander from forest to forest
but have not yet found the healer.
O Mira's lord!
I will be cured only when you are
      my healer.

O Lord, you have kindled the flames of love
and now where have you gone?
You have lit the lamp of love and fled
leaving her who knows nothing but you.
You have launched the boat of love
and left it to drift on the wild sea.
O Mira's lord, when will you come?
I can no longer live without you.

Listen to Hari's footsteps.
From the verandah of my palace
I can see my king coming.
The frogs and the peacocks cry in delight
and the cuckoo sounds her sweet notes.
The clouds rain nectar
in sheer delight
and the earth has decked herself with lush garments
to meet her sweet lord.
O Giridar, Mira's lord and beloved!
Come quickly and
be one with your slave.

If living on fruits and nuts is the way to salvation
then monkeys and cattle would go to heaven before men.
If bathing in holy rivers brings salvation
then the fishes in the Ganges and the Jumna
would gain paradise before men.

A great sannyasi, Sanatana Goswami, refuses to receive Mirabai because she is a woman. "Tell the master," she says to the servant, "that I did not know there was any male in the universe but God. Aren't we all females before HIM?" Sanatana bows low before Mira and touches her lotus feet.

If by a daily bath God could be realized
I would be a whale in the ocean.
If by eating roots and fruits He could be known
I'd gladly be a goat.
If counting rosaries revealed Him
I would say my prayers on gigantic beads.
If bowing before stone images unveiled Him
I would humbly worship mountains.
If by drinking milk one could drink the Lord
innumerable calves and babies would know Him.
If by abandoning one's wife one would find God
would not thousands of men be eunuchs.
Mirabai knows that to find the Divine One
the only requisite is love.

THE LAST DAYS

[Ram Chandra] The present structure of world civilization based upon electricity and atomic energy shall not remain in existence for long. It is destined to fall soon. The whole atmosphere is so much charged with the poisonous effect of absolute materialism that it is almost beyond human control to change it. Godly energy in human form is already at work. It is a fact beyond doubt. The world shall know of him and his work in this respect after some time when events have sufficiently come to light.

I present before the readers a glimpse of the world that is to be, as I see it in my vision. Believe it or not, but this is my reading of Nature in the clairvoyant state. Signs are evident that the destruction of the undesirable elements in the world has already commenced. Such a destruction is accomplished through various means. It may be through war or internal feud, through heavenly calamity such as volcanic upheaval or through similar other causes. The time is now ripe for its final phase, and the world is rushing toward it with headlong speed. The action may come into full swing by the close of the present century, but some of the events enumerated below may take a longer time to come into effect.

The heat of the sun has been gradually diminishing for some time past and it may be a baffling problem for the scientists to tackle, as after some time life on the surface of the earth may become quite impossible owing to insufficient heat in the sun. No solution of it is within their mental approach, in spite of all the material powers at their command. I may assure them that it will not at present diminish to that extent. The present decrease in the sun's heat is meant only to expedite Nature's process of change, and the personality deputed for that work is utilizing it for the purpose. It is an unfailing sign of the imminent upheaval in the entire structure of the world, and after it the sun will again resume its full glow. The same sign will appear again at the time of Mahapralaya [complete dissolution], but as it is a far-off thing, I do not like to dwell upon it here. One thing I may disclose in this connection for the interest of the readers. At the time of Mahapralaya the pole star will deviate a few degrees from its position and will grow a bit hotter. A powerful energy in the form of a gas will begin to gush out from it and will ultimately destroy the world and everything else in existence. The action of destruction will start from the North Pole.

In consequence of the present upheaval, drastic changes will come into effect and the new structure of the world will be quite different from the one we see today. The fate of Great Britain will be sad. A part of it—the southern portion—will sink into the sea. A volcanic energy in the latent state is at work in the heart of London, and in course of time it will burst forth in the form of a volcanic eruption. The Gulf Stream will change its course and the country will become extremely cold. The fate of Europe too will be similar. Smaller countries will lose their existence. The future of Russia is in darkness. She cannot survive. Communism shall have its grave in its own homeland. As for America, she is in imminent danger of losing her wealth, and in course of time she may almost be reduced to paupery. Her power and greatness too will sink along with it. India shall regain her pristine glory, and she will rise to prominence under her own government. Her suzerainty will extend far and wide and the world will look up to her for a beacon light. But she too shall have her share in world upheaval. The germs of rebellion are developing in the country. A part of the country—the eastern portion of Bengal—shall sink into the sea. Volcanic energy is also active and may seriously affect some parts of it. The Deccan plateau may, in the remote future, turn into an island. There shall be enormous bloodshed all over the world, and the loss of life through various causes shall be so great that the world population shall be considerably reduced. The new structure of the coming world will stand on bones and ashes. A type of civilization based on spiritualism will spring forth in India and it shall, in due course, become the world civilization. No country or nation shall survive without spirituality as its base, and every nation must sooner or later adopt the same course if it wants to maintain her existence.

It is the sphere of forms, rituals, and practices of various types we proceed with in our pursuit by the path, cut through mountains of difficulties and obstructions by Nature herself. We march on through different spheres of light and shade of varying grossness, far, far above the sphere of the moon and the sun, growing finer and finer at every step till we attain the highest point of approach.*

A Kaula yogi* may dwell anywhere, disguised in any form, unknown to anyone. Such yogis, in various guises, intent on the welfare of men, walk the earth unrecognized by others. They do not expend their self-knowledge immediately, but live in the midst of men as if intoxicated, dumb, stupid. The mode of yogis is not easily perceivable like the sun or the moon or the stars or the planets in the sky, nor is their mode observable like the movements of birds or fish. Adepts of Kaula yoga speak like the uncouth, behave as if ignorant, appear like the lowly. This they do so that men will ignore them. They talk about nothing at all. Though realized in freedom, the yogi will play like a child; he may handle himself like a moron, and talk like a drunk. Such a yogi lives in a way that the world will laugh at, be disgusted with, abuse, and keep away from. The yogi may go about in different guises, like a well-off man, like a bum, or at times like a demon or a ghost. If the yogi accepts the gracious things of life it is for the good of the world and not out of desire. Out of compassion for all men he will play on the earth. Like the sun that dries up everything, the yogi takes all to himself but is not tainted by sin. Like the wind that blows upon everything, like the sky which covers everywhere, like all who bathe in the rivers, the yogi is ever pure. As water flowing off the land becomes pure when it reaches the river, so do things from the lowly become pure once they reach the hands of the yogi.

[Ishwar Sahai*] The Divine Energy descends only when Nature demands its presence on earth. The coming of the Avatar is not a matter of mere accident but in accordance with some specific plan of Nature. Obviously the purpose of His coming down to the world in human form is to destroy the forces of evil, which are over-predominant in the world, leading to the creation of a chaotic state all around. The coming of the Avatar is inevitable. In the Gita, Lord Krishna says: "When there is a decline of righteousness, and unrighteousness is in ascendance, I come down assuming human form." We must naturally conclude that it is time for the Avatar to come down to earth. Most of the great souls of the world seem to agree that it is just the time for the very zero-hour for the long-expected advent of the Divine personality. But there are a few who, though they believe that he is soon to come, feel somewhat reluctant to accept that he has already come. There are, of course, others who feel convinced that he is already come and is in existence among us this day, silently and imperceptibly. My Guru has said: "Nature now requires a thorough overhauling of the world; and for that purpose I may assure you a special Personality has already come into existence and has been at work for about two and a half years [since the early 1960s]." It is a fact beyond doubt. On the basis of my own personal experience, I may assure the world in all earnestness that the Avatar is in existence in the world today.

The Avatar's advent is not to be proclaimed to the world by the beat of drum, neither by any supernatural phenomenon in the sky nor by any other miraculous means to satisfy the curiosity of the materialistic mind of the people. The most common indication of the Avatar's coming as given by Saint Ram Krishna Paramhamsa is: "When a huge tidal wave comes, all the brooks and ditches become full to the brim without any effort or consciousness on their own part, so when an Incarnation comes, a tidal wave of spirituality breaks upon the world and people feel spirituality almost full in the air."

Swami Vivekananda said in a speech in New York about seventy years ago: "The power has been set in motion which at no distant date will bring unto mankind once more the memory of their real nature; and again the place from which this power will start will be Asia."

To test his presence, let anyone who may, meditate for some time sincerely thinking that he is receiving spiritual impulse from the great personality in existence and feel and judge whether he receives it or not. If he does, it is a sufficient proof of his existence. We can even secure personal contact with Him, if we earnestly so desire. I most earnestly entreat my brethren all over the world not to take my words lightly.

A warning: there may come out dexterous persons making false claims of their being the Avatar. It may perhaps be one of the most difficult jobs to judge such a great personality from his outer appearance or the physical form. Externally, he may be so simple and unassuming that his very simplicity may serve as a veil to his true being. He shall not belong to any nation, race, or religion, though apparently he may have been born within the fold of the one or the other. *His existence is universal.* His entire outward life shall be just like that of an ordinary man.

The Avatar possesses all the godly attributes. He is omnipresent, omniscient, and omnipotent. He can appear in the sun, the moon, and the stars in astral form, all at the same time, in spite of having his physical body at one place only. He is kind, benevolent, just, and merciful and gives everyone his due without reserve. He lavishly bestows his blessings upon the righteous but also punishes and destroys the vicious and the ungodly. His power is unlimited. He can in a moment charge any place, country, or even the whole world with the highest spiritual force so as to bring all men into a state of trance. He can at a single stroke of his will remove or destroy the effect of all the past samskaras of a man and free him from all bondages. When fortunately you happen to find one possessing these supernatural powers, know him not to be an ordinary man but the very Incarnation, Avatar, who has come down for the emancipation of the world.

Mind, learn to see by opening your eyes. All your taste for looking at the beautiful things of the world will vanish forever. Prepare a seat in a lonely corner of your heart and let Him be seated there so you can always look at Him to your heart's content. Your mind will then be free from all sorrow, grief, pain, or hopelessness. You will be swimming in the ocean of love and ripples of joy will rise up in your mind and one day you will reach His abode of bliss and rest there in peace. Therein lies eternal residence and in it you will see young Gaur and by his side Nityananda. You will be thanked and being allowed to serve them, you will be sanctified and live in blissful joy. If the heart of anybody is touched by this loving self and if one can establish relationship, constant relation of love with this blissful self and if he can secure a place in the orbit of the circular dancing of the ever beautiful Lord, he will then taste and realize true love. If you learn to love Him who is immanent and permeating the whole universe, everything will be sweet and full of honey. You will then appreciate that He pervades the whole world and His light illuminates everything. Honey is showered in this world at His gesture, the realization of this fine idea will raise up your heart, you can trace out love and the source of its joy. Otherwise where will you find love in this transient illusory world full of sorrows and where can you find joy? The love and joy you see in this world is nothing but an ephemeral exponent of that divine illusory power inherent in God.

So I say, O mind, you have found gold in the midst of searching brittle glass. No, you have found a jewel. What troubles you then? Do not sit idle building castles in the air with a grievous heart putting hands on your head. Make a garland of this gold and jewel and wear it on your neck. This priceless necklace will swing on your breast and you will be illuminated by the cool shining light of this necklace. It is time for you to accept and welcome that beautiful crystallised image of Absolute Experience. Consciousness and Bliss, you will be blessed in this dark age and be thanked for being born as a man, success in life will then welcome you at every step. Try to understand this image of God and establish relationship with Him. You will then be fortunate being the recipient of this wealth of heavenly love.

When you take your seat under the cool shade of this love tree, all your worries and troubles of life will be evaporated forever. There is cool shade under this love tree even in the midst of the hot desert of Sahara in this dark age. There is no record of the number of men who are saved by taking shelter under this tree. He who will take his seat under this tree will say being elated in joy, "I have been thanked and blessed. There is nothing on earth agreeable or acceptable to me. All my hopes and desires even my penances are at an end and rest here. I have been saved. I have been rescued." Saying this you will begin dancing in joy but uttering "Haribol" [O Lord Krishna!] resounding all sides by its echo. You shall have nothing to say, to speak or get. All shall pass away. Your body and mind will be overflowed in joy by the mercy of your preceptor like the swelling of the ocean. You will be astonished in wonder and maddening in joy you will raise your hands and say, "Gaur Haribol, Hari Haribol." All glory to Gaur, all glory to Hari. Being elated in joyous love, say again and again, "Gaur Haribol, Haribol, Hari Haribol." All glory to God.*

There are two ways of contemplation in Brahman: in sound and in
    silence.
By sound we go to silence.
The sound of Brahman is OM.
With OM we go to the End: the silence of Brahman.
The End is immortality, union, peace.

Even as a spider reaches the liberty of space
by means of its own thread,
the man of contemplation
by means of OM
reaches freedom.

The sound of Brahman is OM.
At the end of OM there is silence, the silence of joy.
It is the end of a journey
where fear and sorrow are no more:
steady, motionless, never-falling, ever-lasting, immortal.

In order to reach the Highest,
consider in adoration the sound and silence
of Brahman.
For it has been said: God is sound and silence.
His name is OM.
Attain therefore contemplation—contemplation in silence
on
    Him.

Power
Infinite
symbol of God
sound
everlasting
sacred
all-containing
original
OM

NOTES

(*Page 16*) The maha yuga, or great age, is composed of 4,320,000 human years. There are seventy-one maha yugas, which make one man-vantara, fourteen of which make one kalpa, which is a day of Brahma. We know that Brahma will live to one hundred years. To cut a long mathematical process short (though we Hindus prefer the long form), we are in the last of the four quarters of the current cycle of the present kalpa and are waiting for Kalki, the tenth avatar of Vishnu, the second member of our triad. Kalki, who is blue, will come riding with a sword in hand on a swift white horse like a blazing comet, to bring about the end of the world by flood or fire. Then a new maha yuga will begin, the ages revolving with their rising and descending races of men, until the end of the kalpa of the day of Brahma, which will culminate in pralaya, the night of dissolution, which is equal to time past. Here the Lord will repose in yoga nidra, or sleep, on the serpent Shesa, the Endless One, until daybreak, when the universe will be created anew and the next kalpa will come. It might be noted that a number of our holy men believe the time of dissolution is here now and that the tenth avatar is among us, in a form we do not recognize; in fact, there are one or two men who claim to be the tenth avatar. Incidentally, the exact age of Brahma is known: he has just completed the fiftieth year of his life. Resolve the contradictions as you will.

(*Page 28*) The Naxalites are a far-left movement, composed largely of students, some workers, a few farmers. It originally began as a peas-ants' protest against rapacious landowners in Bengal in 1966. The original movement is now believed to have split into five groups. They are subject to extreme repression by the government and are involved in much vio-lence, though it appears that many of their "crimes" are actually the work of agents provocateurs and of Goondas and Dacoits calling themselves Naxalites.

(*Page 30*) The five-hundred-year-old man is Babaji. He is said to live in the northern Himalayas, and "has retained his physical form for centuries, perhaps for millenniums." Babaji is "deathless" and bears no marks of age in his body. "He appears to be a youth of not more than twenty-five. Fair-skinned, of medium build and height, Babaji's beautiful strong body radiates a perceptible glow. . . . Babaji can be seen or recognized by others only when he so desires." Sri Paramahansa Yogananda, *Autobiography of a Yogi* (Jaico, Bombay, 1963).

(*Page 33*) Hari Krishna, etc. A prayer to the Lord Krishna. Hari and Ram are names of God.

(*Page 49*) The following verses are freely drawn from various tantric writings.

(*Page 57*) The French scholar Alain Daniélou has an excellent study of mantras (and also yantras and many other aspects of our world) in *Hindu Polytheism* (Bollingen, Princeton University Press, 1964). Daniélou has assembled a formidable collection of references from both Hindu classics and contemporary works. His own insights are admirable.

(*Page 60*) Sir John Woodroffe. Sir John rescued a number of tantric works from obscurity and had them published in English, with notes and often with original Sanskrit texts. Unfortunately his books are hard to find in the United States.

(*Page 62*) Kula pushpa, the tantric term for the menstrual blood of a woman. When a girl reaches puberty she is said to have borne the kula, or flower.

(*Page 68*) Shabad yoga. A specialty of Radha Soami Satsang, which draws upon Sikh mysticism. The terms are largely Punjabi, but the ideas originate in Hinduism, from which Sikhism is an offshoot.

(*Page 69*) Kabir. Apparently born a Muslim, Kabir (c. 1440–1518) drew heavily upon Hinduism as well as Sufism for his mystical poems. He lived in Benares, working as a weaver.

(*Page 100*) Dalai Lama. The Lama's brother, Thubten Jogme Norbu (in collaboration with Colin Turnbull), includes a description of the search in his excellent work, *Tibet* (New York, Simon and Schuster, 1970).

(*Page 104*) Tantra. The mirror in which this book is reflected, tantra is not to be trifled with. The chela approaching tantra stands on the border of the Forbidden Land, which may be entered only with guru. When we awaken Kundalini, who is Kali, we leave ordinary yoga and enter into definitely dangerous ground, where the most esoteric forms of tantric yoga begin.

It is not easy to define tantra, but a facile explanation would be "what extends knowledge." In Hindu tantrism, the Divine Mother, whom we have best known as Kali, is the sum of all the mystery of woman, for every woman is an incarnation of Shakti, with her powers of generation, fecundity, restoration, rest, and re-creation. Man is a butterfly, a fish, a beast, scattering his seed irresponsibly, but woman bears the universe within her womb, with all the enigma of creation. Thus Shakti becomes the focus of tantric yoga, through the worship of Shakti/woman.

I cannot do more than outline tantric practices. Their observance by the uninformed and the noninitiate is dangerous, even fatal. The reader who wants to delve deeper into tantrism (and it can be done only in India) must not only shed his Western ways, but learn Sanskrit and Bengali and perhaps Hindi. Even then, since foreigners are by birth untouchable, they are denied the participation in tantra except symbolically. By improper observance of the rites, which on the surface seem like mere sexual by-play, the worshiper will not only suffer pain at every step but go to hell until the time of final dissolution. What determines the moral character of an act is the intent with which it is done; when a man's intent is bad, so is his act.

Briefly, the tantric yogic rite is the worship of Shakti/woman through the Panch (five) Makaras, commonly called the Five M's. In the Sanskrit terminology they are madya (liquor), matsya or mina (fish), mamsa (meat), mudra (a parched bean believed to be an aphrodisiac), and maithuna (sexual union). The first three makaras are definitely contrary to the Hindu code, as are the last two as practiced in tantra. There are various opinions (among outsiders) about whether the celebration of the five makaras is to be followed literally, i.e., the left-hand path, or metaphorically, the right-hand path. The various tantric manuals, of which there are a number, are usually obscure on this point. In actual practice, observance tends to favor the literal view.

Puja, either individual or collective, plays a central role in the life of the tantric. There are various rituals for daily, fortnightly, and monthly celebrations and for special events like birthdays, holy days, and festivals. The ritual begins with a detailed saying of the normal prayers that any yogi or group of yogis might use. But the second half of the ritual centers on the Panch Makaras. Shakti worship in the left-hand path is significant. The term is vamamarga: vama means both "left" and "woman." The rite may be practiced by a single man alone or by a chakra, or circle, with one Shakti, or the members of the entire circle may each have his own Shakti.

The rites are detailed in the manuscripts, down to the most minute measurements of sacred implements, the yantras, and the saying of mantras, gestures, and so on. The wine, meat, fish, and grain are consecrated in elaborate and time-consuming rites. No more than five cups of wine may be taken, after which maithuna is celebrated. Some manuals include the use of some forms of cannabis indica at the beginning of the rite. The idea of tantric worship has infuriated Westerners, as having other aspects of Indian sexual interest, whether the worship of the lingam, the decorations of various temples, or our marriage manuals. The Abbé Dubois, the eighteenth-century French missionary, whose *Hindu Religion, Ceremonies, Customs and Manners* is a magnificent tribute to our vanishing past, describes the ritual in detail and in a manner in which he left no doubt as to the disgust he felt, ending by saying, "The principal objects which form the sacrifice to Shakti are a large vessel full of native rum and a full grown [Indian] girl. The latter, stark naked, remains standing in a most indecent manner. The goddess Shakti is evoked, and is supposed to respond to the invitation to come and take up her abode in the vessel full of rum and also in the girl's body."

P. Thomas, a South Indian, writing more recently, says that while the rite is "of a sacramental nature, and some priests and texts insist that the worshiper must have his senses completely under control and emotions well regulated, [the reader] may wonder how this is possible for a worshiper with a cup of wine in his right hand and a naked woman on his left thigh."

But the sole purpose of the rite is to arouse Kundalini and to pierce the six mystical chakras, so that She will be led through the sushumna to sahasrara, causing the nectar of union to flow into the worshiper in order to experience the ecstasy of paradise. The Kularnava Tantra stipulates: "In the worship of the Five M's, it is laid down that they are to be used as prescribed purely for the delectation of the Deity. If desire creeps in, then it becomes a sinful act. Thus it makes a large difference whether the worshiper is an enlightened person in the ways of knowledge or is an ignorant man." The wise, adds the Tantra, intoxicated with the spiritual joy of the rite, "do japa, meditate, praise, prostrate, instruct, query, delight themselves during the sessions. But the ignorant wander, roar, laugh, argue, weep, desire for sex."

The rite is far more complex than I have been able to describe in these lines. There are many techniques that enter into it which require training, and are psychologically dangerous for the amateur, one of the most famous being the ability of certain yogis to withdraw their semen after climax (a skilled yogi can also draw water into the urethra as a cleansing measure). But one need not be a tantric to enjoy the divine through sexual union. Pandit Ghildayal, a modern tantric, writes: "Sexual enjoyment is established as an excellent matter. If it is necessary for every living being, if it is a natural act, then its performance is a natural worship, that is to say, it is the worship of the World Mother."

(*Page 105*) Our ideas on food, frankly, irritate me. A yogic manual recommends "milk, barley, dates, fruit, vegetables, wheat, butter, honey, almonds"—all sensible, for "they render the mind calm." But "fish, eggs, meat, chillies, asafoetida" excite passion and are to be avoided, along with "onions, garlic and wine," which "fill the mind with anger, darkness and inertia." The chela "should give up mustard, sour, hot, pungent things, asafoetida, emaciation of body by fasts, etc." The manual in question settles on a diet of either boiled rice and ghee (a kind of clarified butter) or rice with ghee, white sugar and milk. And, "Sugar candy is very beneficial." In short, the preferred diets yogis recommend will lead to malnutrition. I am of the firm opinion that a lot of our holy men are not in meditation but are victims of poor nutrition.

(*Page 105*) The magnetism of the tiger skin. The great Bengal tiger is just about wiped out. We must be ecologically conscious. Why not try real Dynel?

(*Page 110*) Yogic meditation is not the only type, of course. It is interesting to compare the tightly structured practices of za-zen with the more open, "relaxed," and, to me, human techniques of yoga. Soyen Shaku, a Japanese Zen master, has written of za-zen: "Think of your own room as the whole world, and that all sentient beings are sitting there with you, as one. Make a searching analysis of yourself. Realize that your body is not your body. It is part of the whole body of sentient beings. Your mind is not your mind, but a constituent of all mind. Your eyes, ears, nose, tongue, hands, feet are not merely your individual belongings, but one in joint ownership with all sentient beings. You simply call them yours—and others'. You cling to your own being and consider others separate from you. It is nothing but a baseless delusion of yours. Free yourself from all incoming complications and hold your mind against them like a great iron wall. No matter what sort of contending thoughts arise in you, ignore them and they will perish and disappear of themselves. As soon as your thought expands and unites with the universe, then you are free from your stubborn ego. Then you will enter into a condition where there is no relativity, no absoluteness. You are now transcendent, far above both discrimination and equality. You have nothing to receive and there is nothing to receive you. There is no time, no space. There is no past, no future, only one eternal present. This is not the true realization, but you are walking near the palace. Free yourself from all incoming disturbances and hold your mind against them like a great iron wall. Then someday you will meet your true Self as if you had awakened from a dream, and you will have the happiness you could never have derived otherwise. Za-zen is not difficult. It is a way to lead you into your long-lost home."

(*Page 115*) Sai Baba. Swami B. V. Narasimhaswami collected the saint's sayings and the anecdotes about him in a work entitled *Sri Sai Baba's Charters and Sayings*. There is also a three-volume work, *Devotee's Experiences of Sai Baba*. Both are published by the All India Sai Baba Samaj, Madras.

(*Page 122*) "In Quest of Love," by Sri Sri Jibon Krishna Das (Babaji).

A typical Hindu devotional work. Babaji is head of Baranagore Sri Bhagbatacharya Patbari, Calcutta.

(*Page 123*) Preceptor 108 Sree Sreemat Ramdas Babaji Maharaj. The 108 means that Sree is repeated that number of times as a sign of respect. The number 108 or 1008 is a frequent figure in the names of saints and in litanies of the holy. Mother Ganges, for example, has 108 names (Born from the Lotus-like Foot of Vishnu, Dear to Hari, Melodious, Destroyer of Poverty, and so on).

(*Page 128*) *The Saints of India,* published by Nirmalendu Bikash Sen Gupta, Calcutta. Undated.

(*Page 133*) A low-caste man named Tiruppan. There are four castes, divided into two to three thousand subcastes. The lowest, the Sudras, is a mélange of people doing the base and menial jobs—agricultural work, scavenging, etc.—for the benefit of the higher castes. Below the Sudras are the real outcastes, called by Gandhi harijans, the children of God, a term that has not raised them in the eyes of the three higher castes, the Brahmins (priests), Kshatriyas (warriors), and Vaisyas (merchants and artisans). Even the mere presence of a low-caste person can pollute a Brahmin. In the past, low castes and outcastes were sometimes not allowed to use the same roads, wells, or temples.

(*Page 142*) Karapatri. A contemporary tantic swami. The statements are from various of his works, published in Benares.

(*Page 151*) Anandamayee Ma. There is extensive literature about Mother, most of it uncritical, repetitious, unduly adulatory, or poorly written, along with collections of her sayings, and a monthly magazine, *Ananda Varta,* devoted to her cult. Her main ashram is: Shree Shree Anandamayee Sangha, Bhadaini, Varanasi.

(*Page 175*) Divine Light Mission. What look like publicity releases in the following pages actually are. The mimeograph is one of the great weapons in the hands of Satgurudev Shri Sant Ji Maharaj and his team, along with Peace Bomb.

(*Page 182*) "Millions gathered . . ." More of the Mission's press material, concluding with "like wild fire affecting all by its influence."

(*Page 205*) Bedi's version of the Mool Mantra, otherwise known as JAP JI, is quite mystical, free, and poetic. He has had it printed in several works. As contrast I offer three other versions. Gurdip Singh Randhawa and Charanjit Singh: "There is but one God. Eternal Truth is His Name. He is the Supreme Creator. He knoweth no fear; is an enmity with no one. His Being is Timeless and Formless. He is autogenous. Attainable (he is) through the grace of the Guru. [Jap: the Meditations] Supreme Truth—such was He in the beginning; So hast He been through ages all. True He is—O Nanak; Such shalt He be evermore." R. S. Maunder: "By the Grace of the One the Only One/Unmanifest and Manifest the Same/

Always in Contemplation of Himself/The Same as Creation the Same as Law/The Same as Author of the two, PURUSHA soul, spirit/Unencumbered by like or unlike Him/By any other well-inclined or foe/Aid or alliance or obstruction/Without recourse to time existeth Who/Without recourse to cause/Enlightened and Discovered by Himself/The Sole Dispenser of Enlightenment/By the Grace of that One what follows is/For recitation and remembrance e'er/By Nanak write and titled/JAP!./Before and after/Within and without/Confine of time/He ever was and is and so shall be/The True, the Real, the Permanent./The Truth He was, the Truth He is/The Truth He will remain." P. Lal: "By the grace of the Guru! God is one, there is only one God,/God is Truth, He created all things,/God is without flaw, at peace with all things,/Timeless, and Birthless, Being of his/own being./Make known to men by the grace of/the guru! [Jap: the Meditations] Let us repeat His name./As He was in the beginning the Truth,/As He was through the Ages, the Truth,/So is He now, the Truth, O Nanak,/So will He be for ever and for ever."

(*Page 253*) Ram Chandra's prophecy. Given in *Reality at Dawn* published at Shajahanpur, Uttar Pradesh. Ram Chandra writes elsewhere: "I may also say that the momentum of all the creative activities was clockwise; if it now be turned anti-clockwise the universe will begin to dissolve."

(*Page 255*) A Kaula yogi. From Kularnava Tantra, a basic tantric work. Sir John Woodroffe calls it "perhaps the foremost Tantra" of its school.

(*Page 256*) Ishwar Sahai. He is a disciple of Ram Chandra's.

(*Page 259*) "Mind, learn to see . . ." By Sri Sri Krishna Das.

GLOSSARY

There is no standard transliteration of Indian words, which may come anyway from a number of languages—Sanskrit, Pali, Hindi, Bengali, Panjabi and so on. Thus we will find sri, sree, shree, shri, all of which mean the same (roughly "Lord," in the sense of a title of dignity), or asram or ashram. And an Indian glossary is in no way related to an English glossary. To give a few examples (printed in English in the originals):

Braja—Brindabon
Baikuntha—A place in heaven and on going there all mystery is solved.
Bright yellow pigment—Means ochre pigment.
Sabyasachi—A name as he could throw arrows by both hands.
Indelible—Means that cannot be blotted out.
Half (Sree Radha and Krishna with three devotees and a half) —Considered half being a woman.
Eternal being (with his thousand mouths)—Ananta Deb with his thousand heads.
Guru: *gu* signifies darkness; *ru*, what restrains it. He who restrains darkness (of ignorance) is the guru.
Yogi: Because he throbs with the glory of the Mantra due to the practice of *yoni-mudra* and because he is adorable by the host of these gods, *girvana gana* he is called yogi.
Puja: Because it destroys the legacy of previous births, *purvajanma*, because it prevents births and deaths, *janmamrtyu*, because it yields complete fruit, it is called puja.

And so on. But what follows in these pages is an attempt at a more orthodox (in western terms) form of glossary.

AHIMSA. Nonviolence.
AJAPA. Silent repetition (literally "repetitionless repetition"); interior meditation on a prayer or mantra.
AJNA CHAKRA. The topmost of the six chakras; it is also known as the THIRD EYE or the TENTH DOOR.

ANANDA. Bliss.

ARATI. A devotional ceremony in Hindu worship with the waving of
lighted candles and incense before the object of adoration; most
often performed at dawn and dusk.

ARJUNA. The warrior who serves as the foil for LORD KRISHNA's meditation upon the principles of YOGA in the BHAGAVAD GITA. Arjuna, who
also appears in other Indian epics, represents Truth and in some
references is mentioned as the son of the warrior-god INDRA.

ASANA, ASHAN. The posture one assumes in meditation. The preferred
asana is the lotus position, in which the legs are intertwined. It is
very difficult for the average Westerner, and it is suggested that one
sit in the most comfortable posture, with spine straight and head
erect.

ASHRAM, ASRAMA. A monastery or center for holy men and women.

ASTRAL. Pertaining to the heavenly regions, to which the soul may travel
when the adept is in SAMADHI or even asleep.

ATMA, ATMAN. The soul, the self; Supreme Existence or Being that is of
the nature of self-awareness and self-delight.

AVATAR, AVATARA. An incarnation of the Divine. The Divine descends to
earth to protect the righteous, destroy the wicked, and restore order.
An avatar may take various forms, such as KRISHNA or BUDDHA (who
are both avatars of VISHNU), or ANANDAMAYEE MA.

AYURVEDIC. An ancient form of medicine, based on the Vedas.

BABA. An affectionate term for "father."

BABU. A term of respect, something like "Sir" or "Master."

BEL LEAVES. The bel is a sacred tree (especially sanctified to LORD SHIVA).
The leaves are very fragrant.

BHAGAVAD GITA. One of the most famous of all Hindu religious epics
(actually, all epics are religious), in which KRISHNA, eighth avatar
of VISHNU, appears at a time of great social unrest and states various
spiritual, meditative, and mundane courses for mankind to follow,
all of which are forms of YOGA. The name of the work means "Song
of the Lord."

BHAJAN. A religious chant, which oftens produces ecstasy in the singer
and sometimes in the listener as well.

BHAKTI. Devotion or love for God; also worship. The Bhakti movement,
arising out of the BHAGAVAD GITA and similar works, brought man
to a personal worship of God in preference to ritualistic worship,
while at the same time stressing man's divine nature.

BHANG. Hashish or a similar derivative of cannabis indica, the Indian
hemp plant.

BHAVA. Spiritual ecstasy, often highly emotional in character.

BODHI. Enlightenment; enlightened; perfect wisdom.

BRAHMA. One of the three aspects of BRAHMAN (the others being SHIVA and VISHNU). Brahma is associated with the creation of the universe.

BRAHMA RANDHRA (also Brahmandhra). A path running along the vertebral column connecting the muladhara and sahasrara CHAKRAS.

BRAHMAN (sometimes Brahmam). The Supreme Reality conceived of as the One and Undifferentiated, static yet dynamic, and yet above all definition; the ultimate principle underlying the world; the immensity—indivisible existence, knowledge, and eternity.

BRAHMIN. The highest of the four castes, the priestly caste. There are said to be at least seventeen types of Brahmins. The word, to everyone's confusion, is sometimes spelled Brahman.

CHADDAR. A shawl.

CHAKRA, CAKRA. Literally, a circle or wheel. One of the six major mystical centers of the body, through which KUNDALINI rises.

CHELA. A disciple or student of a GURU.

CHENRESIG. The four-armed herdsman, incarnation of the Lord Buddha in Tibet. His special mantra is the famous OM MAN-NI PAD-ME HUM.

CHIP. Slang for rupee, the standard unit of Indian money.

CRORE. Ten million.

DACOIT. A robber. Until the practice was virtually wiped out in the nineteenth century by the English, many dacoits worshiped KALI in her fiercer aspects.

DADA. "Older brother." The term is often applied affectionately to certain holy men.

DEVA. A god. The word is cognate with the English "divine," etc. The root *div* means "to shine."

DEVATA. A goddess.

DEVI. The feminine form of DEVA.

DHARMA. Reality, the way, the law. "The path which a man should follow in accordance with his nature and station in life."

DHOTI. A long cloth (usually of white cotton) worn by men; it is tied loosely about the legs and waist.

DHYANA. Meditation. There are various types of dhyana. The highest is transcendental and leads to SAMADHI, and can be attained only when the composite structure of the ego—the "I am" consciousness—is dissolved. In Hindu teaching the ego is the knot of ignorance.

DIKSHA. Initiation into the spiritual life, effected through the grace of GURU, who represents, *is*, the divine.

DUPATTA. A scarf; it is most often seen in northern India.

DURGA. One of the forms of KALI, who is SHAKTI, Supreme Energy.

FAKIR. A Muslim holy man, a SUFI; roughly the equivalent of a SADHU.

GANGA. The Ganges; the most sacred of India's rivers (which, of course, are all sacred). The Ganges falls from heaven upon the matted hair of Lord SHIVA, in a cave in the Himalayas.

GANJA. Marijuana. A common plant in India (cannabis indica), it is used specifically in certain religious ceremonies and indiscriminately by the majority of the population unknown to the upper classes, who think it is a filthy Western custom only.

GAURI. One of the names of Parvati, who is none other than KALI.

GITA. The BHAGAVAD GITA.

GOONDA. A hooligan; a petty thief.

GOPI. One of the milkmaids attendant upon KRISHNA in his sportive moods as a young man. There were 16,008 gopis. Krishna stole their clothes as they bathed. Each gopi was under the impression that Krishna loved her alone, as indeed He did.

GURU. A spiritual guide or teacher, who represents, *is* the divine and gently guides his CHELA into the higher levels of the spiritual life. Unless the chela is unusually talented and blessed, he must have a guru.

HARI. One of the names of VISHNU. Also spelled Hare.

HATHA YOGA. A heavily physical form of yogic training, the preliminary to higher disciplines like JAPA and AJAPA, and so on.

HINDUISM. The way of life of the majority of people in India. It is more than a religion, and is beyond definition in ordinary terms. It is better called Brahmanism, the religion of BRAHMAN.

ISHT, ISHTA. Literally, "beloved." An isht devata is one's chosen deity, through whom one normally worships.

ISHVARA, ISHWAR (and -*eshwar*, etc.). One of the words denoting the divine. The third form, in various spellings, is attached as a suffix to certain other words, as in Bhuvaneshvari, the Goddess of the Spheres, again KALI.

JAGAD, JAGAT. The world; literally, "that which is going on." The word is often combined with another. Thus a jagadguru is a world, or supreme, guru.

JAMNA. A sacred river which flows into the GANGA. In mystical terms it represents one of the sacred arteries of the body. Also spelled Jumuna, Yamuna, etc.

JAPA. Repetition of a mantra or of the name of God said in meditation either aloud or silently, usually with a fixed pattern of breathing.

JI. An honorific. It can be attached (by others) to one's name as a sign of respect. Among Bengalis a surname ending in -*ji* indicates the person is a BRAHMIN; e.g., Bannerji, Chatterji. Sometimes spelled -*jee*.

JIVA. The individual soul or spirit; the embodied soul; individual consciousness as the eternal aspect of the eternal BRAHMAN.

JYOTI, JYOTISH. Literally, "light," but used in the sense of astrology.

KAL, KALA. Time. It may be used as a name for SHIVA and as the opposite of KALI, who destroys time.

KALI. The Great Goddess, the Universal Mother, SHAKTI. Kali also appears as GAURI, DURGA, Uma, Sati, Parvati, SARASVATI, Bhuvaneshvari, and so on, depending on her aspect. It is likely that many people see the various forms as different goddesses, but in the end all of them are returned to Kali and thence to BRAHMAN.

KALI YUGA. The last of the four basic ages of time in the Hindu calendar (the earlier stages are Krita, Treta, and Dvapara) and the one in which we are now immersed. The present age is the most degenerate. Owing to the general decline of the world, even a moderate amount of spiritual practice will, in contrast, lead to great results.

KALIGHAT. A shrine in Calcutta on a branch of the GANGA, sacred to KALI. It is one of the most revered sites in India.

KALPA. A unit of time which is a day of BRAHMA. The kalpa is 4,320,-000,000 human years. Brahma has just completed the fiftieth year of life.

KARMA. Action or its result. Also (and especially) the law of cause and effect by which actions bear their fruit. We are bound to karma until we realize our true selves. The word is pronounced k'rma. The common Buddhist spelling is kamma.

KAULA. Pertaining to a form of TANTRA.

KHEYAL, KHEYALA. An incomprehensible act of the divine, sometimes playful.

KIRTAN. A type of song which brings religious ecstasy.

KRISHNA. The eighth incarnation of VISHNU, manifested as the Dark One. Krishna is the embodiment of love, of the divine joy that destroys all pain. The love of Krishna for Radha is the theme of the mysticoerotic cults of India.

KRIYA. Activity; action; creative action. Kriya yoga involves astral traveling, bilocation, and other such occult acts.

KUNDALINI. The Serpent Power, which is coiled in the spine of every person and is released after the proper meditation. Kundalini is none other than KALI.

KUTIR. A small hut of bamboo and grass, used for meditation.

LAKH. One hundred thousand.

LILA. Divine play, free by its very nature and beyond physical laws.

LINGA, LINGAM. The male sexual organ, and above all, a sign of SHIVA. Linga shrines are found all over India. The linga is often depicted with the YONI.

LOTUS. A flower accepted as sacred and employed as a symbol of the divine. One bows to a holy person's "lotus feet."

LUNGI. A piece of cotton, usually colored, about two yards long, worn by men as a kind of sarong. It has religious overtones: Muslims prefer the lungi, though Hindus may often wear it. However, Muslims rarely wear the DHOTI, which is exclusively Hindu. The lungi is worn flat and tight instead of pleated and is tied by a knot over the abdomen.

MA. Mother. An affectionate term applied to a holy woman.

MAHA. A prefix meaning "great," "supreme." Cognate with the Latin "major."

MAHABHARATA. One of the great Hindu epics, three and a half times the length of the Christian Bible. Its running theme is the struggle between branches of an ancient family, but under the guise of the histories of epic battles, it is primarily didactic, delivering its messages in the form of stories, songs, poetry, prayers, homilies, discourses, and discussions. The BHAGAVAD GITA forms one section of the Mahabharata.

MAHADEVI. The Great Goddess, that is, KALI.

MAHAPRALAYA. The cataclysmic dissolution of the cosmos into its original substance, after which it will be created again.

MAHARAJ. A term of respect applied to (or taken by) certain holy men.

MAHASAMADHI. The great SAMADHI, which is death.

MAHATMA. Literally, "great soul." A person who has destroyed his ego and realized union with the All.

MANTRA. A invocation, which may be only a single syllable (such as OM) or a longer prayer or chant. Many of the sounds may seem nonsensical. The word is pronounced m'ntra.

MANTRIN. One who says a MANTRA.

MANU. A great Hindu sage and lawgiver. His thinking is codified in the second-century Manu Smriti (Lawbook of Manu).

MATA. Mother.

MATT. An ashram or monastery. Pronounced m'tt.

MAUNA. Silence. Many holy men practice a temporary or permanent period of mauna. Meher Baba's mauna lasted from 1925 until his death in 1969.

MAYA. The technical definition is "the Supreme Divine Power by which the One conceals itself and appears as the many," but the term is more often (and carelessly) used in the sense of "illusion."

MOKSHA. Emancipation from the world; liberation; release from the cycle of birth and rebirth.

MOOL. Root. A mool MANTRA is the original from which other mantras developed. A better spelling is mula.

MUDRA. A gesture of ritual and religious significance. Also a bean.

MULA. The general form of MOOL.

MUNI. A sage.

NABI. A Muslim (or SUFI) prophet. The term is applied to prophets of the Old Testament as well as to those who are specifically Islamic.

NADI. A river. In mystical terms, one of the subtle arteries of the body.

NEEM. A sacred tree.

NIRVANA. Emancipation from the cycle of life. The word does not mean "nothingness" as many Westerners believe. It is a "blowing out" of passion and desire. The word is formed from the negative ni and vana, "desire." The Buddhist spelling is nibanna.

OM. A mantra. OM is the most sacred of all sounds, and contains all sounds. OM represents the divine in all its manifestations.

PADAM, PADMA. Lotus (which see).

PARABRAHMAN. The Transcendental Immensity, the Cosmic Whole. The manifest form of Parabrahman is Bhuvaneshvari (KALI), who supports the trinity of nature, person and time (KALA).

PRASAD, PRASHAD. Food offered to a deity or to a saint. Once it has been accepted, it is sacred and then may be partaken of by the devotee.

PUJA. Ceremonial worship. Puja may be an individual act (said either by someone or by a priest acting on his behalf) or a communal project, such as the great autumn pujas of DURGA and KALI.

QUR'AN. The sacred book of the Muslims, revealed to the prophet Muhammad through the medium of the angel Jibril (Gabriel). Sometimes spelled Koran.

RAJ VIDYA. An advanced form of YOGA, which instills a balanced state of mind in the YOGI, who sits in the "frame with nine gates" [that is, the body], merged with God and seeing the world merely as spectator, not participant.

RAM, RAMA. One of the terms for God; also, an avatar of VISHNU. Actually there are two Vishnu/Ramas, the first being the embodiment of righteousness and the second the embodiment of princely virtues.

RISHI. A seer. MANTRAS are usually revealed to rishis.

RUPEE. The basic unit of Indian currency, divided into 100 paise. The value of the rupee in relation to the U.S. dollar fluctuates wildly, from twenty cents to thirteen. In the 1972 sinking of the dollar the rupee went up to twenty cents again. The street price of the rupee is about a third less.

SAD, SAT. True, truth. Often combined with another word, as sadguru, the most perfect guru.

SADHAKA. A person who is in the process of self-perfection.

SADHANA. Spiritual practices aimed at preparing oneself for self-realization.

SADHU. A holy man, often one who has no fixed abode and wanders about living on alms.

SAMADHI. The state of mind and soul in which the self ceases to function in mundane terms and only Pure Consciousness remains, "revealing itself to itself," in a classical definition. Mystically freaked out, that is.

SAMSARA. The cycle of birth and rebirth. The cycle is perpetuated through ignorance of the true nature of the self and by the dominance of the ego.

SAMSKARA. Literally it signifies purification, consecration, and is cognate with the Latin-derived "sacrament." Meanings are several: (1) a rite of purification, said with certain MANTRAS; (2) rites at various stages of a man's life, such as the taking of the sacred thread, marriage, death, etc.; (3) impressions, dispositions, psychic traces left in the mind after any experience—such samskara may remain from previous births.

SANDHI. The moment of dawn or sunset, which is believed to be especially efficacious for prayer and meditation.

SANNYASI. A man who has renounced the world in order to spend his time in search of the divine. Most often a sannyasi is an older man whose children have grown up.

SANSKRIT. The ancient language of the Aryans, which is now the sacred tongue of Hinduism. It is related to Greek, Latin, Russian, Persian, and so on, and their derivations.

SANT. Holy; a holy person.

SARASVATI. Literally, the "Flowing One." The Goddess of Knowledge, a form of KALI, representing the union of power and intelligence from which creation arises.

SATTVA. Realness, existing-ness. The adjective is sattvic.

SHABAD, SHABDA. Mystical sound or word. Shabad transports one into the endless heavenly spheres.

SHAKTI, SAKTI. Eternal, Supreme Power; manifest energy which is coupled with SHIVA to give birth to the universe. Shakti is most often worshiped as KALI in one of her many forms.

SHASTRA. An authoritative text, usually religious or scientific.

SHIVA, SIVA. One of the three forms of the Supreme Being (see BRAHMAN), the aspect associated both with the destruction of the universe and its creation when coupled with SHAKTI.

SIKH. A follower of Sikhism, a religious movement founded by Nanak (1464-1538), which tried to steer a central path between warring Hindus and Muslims, attempting to combine the best aspects of each into one faith.

SILVER CORD. A mystical tie which links the soul to the body during sleep, SAMADHI, or ASTRAL traveling.

SRI (also Sree, Shri, Shree). An honorific meaning "lord" or "revered one."

SUFI. A Muslim holy man or mystic who approaches the One. In India, Sufism is heavily influenced by YOGA and VEDANTA and the dividing lines are not always sharply demarcated.

SUTRA. Verse; a popular form for many ancient works.

SWAMI, SVAMI. A spiritual leader.

TANTRA. A type of esoteric, often erotic, teaching, most common in Bengal and Tibet, centered around SHAKTI/KUNDALINI.

TENTH DOOR. Another term for the THIRD EYE.

THIRD EYE. The mystic opening of the AJNA CHAKRA, the center located between and slightly above the physical eyes. It is also the site through which the soul leaves in SAMADHI and in death.

UPDESH. Advice.

VEDA. The Vedas are a collection of very ancient sacred texts, composed by the Aryans in the period 2000 to 600 B.C. (but not written down until quite late). They are believed to have been directly revealed by BRAHMAN.

VEDANTA. The concluding form of the VEDAS. The theme of Vedanta is knowledge of the Supreme. We find it best expressed in the BHAGAVAD GITA and the Upanishads, the latter being "secret teachings," which are a reaction to the formalism of the Vedas themselves.

VIRA. Universal; also, heroic.

VISHNARUPA. Universal consciousness.

VISHNU. The third member of the Hindu triad. He is the Inner Cause, the power by which things exist. He is also the principle of duration, of eternal life. When Vishnu sleeps the universe dissolves into its formless state.

VRITTI. A polarization subsequent to the ripening of actions.

YOGA, YOG. Literally, "union" (cognate with the English "yoke"); the union is of the individual ATMA with the universal atma. There are various schools of yoga, running from primarily physical exercises (HATHA YOGA, for example) to JAPA yoga to KRIYA yoga, and so on. Yoga is the primary theme of the BHAGAVAD GITA, where the Lord KRISHNA describes its various types as means of reaching the divine.

YOGI. One who practices YOGA. The plural form is yogins or yogis, and the feminine yogini.

YONI. The female sexual organ, which is normally depicted in combination with the LINGA, since neither functions procreatively alone, the act being both human and divine.

YUGA. One of the four great ages in the cycle of time. See KALPA.

CHILE
INDIA